Europeanism

Europeanism

John McCormick

OXFORD
UNIVERSITY PRESS

OXFORD
UNIVERSITY PRESS

Great Clarendon Street, Oxford OX2 6DP

Oxford University Press is a department of the University of Oxford.
It furthers the University's objective of excellence in research, scholarship,
and education by publishing worldwide in

Oxford New York

Auckland Cape Town Dar es Salaam Hong Kong Karachi
Kuala Lumpur Madrid Melbourne Mexico City Nairobi
New Delhi Shanghai Taipei Toronto

With offices in

Argentina Austria Brazil Chile Czech Republic France Greece
Guatemala Hungary Italy Japan Poland Portugal Singapore
South Korea Switzerland Thailand Turkey Ukraine Vietnam

Oxford is a registered trade mark of Oxford University Press
in the UK and in certain other countries

Published in the United States
by Oxford University Press Inc., New York

British Library Cataloguing in Publication Data

Data available

Library of Congress Cataloging in Publication Data
Library of Congress Control Number: 2010920352

Typeset by SPI Publisher Services, Pondicherry, India
Printed in Great Britain
on acid-free paper by
MPG Books Group, Bodmin and King's Lynn

ISBN 978-0-19-955621-2

10 9 8 7 6 5 4 3 2 1

Preface

In my book *The European Superpower*, published in 2007, I argued that the European Union has all the qualities of a post-modern superpower; that is, one that has the ability to exert influence on a global scale, but with a preference for using civilian rather than military means, and for emphasizing the advantages of soft power over hard power. The book was an attempt to respond to the conventional view that seems to have such a tight grip on the imaginations of so many academics, journalists, commentators, and political leaders: that military power trumps all others, that the United States continues to exert more or less unchallenged power in the world, that Europe is beset with problems and crises, and that China is more likely than Europe to be the world's next superpower.

In the closing chapter of *The European Superpower*, I argued that one of the qualities that has made Europe so influential in the world (even if the level of that influence is not yet fully understood or appreciated) has been Europeanism, meaning the political, economic, and social values that Europeans have in common. These values offer a distinctive set of interpretations of the sources and possible responses to critical problems, while also setting Europe apart from the United States, whose dominating role in shaping the global agenda since at least the end of the Second World War has been so abundantly clear. At the same time, though, I acknowledged that not only was the European model of power difficult to pin down, its significance was also widely doubted. While nationalism may have been on the decline in Europe since the Second World War (or, at least, have undergone a transformation), the majority view is still that Europe is a cluster of sovereign states with separate identities, and few Europeans can say how European interests differ from national interests, or can identify the distinctive features and values of the European project. In other words, Europe is still typically seen as no more than the sum of its parts.

The survey of Europeanism offered in *The European Superpower* was brief and provisional, and intended only as an illustration of some of the arguments I had made in support of the characteristics of the EU as a global actor. Those values and norms needed deeper consideration and more detailed elaboration, and they needed to go beyond an association with the European Union alone. Hence the birth of the idea for this book, which in some respects is an extension of *The European Superpower*. It is prompted by my concern that much of the analysis of Europe's place in the world today seems to be driven by the view that the European project is an accumulation of crises, failures, unmet potential, and fears for the health of democracy and the principle of sovereignty, and that Europeans are still too divided among themselves to be able to move effectively along the same road in search of the same goals. It seems to be almost a given that any attempt to suggest that Europe may be working must be conditioned with a list of the difficulties, handicaps, and obstacles yet to be overcome.

Europe's problems are acknowledged in the chapters that follow, but this study is an attempt to redirect the conversation, and to argue that in spite of the crises, the construction of a Europeanist view of government, economic priorities, social norms, and international relations is well under way. In other words, Europeanism has emerged—and is a legitimate and useful analytical tool—in spite of all the problems. Europeanist ideas have a heritage that pre-dates the construction of the European Union, and have widened and deepened with the impact of European integration, and with broader pressures that have emphasized what Europeans have in common at the expense of what divides them. Prime among the latter has been a combination of the historical legacy of Europe, the subconscious dismay created by its cold war divisions, the disagreements that Europeans have had with external powers, and the rapidly emerging view that Europeans have a distinctive view of the world of the twenty-first century.

Like my arguments in *The European Superpower*, those in this book are unconventional, and are likely to be provocative. I certainly hope so, because if academic research is not ultimately about challenging old assumptions and providing a new perspective, then what is its purpose? Until now there have only been isolated attempts to understand and outline discrete aspects of the European model, and the term *Europeanism* has been used less in the context of what Europe represents than in the context of debates about regional integration. My hope is that this book will encourage both a new assessment of the value and meaning of that term, and new attempts to further tie down what makes Europe and Europeans distinctive.

I have been influenced in my thinking by everyone with whom I have ever had a conversation about politics or about Europe, and I have read multiple literatures in depth, and thus owe my thanks to all those who have been cited in the pages that follow. However, I have generally been less interested in what has been said and written than in what has not been said or written, and so in writing this book I chose deliberately to reflect in isolation. What follows is as much as anything an extended essay, in which I have used data to support arguments, and the work of others to represent competing views, but to which I have appended my own conclusions. This book is designed to provoke and to redirect. Not everyone will agree with my analysis, but if the book encourages a broader approach to understanding Europe it will have succeeded.

As was the case with *The European Superpower*, the present volume benefits considerably from the fact that while I am European, I don't live there. What may seem less obvious to those studying and observing Europe from within may seem more obvious to the external observer, particularly one living in the United States. I continue to hear and read arguments made in favour of sustaining and exploiting the transatlantic alliance, and yet much of what I see and experience in the United States convinces me that Americans and Europeans—while agreeing generally on the overall goals of democracy and capitalism—differ on most of the details. I have far less optimism than most that Europeans and Americans can continue to agree, because the differences in their norms, values, and perspectives are just too adundant. These differences also make the similarities among Europeans that much more apparent, and have helped inspire the arguments that follow.

My thanks to Dominic Byatt for his help and encouragement, and to the production staff at Oxford University Press for their fine work. My thanks also to an anonymous reviewer who made a number of helpful comments that I took on board, and to the audiences at several presentations that I made on both sides of the Atlantic on themes that were later developed in the chapters that follow. As always, the book is dedicated to Leanne, Ian, and Stuart for helping keep it all real.

Contents

Contents

List of Figures

Map

List of Tables

Acronyms and Abbreviations

BRIC	Brazil, Russia, India, China
CFSP	Common Foreign and Security Policy
ECHR	European Convention on Human Rights
ECSC	European Coal and Steel Community
EEC	European Economic Community
EFTA	European Free Trade Association
EPC	European Political Cooperation
ESM	European Social Model
EVS	European Values Survey
GATT	General Agreement on Tariffs and Trade
GDP	gross domestic product
IMF	International Monetary Fund
NATO	North Atlantic Treaty Organization
ODA	official development assistance
OECD	Organization for Economic Cooperation and Development
SEA	Single European Act

Introduction

Europe is a region of contradictions. It seems to be well embarked upon a voyage of perpetual peace, its people are wealthier and healthier than at any time in their troubled history, its political values have become a democratic example to the rest of the world, and since 1945 it has set aside its most serious political and cultural divisions in order to build the world's most successful example of regional cooperation: the European Union. And yet its achievements are routinely questioned and challenged. Europe, claim the sceptics, has failed to capitalize on its political and economic potential, and has struggled to live up to its own aspirations for economic openness and productivity. It has failed to carve out a new role in the world, and is not bearing its share of the burden of critical security challenges. Its governments are often unable to set aside policy disagreements for the greater good, and regularly ignore public opinion when making their collective decisions. As though all this is not enough, Europe is failing to adapt to its new ethnic and religious diversity, and faces demographic problems arising from its shrinking and aging population.

For the optimists, the construction of a United States of Europe is well under way, and we can look forward to the day when its residents truly consider themselves European, when they will carry European passports with them on their travels, and when Europe will have enough confidence and power to offset American and Chinese influence in the world. For the pessimists, the European Union is a deeply defective non-state actor whose member states are being carried along on a powerful political tide to an uncertain destination. Europe's leaders make unrealistic claims for the region's new global role one day, and overlook remarkable achievements the next day. Meanwhile, most ordinary Europeans remain bemused and confused, some engaging happily with the European project, others opposing it with vigour, and the majority turning away with shrugs of indifference. Most freely admit that they understand neither the dynamics nor the significance of the European Union, nor their place in the broader concept of Europe. Suspended between the once-was and the yet-to-be, and between the confusing and the unknowable, the personality of contemporary Europe is more actively discussed than ever before, and yet continues to defy attempts to pin it down. We cannot even agree on the distinction between Europe and the European Union.

Perhaps there would be less confusion if there was more certainty about what Europe represented and what it meant to be European, and more sense of solidarity and connectedness among Europeans. Raised on a diet of nations and states, only a handful of Europeans are willing to consider themselves as such, while the rest either identify exclusively with states, or have dual loyalties to states and to Europe. But even among those with the strongest sense of association with Europe, it is not always clear what being European means. There is the geographical entity that is Europe (although its eastern limits are debatable), and the political and economic entity that is the European Union (which has failed to much excite public opinion). But all the remaining points of reference are missing: there is no European state, no European nation, no European language, no European government, no European people, no European religion, no European citizenship, no European passport, no European army, no European police force, and no European culture.

This, however, does not mean that a sense of solidarity is missing altogether—what we find depends upon where we look. Given the unique and unprecedented nature of the European experiment (for which read European integration as represented mainly but not exclusively by the European Union), perhaps the usual points of reference do not necessarily apply. Perhaps instead we should be looking to identify common values, preferences, predilections, and propensities across Europe's communities, nations, and states. In other words, are there ideas and qualities that define what it means to be European, and that generate expectations among those who deal with Europe and its residents? Is there a distinctive set of values and preferences that drive choices and preferences in Europe? Is there a brand, a model, or a paradigm that is distinctively European? Is there, in other words, such a thing as Europeanism?

These are the questions this volume seeks to address. Shaping the answers is a little like trying to finish a jigsaw from a box whose lid has been lost. The pieces are all there, we have numerous clues as to how the finished design might appear, and parts of the puzzle have already been completed and discussed. But nobody has yet tried to speculate on the finished design. All we have been offered—whether by political leaders, commentators, scholars, or the media—is a cluster of mainly unconnected suppositions and theories, along with a host of opinions about what Europe is not rather than what it is. A clear sense of the qualities of Europeanism is missing from the debate, if understood to mean the political, economic, and social norms and values that define Europe and the European experience; that shape European public preferences and proclivities; that drive the attitudes of Europeans towards each other and towards others; and that guide European views about their place in the world.

Some of the features of Europeanism are abundantly clear and little disputed. So when the Maastricht treaty proclaims that the European Union is founded 'on the principles of liberty, democracy, respect for human rights and fundamental freedoms, and the rule of law', it is hard to disagree. And former Czech president Václav Havel states the obvious when he lists the 'basic set' of Europe's values as including 'respect for the unique human being, and for humanity's freedoms, rights and dignity; the principle of solidarity; the rule of law and equality before the law; the protection of minorities of all types; democratic institutions; the separation of legislative, executive and judicial powers; a pluralist political system; respect for private ownership and private enterprise, and market economy; and, a furtherance of civil society'.[1] But while these are all European values, they are also American, Japanese, Indian, and Australian values. What we must instead seek out are the norms and values that are particularly felt, respected, developed, embraced, represented, or promoted by Europeans, and associated most closely by others with Europe.

Association is the key. In spite of the removal of political, economic, social, and cultural barriers under the auspices of the European Union, few Europeans are yet ready to define themselves as such. Polls find that less than 5 per cent of Europeans self-identify exclusively as Europeans rather than as citizens of their home state, or as citizens of both Europe and their home state. Imagine a European travelling abroad who is asked where they are from, or to identify their nationality. They are expected to answer that they are Dutch, or Spanish, or Czech, or Latvian. If they answer 'I am European', they are likely to cause much scratching of heads and demands for explanation. But the balance is changing. While it is not yet possible, legally speaking, for a European to renounce citizenship of a state and to become a citizen of Europe, there is a new sense in Europe that it is both possible and desirable to associate not just with states and nations but also with the larger idea of Europe, with an emerging European consciousness, and with a set of values that are quintessentially European.

The European Union has made numerous attempts to encourage this trend, as when the European Commission argued that EU cultural policy must contribute to strengthening and expanding the 'European model of society built on a set of values common to all European societies'.[2] Meanwhile, political leaders in Europe's states couch their arguments in European terms, and speak of the new role played by European interests in defining state priorities. While the building of common policies has had a telling effect on the development of a European consciousness, far more important in this process have been the changing perceptions and experiences of ordinary Europeans. Building on the foundations of a shared historical heritage, with its distinctive ideas about the public role of government, science, culture, and religion, and responding to the changing circumstances in which they have found themselves, Europeans since 1945 have been setting aside their national and state priorities in the interests of working with their neighbours to understand what they have in common, and to pursue shared goals. They have done this both consciously and unconsciously, with three forces in particular providing encouragement.

First, the state has been retreating more rapidly in Europe than anywhere else in the world. It was born in Europe, and its authority is still felt (more strongly today than ever, some would argue) through law, regulation, taxation, and the provision of welfare and social security. But identification with states has declined as Europe's internal borders have become more porous, as the reach of European law and policy has widened and deepened, as cross-border initiatives have grown in number and reach, and as Europeans have mingled with their neighbours. Elite-led Europeanization has paved the way, to be sure, but Europeans have also been voluntarily reinventing themselves. The attractions of the realist view of the world (with its emphasis on the self-interest of states) have weakened at the expense of post-modernist views that value cosmopolitanism, personal mobility, multiculturalism, peace, communitarianism, new attitudes towards the role of science, opposition to war, social spending rather than military spending, mass communications, and sustainable development. Europeans have made political, economic, and social connections that have redefined the way they regard the state, each other, and their place in the world. Identification with states is being replaced with a new interest in the collective interests, views, and priorities of Europe.

Second, the changes wrought by the end of the cold war have redefined the political, economic, and social meaning of Europe. Where once there were two antagonistic ideological blocs, whose interests and priorities were entirely separate, and whose peoples and cultures were mysterious and foreign to one another, a new pan-European awareness is emerging. The east (or central Europe, as some prefer to call it) has not yet entirely adapted to the political and economic norms of the west, and the west is still not entirely sure how to view the east, but at no time in the history of Europe have so many Europeans been so clearly moving along the same path, carrying so little in the way of philosophical, religious, political, or ideological baggage. What unites Europeans is today more important and obvious than what divides them, and the growth of a new generation of Europeans who think in European terms is well under way. Corporate boards plan for the European marketplace, political leaders work together on shared problems, foreign policy interests are defined in European terms, and Europeans move to live and work in neighbouring states without a second thought. The rise of the Erasmus generation has been symbolic of the change: nearly two million students have studied abroad in Europe since the launch of the Erasmus student exchange scheme in 1987.

Finally, external pressures continue to play the same critical role that they always have in helping Europeans define themselves. Once it was the Persians, the Arabs, and the Ottoman Turks. Then it was the threats posed by straddling the frontlines of the cold war. While eastern European differences with Soviet values and aspirations were always clear, the discomfort often felt by western Europeans with their American allies was less obvious. From the Berlin crisis through Korea, Suez, Cuba, Vietnam, and the Middle East, the Atlantic alliance was one of convenience rather than always of conviction. Then came the perfect storm of the Bush/Cheney years: first the 9/11 attacks brought Americans and Europeans together in common cause as never before, and then the 2003 invasion of Iraq drove them apart as never before. Today, transatlantic tensions—long known by a minority and suspected by many others—have become abundantly clear, and while optimists continue to argue that the differences can be resolved, and that the abiding importance of transatlantic ties remains clear, others are not so sure.

In spite of these new realities, believers in Europeanism are not easy to find. How, it is reasonable to ask, can we identify common values among a group of forty sovereign states, containing dozens of different nationalities; speaking dozens of different languages, with histories that have often been quite different; that are still divided by religion, culture, and competing social attitudes; whose internal links are often still troubled; and where doubts about efforts to cooperate still abound? Eastern Europeans seem to be particularly sceptical, if the views of the Slovenian essayist and poet

Ales Debeljak are any reflection. Western and eastern Europe, he argues, are still too divided and distant from one another to make possible the development of a common identity. Although Europeanism needs to be 'contemplated and imagined', as an 'orderly constellation of aspirations, values, images, attitudes, convictions, and concepts that, when success-fully welded together, provides sources of individual inspiration and grants meaning to collective behaviour', it is far from well developed. It cannot be an effective unifying idea, he suggests, unless it 'wilfully and systematically reaches into the heritage of all European nations'. But this would in turn demand inter-generational continuity, perpetuated by distinct ethnic traditions, and reinforced by a shared memory and the expectation of a common future. For now, he concludes, Europeanism is little more than the kind of 'invented tradition' described by Eric Hobsbawn.[3]

Speaking before the European Parliament in 1994, Czech president Václav Havel argued that while the European Union had a 'spirit' from which its founding principles had grown, this spirit was difficult to see because it was hidden 'behind the mountains of systemic, technical, administrative, economic, monetary and other measures that contain it'. Thus, he concluded, the most important task facing the European Union was to develop 'a new and genuinely clear reflection on ... European identity, a new and genuinely clear articulation of European responsibili-ty, [and] an intensified interest in the very meaning of European integra-tion in all its wider implications for the contemporary world'. This, he suggested, might take the form of a charter 'that would clearly define the ideas on which [the EU] is founded, its meaning and the values it intends to embody'.[4] In another speech before Parliament six years later, Havel argued that most Europeans never thought about the idea of being Euro-pean, and were surprised when asked by opinion pollsters to declare their European affiliation. 'Conscious Europeanism', he concluded, 'seems to have had little tradition on this continent'. But he also saw welcome signs that European self-awareness appeared to be on the rise, and argued that this new development was particularly critical given the multicultural and multipolar nature of the world, in which the ability to recognize one's own identity was the primary prerequisite for a coexistence with others.[5]

From the era of nineteenth-century nationalism through to the end of the cold war, Europeans were deeply divided, and too focused on domestic priorities to consider the bigger picture. But since the end of the cold war, the rejoining of east and west, and the fallouts with the Americans, there has been a rebirth of the idea that Europe is distinctive and that it is a region bound by common values. That many European states still remain outside the European Union (for now, at least), and that there is no agreement on where to place Europe's eastern border, does not matter as much as it might seem. The European Union exerts an irresistible influence over neighbouring non-member states, where public debates are often coloured and driven by how those states should relate to 'Europe'. Europeans—both inside and outside the European Union—have become more conscious of what they have in common, obliged as they have been by the process of building the European Union to debate more vigorously what it means to be European, and where the European project is headed.

But Europe will be unable to move ahead constructively with its attempts to build shared institutions and policies, to improve its economic prospects, to capitalize on its human and intellectual resources, or to participate effectively in the solution of international problems, until Europeans appreciate what they have in common. Havel's suggestion for the development of an EU charter of identity is not the path to follow, because such a document would almost certainly be replete with the kind of grand and yet often shallow declarations that committees—particularly those associated with the European Union—are so adept at producing. More effective would be a public debate about the nature of Europeanism, to which scholars of the European Union could contribute if they could briefly set aside their fascination with treaty articles, theory, and grand concepts, and look instead at the values, qualities, norms, and goals that delineate—in practical terms—the European experience.

An attempt to move the debate along was sparked by events leading up to the March 2003 invasion of Iraq. Outraged Europeans turned out in their hundreds of thousands at anti-war demonstrations held on 15 February in London, Berlin, Paris, Rome, Madrid, Barcelona, and other cities. Former French finance minister Dominique Strauss-Kahn saw the birth of a new 'European nation'[6] in the demonstrations, and the philosophers Jürgen Habermas and Jacques Derrida were inspired to write an article for *Frankfurter Allgemeine Zeitung* in which they hailed 15 February as signalling the birth of a 'European public sphere'. Arguing that Europe had undergone a reaction to nationalism, and that new values and habits had given contemporary Europe 'its own face', they now saw an opportunity for the construction of a 'core Europe' (excluding Britain and Eastern Europe) that might be a counterweight to the international influence of the United States. In an attempt to explain what Europe represented, they listed six facets of what they described as a common European 'political mentality':

- Secularization.
- Trust in the state and scepticism about the achievements of markets.
- Realistic expectations about technological progress.
- Welfarism.
- A low threshold of tolerance for the use of force.
- Multilateralism within the framework of a reformed United Nations.[7]

Although the article was provocative, it was only a modest start and much more had to be done to fill in the details. The differences over Iraq were something of a wake-up call, obliging Europeans to think more actively about what they had in common and where they differed with American leadership. And while European integration had paved the way, we are dealing here with far more than the efforts of the European Union, and are instead faced with the challenge of understanding the cumulative effects of the European historical experience, and of deciding where Europe sits within the framework of contemporary political, economic, and social understanding. While much has been said and written about discrete aspects of Europeanism as it relates to social expectations, economic priorities, secularism, multiculturalism, and foreign policy, no one has yet synthesized all this work into a systematic statement of the content, meaning, dimensions, and qualities of Europeanism. This volume is an attempt both to provide that synthesis and to redirect the focus of the debate. It acknowledges that we are looking to some extent at a moving target, and that the extent to which Europeanist qualities can be identified varies from one state to another, and even from one community to another. But it also argues that European values have a longer history than is often recognized, that they are central to the definition of Europe and its place in the world, and that it is critical that we now identify and understand those values for what they are.

Three explanatory notes are needed. First, it is important to make a distinction between Europeanism, Europeanness, and European identity. At its simplest, Europeanism is a noun denoting a set of values and beliefs while Europeanness is an adjective implying a measure of the extent to which those values and beliefs have been adopted. Thus we see reference to the extent to which Turkey has (or has not) advanced along the path of Europeanness as it is considered for EU membership, or the extent to which internal migration within Europe is helping encourage a greater feeling of

Europeanness, or the results of polls that find a greater sense among Europeans of being European rather than of only being citizens of their home states. Europeanness comes in different degrees, whereas Europeanism—although its constituent qualities may change—is an absolute. Meanwhile, any discussion about Europeanism will inevitably raise the question of European identity, but this also is only a part of the bigger picture. While identification with Europe means a sense of belonging or a sense of association with Europe as distinct from (or in addition to) an association with a state, a nation, or a religion, Europeanism provides the reference point by which identity can be measured and understood.

Second, it is important to be clear about what we mean by 'Europe', a term that has always had indistinct geographical, historical, political, and social boundaries. Europe is neither a state nor a continent, and establishing its limits has been complicated in recent decades by the distinctions made between Europe and the European Union, and debates about which states on the margins of Europe might be considered European. Conveniently, coastlines establish the southern, western, and northern limits of Europe, but the eastern borders have always been problematic, with questions about where Turkey, the Balkans, and the Caucasus states fit, and whether Europe ends at the border with Russia or spills over into Russia. Borders are changeable and permeable, and this has been as true with demarcating the territories of European states as it has with defining the eastern limits of Europe. For Delanty and Rumford, Europe is best defined as a 'civilizational constellation', a label that shifts the focus away from states and borders and stresses instead the civilizational basis of European history and takes account of its constantly changing relationship with the east.[8]

For present purposes, little distinction is made between Europe and the European Union, on the basis that the political, economic, and legal impact of the European Union has been felt throughout the region. In spite of regular references to the European Union in the chapters that follow, this analysis is not solely about the European Union. It is instead about the qualities that make all of Europe distinctive, while acknowledging that the European Union has been the critical motive force in encouraging, shaping, and confirming those qualities. While the ambiguities of Europe's eastern borders are recognized, the focus of the analysis that follows will be the experiences of those who live within the territory of Europe's forty contemporary sovereign states (see Map 0.1). Of these, twenty-seven are today members of the European Union and have been subjected to the

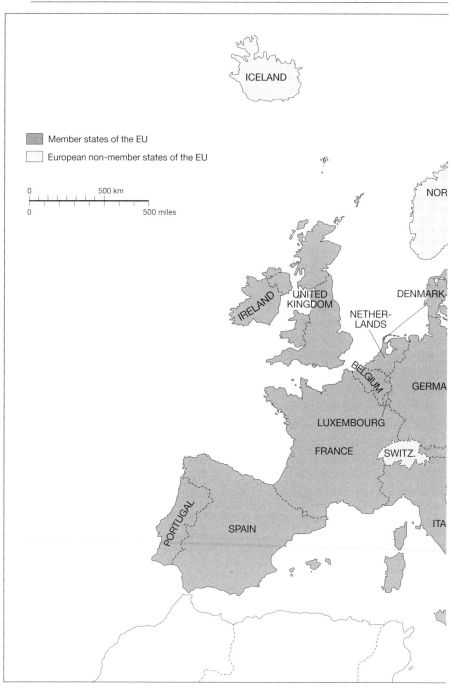

Map 0.1 Europe today

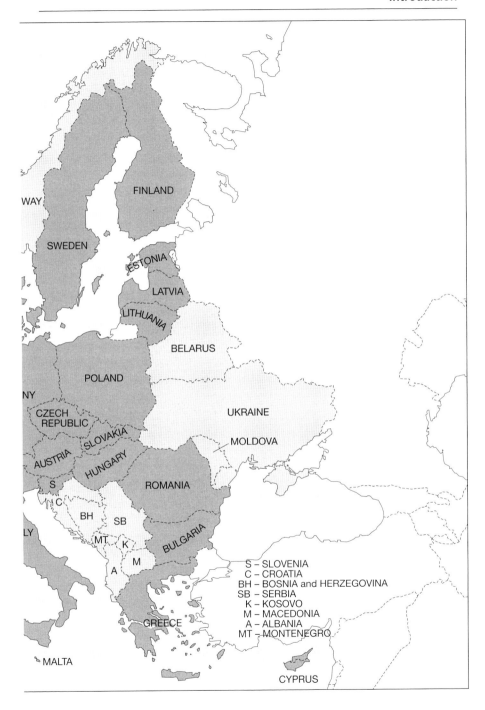

S – SLOVENIA
C – CROATIA
BH – BOSNIA and HERZEGOVINA
SB – SERBIA
K – KOSOVO
M – MACEDONIA
A – ALBANIA
MT – MONTENEGRO

pressures and influences of what might be termed inclusive integration. Of the remainder, twelve either have aspirations to join the European Union or have policy agreements with the European Union that have had the effect of changing much of their domestic policy and body of laws, thereby subjecting them to the pressures and influences of what might be termed exclusive integration. This leaves just one state outside today's core Europe: the authoritarian politics of Belarus make it the one clear, remaining exception to most of the general rules that apply to Europe. As for Turkey and Russia, neither is regarded here as playing an inclusive role in the definition of Europeanism; their histories have often overlapped with those of core Europe, and Turkey may one day join the European Union, but the impact of both states on European ideas has been mainly from outside rather than from within.

Finally, what follows is influenced by the methods of comparative study, in which differences and similarities between Europe and other parts of the world are used to draw attention to the distinctive qualities of Europeanism. There is particular emphasis on comparisons with the United States, prompted mainly by how Europe and the United States are so similar in many ways and yet so different in others. We have long been led to believe that the two actors have so much in common that they are the primary components of the 'West'; indeed, a 2008 Eurobarometer poll found that a plurality of Europeans (44 per cent) believe that there are no common European values, only global Western values. At the same time, 61 per cent of those asked were of the view that comparison with other parts of the world made it easier to see what Europeans had in common.[9] The rising awareness of transatlantic differences has not only raised numerous questions about the value of the West as an analytical concept but has also drawn new attention to what Europeans have in common. George Bernard Shaw once described England and America as two countries divided by a common language, but we might as easily describe Europe and the United States as two regions divided by common political, economic, and social values.

The study begins with an examination in Chapter 1 of the broad themes in the evolution of the idea of Europe and of how Europeans have been defined. It argues that Europeans were for centuries understood less on their own terms than in relation to outsiders. Christianity provided a critical early defining force, as did external threats from the Persians, the Arabs, and the Ottoman Turks. But Christianity was never a unifying force, and indeed Europe was for centuries divided by religious wars, and territorial authority was exerted by aristocrats and the church. It was only in the seventeenth century that the modern state system began to emerge, soon to be overlaid by national divisions that created a complex and troubled political dynamic. In the nineteenth century, nationalism evolved from a cultural into a political force, Europe was held hostage to great power rivalry, and the accumulating tensions spilled over into the two world wars. Until 1945, European history was one of divisions compounding divisions, and there was little sense of a common European mission or purpose, and few signs of a Europeanist ethic.

Chapter 2 focuses on the changes that have redefined Europe since 1945. The two core internal influences were initially the search for a lasting peace, which meant addressing the causes of conflict, and the need to rebuild European economies and bring prosperity to its peoples. In both causes the United States played a critical role, at least in the west, while cold war divisions illustrated the extent to which Europe was being made to pay for its historical failures. The three core external influences on the redefinition of Europe were the military insecurity posed by the Soviet threat, the economic insecurity caused by the decline of Europe's global advantages and the rise of foreign competition, and the political pressures arising from philosophical and ideological divisions between western Europe and the United States. Transatlantic tensions grew coincidentally as the first steps were taken along the path to European integration. While the grasp of the new Europe exceeded its reach during the 1990s, the combined effects of the dispute with the United States over Iraq and the eastern enlargement of the European Union helped shed new light on the common goals and values of the new post-national Europe, giving new definition to the outlines of Europeanism.

Chapter 3 assesses Europeanist attitudes towards the state. It argues that regional integration has combined with changing views about Europe to weaken the authority of the state, and that the meaning of *nation* and *nationalism* in Europe have both undergone a metamorphosis. Where Europeans once closely identified with states and nations, the former have seen many of their powers reduced by the effects of a pooling of sovereignty in the European Union, and attachments to the latter have been transformed as the assertive political nationalism of the nineteenth and early twentieth centuries has been replaced by today's more benign cultural nationalism. The meaning of citizenship has changed, patriotism is regarded with some scepticism, and Europeanism has adopted strong cosmopolitan qualities: Europeans increasingly believe that local, European, and global concerns cannot be separated. As identity with states declines and the meaning of nationalism changes, Europeanist loyalties have switched to ideas and values.

Chapter 4 looks at the common features and qualities of politics in Europe. It opens with a discussion about political culture, and about the difficulties of defining this term, and then of determining the forces that have been the most telling in the formation of a European political culture. It then outlines some of the core features of European political culture, including collective responsibility and communitarianism, the pragmatic views regarding the possibilities of democracy, and the changes in the patterns of political participation. The second half of the chapter focuses on the institutional and procedural character of the European parliamentary model, and on what it has meant for the character of the government in Europe, and how it impacts Europeanist views on the dynamics of politics. It ends with a brief assessment of the prospects for understanding and defining the European political space.

Chapter 5 examines the economic facets of Europeanism. It notes the irony in, on the one hand, the declining identification with states as territorial and political entities discussed in Chapter 3, and, on the other hand, the Europeanist expectation that the state as a functional mechanism will intervene to regulate, to redistribute income and wealth, and to follow policies designed to encourage economic growth. Above all, Europeans are welfarists; the modern welfare state was born in Europe and it has achieved its greatest reach and its most telling effects in Europe, where equality of results is favoured over equality of opportunity. More than is the case anywhere else in the world, Europeans expect the state to intervene in the economy in the interests of encouraging a level playing field, and believe that success is a matter less of personal choices than of community arrangements. Europeanism also means an emphasis on civilian–industrial endeavour in contrast to the military–industrial flavour of the American economy, and a concern for sustainable development: production and consumption that occurs with deliberate concern for the management of natural resources and for the effect on the quality of the natural environment.

Chapter 6 focuses on European society, arguing that the European Social Model—while interesting as a reference point for analysis—is too driven by economic factors to shed as much light on European social norms as it might. The chapter instead focuses on four sets of issues that bring out the social facets of Europeanism more directly: the causes and effects of Europe's declining population numbers, the changing definition of the European family (fewer marriages, fewer children, more children born outside marriage, and smaller households), the changing European work ethic with its emphasis on greater leisure and more enjoyment of the rewards of labour, and the nature of approaches to criminal justice. The chapter argues that Europeanism favours quality over quantity, and that Europeans are less focused on accumulation and consumption than on pursuing post-modern objectives.

Chapter 7 attempts to assess some of the core values of Europeans, focusing in particular on four areas where the Europeanist perspective is notably different from that in any other part of the world. It looks first at multiculturalism, arguing that claims of a multicultural crisis in Europe overlook the fact that the region has a long tradition of recognizing and integrating multiple different cultures. What has changed of late has been the addition to the mix of race and of Islam, which has brought out some of the less desirable qualities in European thinking. It then looks at the role of secularism in European society, arguing that while religion is growing almost everywhere else in the world, its role in Europe is declining. The third case in the chapter is capital punishment, on the abolition of which Europe is taking the leading role, in spite of equivocations among Europeans themselves on the issue. Finally, the chapter looks at the rather more ambiguous issue of life satisfaction, asking what change has meant for European perceptions about personal goals.

Chapter 8 examines the qualities of Europeanism as they relate to perceptions about relations between Europe and the rest of the world. After centuries of assertion—expressed most obviously by colonialism and imperialism—post-war Europe has fundamentally altered the way it sees itself in the world. Europeans have emphasized peace and cooperation in their dealings with each other, while on the global stage they have switched away from reliance on military means of expressing power towards civilian means. They have also adopted a combination of hard and soft power tools, now increasingly described as 'smart power' or an adept use of a balance of coercion and encouragement. Europeanism champions internationalism, engagement, diplomacy, and multilateralism, not—as some would have us believe—because they no longer can afford large militaries, but because their history has suggested to them the futility of a reliance on militarism and instead encouraged them to seek the achievement of perpetual and positive peace.

The argument made in the pages that follow is that there is a distinctive set of values, norms, ideas, and positions that mark out European attitudes, and that rather than focusing on the effects of European integration alone, we should work to achieve a broader understanding of how and why Europe has been transformed since 1945. Where once the region was internally divided, its communities fighting with one another over territory, religion, and national identity, today it has become clear that Europe has set aside its most damaging internal divisions and that Europeans have come to think and act alike on a wide range of issues. Europeanism offers us a means of understanding the way that Europeans think and organize the world around them, and—as a key to appreciating the impact of regional integration on Europe's changing place in the world—deserves to be more thoroughly studied.

1

The Idea of Europe

Understanding contemporary Europeanism demands that we first place the development of European ideas and identity in its longer historical context. Whatever else we think about European integration, its great achievement since 1945 has been the manner in which it has brought a close to the chronicle of strife, conflict, and war that has for so long troubled the region, and has encouraged Europeans to rise above the forces that have divided them, and to better understand what they share and have in common. These forces took different forms, the dynamics of division changing with the evolving balance of political, economic, and social influences that for so long defined relations among the kingdoms, empires, and then the states of Europe. Among those influences were religion, external threats, philosophy, the competition to build empires, and nationalism.

Although historians are divided on the question of when modern Europe was born, a loose consensus has settled on the Renaissance, the period spanning roughly the fourteenth to the seventeenth centuries when politics, society, art, culture, and technology were transformed, paving the way for Europe's emergence as a global leader in almost every field of human endeavour. Democratic government took its first tentative steps, state borders took on a new permanence, economic systems and structures were transformed, trade routes expanded, new patterns of social relations evolved, advances were made in science and technology, and the age of European colonialism was born. By the beginning of the twentieth century, Europe sat astride the earth with the most powerful militaries, the biggest economies, the most advanced technology, and an overwhelming sense of its own political, moral, and cultural superiority.

But then Europe entered the most turbulent period in its history, the broad sweep of which has never been short of tumult. The decade prior to the outbreak of the Great War was a time of relative peace, stability, growth, and progress, but these were also what Blom has described as the 'vertigo years':[1] the old order—as it had so often before—was giving way to the new, and the expanded nationalist and imperialist tensions of the nineteenth century were about to spill over into the most cataclysmic war the world had ever known. That war was followed by an uneasy peace, and by economic depression, political dysfunction, and the rise of fascism, sparking an even more bloody war that drained much of Europe's remaining power and energy, leaving the region politically divided, and in thrall—for the first time in its history—to the control of external powers. Between 1914 and 1945, argues Duroselle, 'there was no Europe', a destructive combination of nationalism, imperialism, and fascism undermining the region materially and intellectually, assuring an almost continuous state of civil war.[2] After 1945, Europe imploded, divided into two hostile regions, distracted by the difficulty of understanding the challenges posed to its identity by the war, its energies consumed by political and economic reconstruction, and obliged to follow the lead of the two superpowers.

How different twentieth-century Europe might have been without the intervention of two world wars we can only imagine: the era of colonialism would surely have ended regardless, and the expansion of human rights and the welfare state that had begun before 1914 would have continued, but relations among European states would have evolved quite differently, and Europe's place in the world would have been more certain and confident. As it was, the wars confirmed the dangers inherent in the volatile mix of nationalism and new military technology that greatly expanded the prospects for death and destruction. Meanwhile, the post-1945 division of Europe was to show Europeans just how much they had lost since 1914, and how much they stood to gain from working and thinking together rather than being constantly at odds with one another.

Philosophers and idealists had long spoken and written of the advantages to be gained by a cooperative Europe, but it was not until 1945 that a wider and more receptive audience was willing to hear their case. Europe might have been divided in the past, but Europeans had more common interests and shared experiences than they often appreciated. They usually defined themselves in local terms, but the sense of a shared destiny was always there, bubbling under the surface, its significance ebbing and flowing with the changing fortunes of kingdoms, empires, states, and nations. After 1945, the circumstances were right and the time was ripe for a new assessment of what Europeans had in common, of how cooperation might be achieved, and of how the definition of Europe might achieve a new clarity. But how did they arrive there, why did it take them so long, and what role does Europe's past play in understanding its present? How, out of this background of constant change and frequent conflict, can we identify the common themes in today's Europeanism?

The birth of Europe

Even the briefest review of an historical atlas will quickly reveal that the geopolitical dimensions of Europe have been in an ongoing state of flux and transition stretching from the time when 'geopolitics' first began to have any meaning until the present day. Of course, the same can be said for almost any part of the world, but the recorded history of Europe is longer than most, and unlike—say—China or India, Europe's internal changes have had global consequences. As Europe's boundaries have changed, so the nature and control of political authority has been revised and reinvented, states and nations have jostled for control, empires have risen and fallen, and since 1945 we have seen the ideological divisions of the cold war, the rise of the European Union, and adjustments to the borders of Germany, the Balkans, and Czechoslovakia. Even today, additional EU enlargement is planned, Kosovo and Montenegro are emerging as new states, and several more potential new states may be in the pipeline, including the Basque country, Flanders, Wallonia, and Scotland. It has been argued that all maps are fictions, and that the political maps of pre-modern Europe should be treated with particular caution,[3] but the changing lines of these maps make the forceful point that this is a region of constant metamorphosis.

Perhaps fittingly, the origins of Europe are commonly traced to a myth. Europa was a Phoenician princess who was abducted by the god Zeus disguised as a white bull, and taken from her homeland in what is now Lebanon to Crete, where she was ravished by Zeus and became queen. Or, depending upon which story is given the most credence, she was abducted by merchants from Crete in a ship with the shape of a bull, and later married the King of Crete. Whatever the details, the Trojans later took their revenge by seizing Helen, another daughter of Zeus and wife of the Spartan king Menelaus, whose brother Agamemnon took an army in pursuit, sparking the Trojan War. Europa herself was from what was later known as Asia Minor, and her abductors were what we now call Europeans. These mythical events are often cited as the beginning of a hostility between the two regions that helped define Europe as being distinct from the

Asian continent of which it is a part. The Trojan link continued with Aeneas, son of Aphrodite, who fled Troy after its collapse at the hands of Agamemnon, and settled in Latium (present-day Italy) and was later credited with the founding of Rome.[4]

It is unclear exactly when the term *European* was first applied to a specific territory or its inhabitants, but it most likely occurred some time in the fifth century BC when Greeks settled the Ionian Islands and first came into contact with the Persians. Giving birth to what would become a long tradition, Europe was defined less by what it was than what it was not:[5] it was not the Persian Empire, which was then expanding westward, finally resisted by the armies of the Greek city states between 499 and 448 BC. Greek authors such as Aristotle were prompted to make a distinction between their languages, customs, and values, and those of the inhabitants of Asia (as represented by the Persians) and the 'barbarians' who lived to the north. For some Greeks, Europe meant only the region in which they lived, characterized by a strong civilization based on freedom and democracy, and classical Greek maps represented the known world as being divided into Asia, Europe, and Libya (Africa), with the boundary between Europe and Asia indicated by the River Don and the Sea of Azov.[6] The same division was reflected in the T-and-O map drawn by the seventh-century scholar Isidore of Seville, with Asia in the top half and Europe and Africa in the two lower quarters.

If it was the Greeks who first gave Europeans a name, it was the Romans whose regional hegemony (approximately 200 BC to AD 400) first brought much of Europe under what Cornell and Matthews have described as a 'single cultural complex'.[7] The Roman Empire was also a single legal complex, based on the foundation of principles that protected life, property, and individual rights. Roman domination also brought with it a common language (Latin), a common administrative system, and—following the adoption of Christianity in AD 391—a common religion, which eventually spread from its Roman base to the rest of Europe. But because the Roman Empire was centred on the Mediterranean it was not solely European, and because it was an empire it did little to foster a common sense of belonging among the peoples who came under its sway. Middle Easterners and North Africans may have regarded the inhabitants of Europe (who they referred to as Franks or Romans) as distinctive, but shared interests and identities were far from the minds of the inhabitants of Europe themselves. They were even less evident when northern barbarians invaded a collapsing Rome during the closing years of the fourth century AD, and Europe dissolved into feuding kingdoms and was traversed by invading Huns, Vikings, and Magyars.

The Early Middle Ages (approximately AD 500–1050) saw three crucial developments that brought about a change in perceptions. First, a common civilization emerged with Christianity as its religion, Rome as its spiritual capital, and Latin as the language of education. Then came the expansion of Frankish power between 481 and 768 (from the start of the reign of Clovis I to the end of the reign of Pippin), opening with a base in the area of what is now western Germany, Belgium, and the Netherlands, and expanding to cover almost of all of what is now France and the northern half of Italy. Finally, the internal meaning of Europe was given new clarity by external threats, this time from the Arabs. Emerging out of the Arabian peninsula in the seventh century, the Arab empire expanded west across North Africa, and during an eight-year campaign at the beginning of the eighth century brought most of the Iberian peninsula under its sway. The Arabs (and Islam) were turned back only in 732 with the victory of Charles Martel near Poitiers in west-central France. Whether or not the battle halted the Islamic advance, and thus saved Christian Europe, is a point much debated by historians, but it certainly confirmed the reality of Frankish domination of much of continental Europe.

Although forces under the command of Martel were described by contemporary chroniclers as European,[8] the term would not become more widely used until after 800. In that year, Martel's grandson Charlemagne (king of the Franks from 768) was crowned Holy Roman Emperor by the Pope and hailed in poems as the successor to the Roman emperors, and king and father of Europe; he is still seen today as symbolic of the idea of Europe. Charlemagne's campaigns against the Arabs, the Saxons, the Bavarians, the Avars, and the Slavs expanded the Frankish Empire so that by the time of his death in 814 the Carolingians controlled most of what are now France, Switzerland, Austria, southern Germany, and the Benelux countries. (Champions of European unity in the 1950s liked to point out that this area coincided closely with that of the six founding member states of the European Economic Community.) Following Charlemagne's death, the territory was soon divided up among his sons, and while the Holy Roman Empire persisted until the middle of the fourteenth century, modern maps of early twelfth-century Europe reveal a complex patchwork quilt of kingdoms, duchies, and fiefdoms, interspersed with clusters of church lands.

If the birth of Europe had been accompanied by the emergence of a common civilization with Christianity as its guiding philosophy and

Rome as its spiritual capital, it was not until the early Middle Ages that it became more geographically united. Where western and northern Europe had been regarded as peripheral during Roman times, there was now a shift that would ultimately result in the focus of culture and power moving north. Europe as a whole underwent a process of Christianization, and just as religion had helped define Europe in the face of Arab expansionism in the eighth century, so it was to continue in this role as Christian armies gathered from across the region to participate in the first Crusades, launched in the late twelfth century. From the eleventh century to the fifteenth century, Europe was known in common parlance as Christendom.[9] This not only gave it a separate identity from Islam, its critical external competitor, but also drove thinking about the principles upon which Europeans might relate to one another. For example, protecting Europe from itself encouraged the French advocate Pierre Dubois—despondent that war seemed to be endemic in Europe despite the teachings of Christianity—to suggest in 1306 that the princes and cities of Europe should form a confederal 'Christian Republic' overseen by a permanent assembly of princes working to ensure peace through the application of Christian principles. In the event of a dispute, a panel of nine judges could be brought together to arbitrate, with the Pope acting as a final court of appeal.[10]

While most of Europe has for much of its recorded history been ruled by monarchs, and freedom was long enjoyed only by the privileged few (and even then freedom was defined quite differently from the way we define it today), Pagden argues that Europeans have always pursued approximately similar political ends. In spite of its limited reach, the principle of liberty was long a vital feature of European political society, tracing its roots back to the republican and democratic traditions of ancient Greece. Furthermore, governments have long subscribed to the view that freedom of choice and respect for the rule of law are essential to the success of democracy and society. In spite of their number and powers, European monarchs—unlike their contemporaries in Asia and Africa—generally accepted the principles that their subjects were free persons, that rulers were subject to a higher legal order derived from God, and that power was conferred on monarchs through a contract with the people. In short, monarchs may have had considerable power, but it was not unlimited.[11]

In spite of the early indications of common values, the identity of Europe was still uncertain, and during the late Middle Ages it was once again tied to Europe's need to protect itself from external threats. This time it was the Ottoman Turks,[12] whose gains in Asia Minor were to have implications for

Europe's sense of itself and for the development of its global interests. The Turks captured Thessaloniki from the Venetians in 1387, triumphed over the Serbs at the Battle of Kosovo in 1389, and captured Constantinople in 1453. These events continued to encourage the view that Europe and Christianity were virtually synonymous, and that Europe should respond by reviving the Holy Roman Empire and the supremacy of the papacy.[13] It was also Ottoman control of the eastern Mediterranean that was to help spark European attempts to find an alternative trade route to the Indies, which was to lead in turn to the first wave of European imperialism. That greater confidence attached to the idea of Europe as a geographical term was meanwhile reflected in the publication of the first maps depicting Europe alone.[14] As the age of exploration dawned, the addition of more detail to the shape and extent of Africa combined with the 'discovery' of the Americas to change the frame of reference. What the Europeans found as they studied their neighbours convinced them that Europe was superior and that its peoples had a 'civilizing mission' underpinned by Christianity.

Economic and social changes were meanwhile taking place that would further strengthen the European sense of identity and confidence: the growth of commerce, agricultural production, and population; the evolution of towns into centres of intellectual and commercial life; the emergence of a new class of merchants; and the imposition by monarchs and the aristocracy of greater control over their territories. Intermarriages among the dynasties of Europe created a ruling network to which key social groups were tied through clientelism, the whole edifice held together by the idea of a European Christian commonwealth. This is not to suggest that there was a common European identity or culture, however; far from it. The peoples of the region known geographically as Europe still had little in common beyond shared religious and economic ideas, common political beliefs, and shared external threats. Europe was patently multicultural, and its different communities had quite different social organizations and spoke different languages. And before the age of personal mobility and mass communication, the vast majority of Europeans were barely aware of a world outside their own villages.

Most significantly, religion—in spite of its prominence as a political and social phenomenon—was never a unifying force for Europeans,[15] and in fact was at the heart of many of their bloodiest and longest internal squabbles and wars. Although Europe and Christendom were synonymous to outsiders, Europeans were divided first between the Latin and Orthodox churches, and then between the Catholic and Protestant churches. Famines, the Black Death, and the Hundred Years' War (1337–1453) provided a turbulent background to the emerging power of monarchs and challenges to the authority of the papacy, which in turn paved the way for the Reformation, the expression by Protestant churches of their independence from the Roman Catholic Church, and an almost constant state of religious warfare throughout the sixteenth and early seventeenth centuries. What are now Austria, Bohemia, Denmark, England, France, Germany, Ireland, the Netherlands, Scotland, and Switzerland were all impacted.

Religion had become such a clear source of division by the end of the sixteenth century that those few idealists who had considered the prospects for a united Christian Europe now abandoned thoughts of unity based on a common religion, and instead looked to unity as a means of addressing the religious causes of conflict and the growing threat of Habsburg power. These were the motives, for example, behind the Grand Design outlined in 1598 by the Duc de Sully, chief adviser to King Henry IV of France. He proposed replacing the existing network of European kingdoms and fiefdoms with fifteen new states that would be sovereign but that would also cooperate in a European league of nations. A European Senate would be created, with sixty-six members serving three-year terms, and it would be responsible for making law, settling disputes, preserving peace, and managing the league's army and navy.[16]

But de Sully's plan came to nothing and the prospects for a common European sense of identity were undermined by a new phenomenon that would once again redraw the map of Europe: the growing powers and authority of the state. Its new role was encouraged by the end of the large-scale migrations which had contributed so much to the constantly changing identity of Europeans during the early Middle Ages. With Europeans now settling down, social structures became more regularized, the benefits of education spread, technology was standardized, and political relationships changed. The result was a strengthening of political authority and the replacement of the patchwork quilt of lands tied to monarchs, aristocrats, and the church with a more regularized—but still often politically divided—network of states.

States, science, and empires

The debate over when and how states emerged is long and contentious, and this is not the place to add to it. Suffice it to say that there is general agreement on two points: that the modern state system was born in Europe, and that confirmation of its permanence can be dated to the 1648 Peace of

Westphalia, which brought to an end decades of war, confirmed many territorial adjustments, marked the beginning of the end of the absolutist era of European government, and gave a new prominence to the idea of state sovereignty. Prior to the growth of states, argues van Creveld, there existed government but not states, and a wide variety of political communities that he classifies into tribes, city states, and empires.[17] But this rather overlooks the history of city states in Greece, and of the absolute monarchies of the Middle Ages, which functioned much like states; Tilly has argued that there were as many as 500 states in existence in Europe in 1500.[18] These were not states as we know them today, however, and it is important to appreciate that states had little impact on the mass of the European population prior to the late eighteenth century, at which point they began to occupy and even create the 'national space' of today's European states.[19]

The political complexities that characterized the feudal era now took on new patterns as three sets of forces shaped the outline of modern states: the struggle for power in Europe between the church and the monarchs, the demands by key social groups that they be involved in making decisions, and the consequences of the competing forces of religious and secular ideas. The result was that the influence of the church and of organized religion declined, and the informal, often arbitrary, and occasionally violent means by which decisions were made and implemented by monarchs and aristocrats began slowly to be replaced by the apparatus of the modern state as we know it today: elected representatives, permanent bureaucracies, structured legal systems tied to courts and the police, taxes, standing armies, and a formalized system of authority built on territory, independence, and legitimacy.

While much of the rest of the world was organized into empires, argues Jones, Europe 'became a single system of states in which change in one cell affected the others'. There had been no real empires in Europe since the end of the Roman era, and when the new European empires eventually came, they would be in the form of the overseas possessions of Europe's great powers.[20] The modern state began to take form as political and economic control was centralized in the hands of Europe's most enduring dynasties, including the Bourbons in France, the Tudors in England, and the Habsburgs in Spain. Political boundaries achieved new clarity, and the fragmentation of the feudal era was replaced with a more definite delineation of control, expressed through the creation of systems of taxation, the establishment of standing armies, and the necessity for diplomatic representation. But still there was no sense of Europe; the residents of Europe still associated themselves with whichever authority happened most obviously to impact their lives, the only difference being that where once it might have been the church, or an aristocrat, or a monarch, it was now becoming the state.

Complications were created, however, by a mismatch between states and nations, and by peoples speaking different languages and having different religious affiliations coming under the jurisdiction of the same territorial authorities, or being divided between two or more such authorities. Illustrating the new pressures, a revolt broke out in 1568 in the Seventeen Provinces of the Low Countries against the rule of the Spanish, sparking what would become the Eighty Years' War. During this conflict, the Dutch first asserted their independence and then fought for recognition of the independence of the United Provinces. In 1618, a struggle between German Catholics and Protestants fed into ongoing rivalry between the Habsburgs and the Bourbons to spark the Thirty Years' War, until then one of the most destructive conflicts yet among Europeans.

Peace treaties signed in Osnabrück and Münster in May and October 1648—and known together as the Peace of Westphalia—brought an end to both wars. The Peace recognized the rights of princes to determine the religion of their own states; removed barriers to trade and commerce; gave *de jure* confirmation to the independence from the Holy Roman Empire of the Netherlands, Switzerland, and the northern Italian states; and made adjustments to the boundaries of Sweden, France, and the German states. In short, it created a new political order in which the lines of authority were reordered, such that after 1648 the critical dynamic in the regional politics of Europe was to be relations among states. They still fought and competed with one another, it is true, but there were now fewer and more consistently regulated protagonists in the struggle, and Voltaire was moved to describe Europe as a 'kind of great republic divided into several states ... [united by] the same principle of public law and politics, unknown in other parts of the world'.[21] Politics also became more secular in character, and there was a new emphasis on the need to maintain a balance of power among states.

For Jones, enough states were created of similar strength 'to resist the logical conclusion of the process of conquest and amalgamation: a single unified European state'.[22] And yet there were still those idealists who felt that peace and prosperity could best be achieved in Europe through cooperation and the creation of a political or economic league. In 1693, against the background of the Nine Years' War, during which the Grand Alliance attempted to restrict French political ambitions, William Penn published his *Essay Towards the Present and Future Peace of Europe* in which he proposed the creation of a European diet or parliament that could be used for dispute resolution, with states given votes in proportion to their economic power (Germany would have twelve, France ten, England six, and so on) and decisions being reached on the basis of a three-quarters majority vote.[23]

In 1717, the Abbé de Saint-Pierre published his *Project for Settling an Everlasting Peace in Europe*, in which he argued for free trade and proposed the creation of a European Senate. Meanwhile, Jean-Jacques Rousseau wrote in favour of a European federation, and Jeremy Bentham, in *A Plan for an Universal and Perpetual Peace* (published in 1789), wrote of the need to address the tensions between Britain and France, the key step in the direction of which should be the abandonment of foreign dependencies. But the intellectual basis for the development of democratic peace theory that would follow, and for the changes still taking place in Europe today, was provided by Immanuel Kant and his *Thoughts on Perpetual Peace*, published in 1795.

Kant argued that it was the duty of mankind to end violence and enter into a universal cosmopolitan peace.[24] He outlined the conditions he considered necessary, including the abolition of standing armies, an agreement that states would not interfere with the constitutions or government of other states, the employment during war of methods and actions that would not undermine confidence in the subsequent peace, the absence of peace treaties that contained the tacit prospect of future war, and a system of national laws founded upon a federation of free states. Although Kant (like Bentham) was not restricting himself to Europe, his suggestions clearly had their most immediate application in Europe, then unsettled by the fallout from the French Revolution and the building pressures that would lead to the Napoleonic wars of 1803–15. The notion of cosmopolitanism is today key to understanding Europeanist views about relations between individuals and authority—see Chapter 3 for more discussion.

Kant's ideas also happened to represent the emerging thinking of the Enlightenment, which Kant himself described as 'man's release from his self-incurred tutelage', by which he meant 'the incapacity to use one's own understanding without the guidance of another'. In contrast to the principles of acknowledging religious authority and absolute political power that had prevailed during the Middle Ages, intellectuals now argued that reason—not religion—should be the primary source of authority in political and social life. Where there had once been a sense of Christian community, now there was more a sense of a European community. Demands were made for individual rights and liberties, and for recognition of the importance of self-government, natural law, and common sense, marking a departure from aristocracy and the ties between religion and government. At the same time, the term *civilization* entered the French and English languages, describing the Enlightenment belief in progress. The expression 'European civilization' was soon used for the first time to suggest that Europe was the embodiment of the highest stage of progress, and Christendom was replaced by civilization as a synonym for Europe.[25] Meanwhile, atheism and agnosticism spread, and religion continued to be battered during the nineteenth century by the age of scientific discovery.

Following the Black Death of the fourteenth century, the population of Europe began its steady growth, the result of improved nourishment and an increase in the birth rate. The agricultural revolution introduced new crops and advanced agricultural practices, and improved the productivity of land. Urban populations expanded, transportation systems improved, labour was made available for different kinds of work, there was a growth of cottage industries, and overseas trade encouraged production and consumption. The scene was now set for the industrial revolution, which was born in Europe thanks to a fortuitous combination of factors: political stability that reduced risk, encouraged investment, and sustained trade; a higher level of personal wealth and education than was found elsewhere in the world; moderate rates of population growth; and technological advances that led to breakthroughs in the textile and iron industries. The rise of cities and the slow increase of class mobility now changed political expectations and relationships.

As the authority of European states achieved more permanence, several of those states—notably Britain, France, Spain, Portugal, and the Netherlands—embarked upon the construction of overseas empires. Where Europe had once had to defend itself against foreign encroachment, it now became the encroacher, the struggle for control at home translating into a struggle for control overseas. Initially, the primary motives were economic and social, but as time went on it became a matter of asserting political power and of keeping up with other states; the era of new imperialism, or 'empire for empire's sake', dawned in the nineteenth century, and was reflected in the 'great game' played out between Britain and Russia in central Asia, and in the scramble for Africa (with an attempt made to divide the spoils at the Congress of Berlin in 1884–5). Imperial conquest also allowed Europe to export its values, hence Pagden concludes that European expansion and imperialism 'were widely conceived in terms of the triumph . . . of one political system, belief, and (crucially) one vision of the world over all others'.[26]

Colonies had been won and lost before 1800, but it was the growth of European global power during the nineteenth century that altered Europe's perception of itself and of its place in the world. Where once Europeans had squabbled among themselves, or worried about encroachments from outside, they were now exporting their views to the rest of the world, and coming to dominate and shape that world. The extent of expanding European influence is reflected in four compelling sets of data:[27]

- Between 1800 and 1914, European settlement or colonial control expanded from 35 per cent of the land area of the earth to 84 per cent.
- Between 1800 and 1900, the European share of world manufacturing output grew from just over 28 per cent to 62 per cent (with Britain and Germany alone accounting for half the European total).
- Between 1820 and 1900, the European share of global gross domestic product grew from 49 per cent to nearly 90 per cent.
- Between 1816 and 1880 the size of the militaries of Britain, France, Germany, and the Habsburg Empire grew from 737,000 to nearly 1.5 million personnel (compared to a growth of the US military from 16,000 to 36,000).

The rise of Europe from relative backwardness to global domination has been described by Jones as the European miracle. Europe, he argues, was 'a minor region that generated economic growth when other, larger societies did not', helped by a combination of an environment that was conducive to regional specialization, political developments that checked the arbitrary use of power, and competition among multiple political units.[28] Thanks to this confluence of circumstances, Europe by the end of the nineteenth century stood astride the globe in its political, economic, military, and social reach. Russia and the United States were far bigger and more richly endowed in land, people, and resources than any single European state, but it was the great European powers—primarily Britain, France, and Germany—that now ensured the spread of European ideas and priorities to most of the rest of the world, whether China, India, the Middle East, or Africa. The era of European dominance was accompanied by European migration overseas, the bulk of those leaving destined for the United States, but many others with their sights set on Canada, Australia, New Zealand, and Brazil. But while Europe was both powerful and assertive, it was still far from united. Imperialism had the effect of diverting Europeans from thinking about their common values, the prospects for which were further undermined during the nineteenth century by the rise of another divisive home-grown force: nationalism.[29]

The rise of nationalism

The term *nation* is hard to pin down, Seton-Watson concluding that it defies 'scientific definition' in spite of the fact that nations clearly exist.[30] For present purposes, a nation is defined as a group of people who have common characteristics that encourage them to identify with each other, to sustain that identity, and to differentiate themselves from other groups. These characteristics are sometimes real, sometimes imagined, and may include language, ancestry, history, culture, territory, religion, symbols, and/or myths. The key is identity, and the importance of the willingness of all members of the group to empathize with the traditions and interests of the group. In turn, identification means an association and comfort with, and support for, the values and norms of the group. These feelings can in turn evolve into nationalism, which—suggests Breuilly—has three core elements: the existence of a nation with an explicit and peculiar character, a belief that national interests and values take priority over all others, and the accumulation of as much independence as possible for the nation.[31] Nationalism is a belief that the shared qualities of the nation are valuable and worth preserving, that one's nation should be differentiated from others and may be superior to others, and that the national interest can and should be promoted and protected from others, even if it leads to controlling the movement of non-nationals, promoting national economic interests, expanding territory, or attacking others in order to protect the home nation.

For Anderson, however, a nation is no more than an imagined political community, because while its members will never know or meet most of their fellow-members, 'in the minds of each lives the image of their communion'.[32] The nineteenth-century French philosopher Ernest Renan described a nation as 'a soul, a spiritual principle' made up of the past in the form of a legacy of memories, and of the present in the form of a willingness by individuals to live together and to continue to value their heritage, which is seen as the product of a long history of sacrifice that must be remembered.[33] He also argued that memories were ephemeral, that just as they began so they would come to an end, and that in the European case they would 'probably' be replaced at some point by a European confederation.[34] For the Czech philosopher Ernest Gellner, 'nationalism is not the awakening of nations to self-consciousness: it invents nations where they do not exist'.[35] National identity is clearly based heavily on myth, and on a selective assessment and retelling of history. In short, then, nation and nationalism are both constructs that exist more in the human mind than in reality, which suggests that their health and well-being is a matter of choice.

In spite of the many questions that surround the meaning of nation and nationalism, and the difficulties involved in identifying the features of national culture, both played a critical role in defining the dynamics and qualities of political control and of understanding 'the other' in Europe from the early nineteenth century through to the end of the Second World War. The nation became the principal source of political legitimacy in Europe,[36] and nationalism became the glue that governments used to extend and define their power. But nationalism took different forms, and had occasionally different roots and purposes. In some cases it was defined by territory and ethnicity, and was used to encourage a common sense of identity in a culturally diverse environment, or to promote the interests of dominant ethnic groups. In other cases it was defined by purpose, hence the three-way distinction made by Breuilly:

- Nationalism aimed at unification, prime among the cases being those of Italy and Germany in the nineteenth century.
- Radical nationalism used by opposition forces intent on moving state and society in a particular direction, as in the case of fascist movements in Germany, Italy, and Spain between the two world wars.
- Separatist nationalism of the kind found among many nineteenth-century independence movements, or among separatists more recently in Britain, Spain, Belgium, and the Balkans.[37]

Nationalism can also be defined by goals, and thus we can make a distinction between defensive nationalism, which is primarily cultural and works to protect the heritage and identity of national groups, and assertive nationalism, which is primarily political and is based on the idea of superiority over others and of asserting the interests of dominant nations over subject nations or those defined as posing a threat. To this list can be added the kind of everyday, endemic 'banal nationalism' described by Billig, which does not threaten the state through demands for separation, but is instead limited to the sense of belonging generated by flags, sporting events, national anthems, popular expressions, and the sense of community generated by the mass media.[38]

The roots of European nationalism can be found in the Enlightenment rejection of divine law—by which God's authority underpinned the political roles of monarchs and the church—and its support of natural law, where sovereignty lay with the people. The spark for the end of the old political order in Europe, and for a reassessment of the manner in which societies should be organized politically, was the French Revolution, which relates to the rise of the nation in much the same way as the Peace of Westphalia relates to the rise of the state. Intellectuals across Europe had questioned the monarchical order, and encouraged instead the collective ideas of national self-determination, the rights of man, and the promotion of equality and liberty, ideas that were now put into practice by French revolutionaries. They feared a reaction from other European states, while also being enthused about the idea of spreading their revolutionary ideas to those states: thus revolutionary ideas inevitably evolved into nationalist ideas.

The French revolutionary wars saw these views given violent expression, but it was assertive French nationalism that was at the heart of these wars, and it was Napoleon's attempts to build a European empire that—by encouraging resentment at French influence in Europe—generated a defensive nationalist response in Germany, Italy, and the Netherlands, and even to some extent in Britain. Dunkerley et al. argue that 'for populations that resented being tied to others by virtue of sharing the same territory, nationalism became—and remains—a potent ideology'.[39] It continues to help explain some of the scepticism and resistance that still attaches today to the idea of European unity, challenged most often by those who hold most strongly to the myth of the nation.

Much like the Peace of Westphalia, the 1815 Congress of Vienna brought to a close an extended period of war and further rearranged the boundaries of states, including those of Russia, Prussia, the Netherlands, Austria, and Bavaria. Although it laid the foundations for a general peace in Europe that would last almost a century, the Congress also represented a triumph for traditional monarchies, and promoted a conservative order that emphasized structure, tradition, obedience, and a resistance to revolutionary ideas and demands for civil liberties. But this conservatism ran counter to the new dynamism of European society, now undergoing rapid economic, social, and technological change. Seeking some stability against a background of social turmoil and challenges to traditional religious values, many Europeans sought refuge in national identity. Hegel argued that against the background of a decline in monarchical power, it was to national identity that Europeans should turn as an alternative. The ideal was the creation of nation-states, where nations governed themselves and the boundaries of states and nations coincided. For Jones, the nation-state 'is a purely European form which has been exported to parts of the world that had hitherto known only tribalism'.[40] From the late eighteenth century, it became—argue Dunkerley et al.—'*the* model for organizing political space in Europe'.[41]

Nationalism was born as a cultural movement, with an emphasis on history and the promotion of national languages in the face of the elite domination of French and Latin. But it then became political in reaction to the rise of the French threat after the revolution, and evolved into liberation movements on the back of expanding resentment at foreign rule. This was no assertive nationalism, however, but espoused the need for all Europeans to achieve nationhood and to live peacefully in a Europe of free peoples. In Belgium, Greece, Hungary, Ireland, and Italy, nationalism came to be seen as a means of encouraging resistance in common cause against foreign rule, and was expressed in the independence of Greece from Ottoman rule in 1832 and then of Belgium from Dutch rule in 1839.

Nation and nationalism meant little to peasants or workers lacking either education or personal mobility; both concepts were instead championed by the urban middle class, and resisted in turn by conservatives who saw them as threats to the loyalty previously directed at monarchs and the church.[42] Where local and regional identity had once prevailed, the revolutions of 1848 represented the expression of national identity through much of central continental Europe; led to demands for independence in Germany, Hungary, Italy, and Poland; and sparked worried conjecture about the prospects for nationalist uprisings elsewhere. Where religion and states had once been the major sources and causes of division and conflict in Europe (as well as the prime targets of loyalty), they had—by the mid-nineteenth century—been joined and even to a large extent supplanted by nationalism.

At least two different strands of nationalism were now at work. In the cases of Italy and Germany, the primary motive—as we have seen—was unification and the attempt to overcome political and philosophical divisions in the interests of building a nation-state. This is what Anderson describes as 'official nationalism',[43] which emerged in response to popular nationalism. It resulted in the creation of two powerful new nation-states whose presence fundamentally altered the nature of inter-state relations within Europe. Elsewhere, meanwhile, the primary motive behind nationalism—as we have also seen—was separation; hence in the Austrian empire there were demands for self-rule from the Magyars and the Czechs, while the Ottoman Empire saw rising nationalist demands from Bulgarians, Greeks, Romanians, and Serbs.[44] The Hungarian independence movement dated back to the early eighteenth century, and its demands had spilled over into war in 1848–9, Bulgarian autonomy and Romanian independence were both recognized in 1878 (but independence would not come for Bulgaria until 1908), and the creation of Czechoslovakia in 1918 was the culmination of a long struggle by the Czechs and the Slovaks against the Habsburgs.

States now actively exploited nationalism both to exert greater control and to create a sense of 'us versus them'. National languages were promoted, and minority languages suppressed where necessary; work proceeded on the standardization of regulations, laws, educational systems, and transport networks; symbols such as flags and anthems were championed as a means of encouraging identification with the state; and propaganda cultivated a fear of threats from neighbours (a myth that is still reflected today in the opinions often held by the British and the French about each other, or in the residual nervousness that many still feel about the Germans). Dunkerley et al. argue that national unity was often an illusion, overlooking as it did the social divisions and conflict that troubled many European states. But loyalties to the state and the nation were strong enough to ensure that when a new European war eventually broke out in 1914, xenophobia and national rivalry could be exploited to generate strong feelings of national identity, and millions of men would be willing to fight for their country.[45]

The Franco-Prussian war of 1870–1 ended the continental dominance of France, and opened a new nationalist rivalry that swamped idealistic notions of a belief in Europe. 'Whoever speaks of Europe is wrong', declared Otto von Bismarck; 'it is a geographical expression'. For Bismarck, German unification took place in the primary interests of the German people, and certainly it had little support anywhere else in the region. The decades leading up to the First World War are often seen as a golden age for Europe, with a general prevalence of peace and prosperity, the spread of education, rapid economic and social change, urbanization, rising wages, scientific advances, an expanding middle class, and a rising belief in European civilizational supremacy. But this was also the era in which nationalism took its firmest grip on European imaginations; Baycroft describes the period between 1870 and 1914 as 'nationalism's popular phase'.[46] In spite of the peace that prevailed after 1871, Bond sees the era as one characterized by 'the formation of ominous alliances, desperate arms races and increasing expectation of an eventual Armageddon'.[47]

Nationalism and imperialism overlapped to create a volatile cocktail, the latter being an extension of the former and being used to express the superiority of the nations engaged in building empires. Britain was an exception to the general rule, because much of its empire pre-dated the era of nationalism, and had been built mainly for economic and commercial reasons. This did not discourage attempts in Britain at the end of the nineteenth century, however, to associate the empire with national identity, national success, and superiority, nor to continue expanding the reach of the empire. But where Britain had been largely untainted by national humiliation (or else had adeptly turned defeat into glory, as in the case of the charge of the Light Brigade during the Crimean War, or the murder of Gordon at Khartoum in 1885), the French and the Germans built empires mainly in order to affirm themselves and to compensate for losses, defeats, or weakness. For the French it was a question of rebuilding confidence after their defeat in the Franco-Prussian war, and also of promoting French language and civilization. For the Germans, meanwhile, it was a question of solidifying political power at home by further demonstrating the glory of the German nation.[48]

The volatile cocktail of national competition, secret deals, state interests, and unresolved disputes that had been mixed in Europe in the closing decades of the nineteenth century eventually spilled over into the Great War, the immediate spark for which was nationalism: the assassination of Archduke Franz Ferdinand, heir to the Austro-Hungarian throne, by a member of Young Bosnia, a group seeking the independence of the South Slavs from Austria-Hungary. The war began as what has been described as 'a traditional European war',[49] but is better understood as the first phase of a European civil war whose articles of dispute were not finally resolved until 1945. It dealt a heavy blow to European self-confidence, and two events in 1917—the entry into the war of the United States and the revolution that same year in Russia—can now be seen as early signs that the balance of world power was about to shift outside Europe.

The illusion of peace

The brutality of the Great War created an atmosphere in which the 'victors' sought revenge and reparations over the 'losers', paving the way for arrangements in which further losses were—we now know—all but guaranteed. The terms of the 1919 Treaty of Versailles emphasized the core principle of national self-determination, and continued to reflect concerns about the balance of power. It is significant that the three great continental European dynasties—the Habsburgs, the Hohenzollerns, and the Romanovs—were now gone (as was the Ottoman Empire), and Europe had emerged as a region of nation-states.[50] Eight of Woodrow Wilson's

Fourteen Points focused on territorial adjustments, so once again the map of Europe was redrawn, with the demise of Austria-Hungary; changes to the borders of Belgium, Bulgaria, Denmark, France, Germany, Romania, and Russia; and the addition of Austria, Czechoslovakia, Estonia, Hungary, Latvia, Lithuania, Poland, and Yugoslavia as independent political entities.

Opinion is divided on how harmful the treaty was to Germany. For the British diplomat Harold Nicolson, the atmosphere and passions aroused by war meant that 'it would have been impossible even for supermen to devise a peace of moderation and righteousness'. The result, he lamented, was that instead of the creation of a new order, 'the new order had merely fouled the old'.[51] While most assessments argue that Versailles imposed crippling economic burdens and created a level of resentment that fed in to the rise of Hitler, some have argued that Germany at least emerged in one piece rather than being occupied or broken up, and others have suggested that the terms were more lenient than those that Germany would have imposed on the Allies if it had won the war.[52]

But the inter-war years were little more than a truce in the fighting, and the peace created by Versailles was, as Marks has put it, illusory.[53] There was no firm foundation for that peace, she argues, because three of the four strongest continental powers (Germany, Italy, and Russia) were deeply dissatisfied with the status quo, and viewed the small nations on their borders as 'tempting morsels to be devoured at the first opportunity'. Europeans and their leaders became aware that the post-war structure lacked solid foundations and provided little security, and the era was marked by the collapse of democracy in many states, by political and social instability, by precarious economic prosperity, by the disintegration of the League of Nations, by the illusion that Hitler could be tamed and that he meant what he said, and by the problem that 'the political fragmentation inherent in the post-war peace settlement was either too great or not great enough', and that there was no economic integration of the kind that might have compensated for the political fragmentation. Above all, there was an eruption of political and ethnic nationalism. This left behind, concludes Marks, a host of small and relatively weak states created partly out of defunct empires, generating a potentially explosive situation.

The decline of Europe's global role had also set in. Entering the Great War, the great world powers had all been European, but in the aftermath of the conflict they found themselves saddled with large debts, unsettled economies, social change, and unresolved political disputes. It was also beginning to be clear that colonialism could be neither maintained nor justified indefinitely; Britain in particular was feeling the earliest pressures for change from India, Egypt, and some of its African colonies. Japan and the United States had meanwhile both emerged from the war as great powers, and while Russia was still weakened by severe domestic problems, its revolutionary model was attractive to many. The European order had risen, fallen, and been reformulated repeatedly over the centuries, but at no time had it experienced such overwhelming pressures as those generated by the fallout from the Great War. It took another war to finish the job and to finally convince Europeans of the need to resolve the disputes that had for so long divided them, but the first great step in changing Europe's understanding of its place in the world—and of the role played by states and nations in Europe's definition of itself—had been taken in 1914–18.

In spite of the forces working against them, or perhaps because of those forces, which they might have regarded as all the more justification for the merits of cooperation, Europe's idealists continued to lobby for a rejection of national identity and its replacement by a broader regional consciousness. As so often before, their thinking was prompted by a desire to remove the causes of conflict, but where their predecessors had been working in a vacuum of public interest, the horrors of the Great War now created a wider audience that better understood the dangers of nationalism and was more receptive to the idea of European cooperation. Although the call to arms in 1914 was based on fighting for the preservation of national interests, the sacrifices can now be seen as having been made in the interests of building a new European consciousness.

The creation of the League of Nations seemed to offer some hope; it ultimately failed in its core objectives because none of its members was willing to commit themselves to the concept of collective security, but it was the first such international organization of its kind, and thus at least provided a model for what might be possible. But its failure may also have created more pessimism for the prospects of achieving peace through the work of international organizations. Whatever the leaders of the great powers were thinking, the leaders of smaller states that were tired of being caught up in big power rivalry decided to take the first practical steps towards economic cooperation. Thus, Belgium and Luxembourg created a limited economic union in 1922, under which economic barriers were removed and the exchange rates of their two currencies were fixed relative to each other. In September 1930, the governments of the Netherlands, Denmark, Norway, and Sweden agreed upon the Dutch–Scandinavian Economic Pact, designed to coordinate tariff policies and promote trade. Three months later, the four Pact members and the Belgium–Luxembourg Economic Union promised not to raise internal tariffs without first notifying and consulting each other. These latter developments were encouraged more by the need to take action in the face of the Great Depression than to promote European cooperation for its own sake, but they represented a key departure from earlier practice.

Looking at the bigger picture, one of the most convinced champions of European unity was Richard Coudenhove-Kalergi, who in 1922 co-founded—with Archduke Otto von Habsburg—the Pan-European Union, an organization designed to help reverse the internal decline of Europe. Europe's post-war problems had convinced him that the only workable guarantee of peace was political union, and he outlined his ideas in his manifesto *Paneuropa*, published in 1923. His arguments were based on the belief that Europe was a natural entity that could become a significant global force, and on the fear that unless substantial changes were made to the way it was organized politically, it might well descend once again into nationalistic conflict.[54] The solution he proposed was a new emphasis on large-scale cooperation, but changes in Europe could not happen in isolation from those in the rest of the world, and Coudenhove-Kalergi felt that the best hope for world peace lay in the creation of five 'global power fields', including Paneuropa. This would consist of continental Europe and its colonies, but would exclude Britain, which he felt was powerful enough (along with Australia, Canada, India, and its colonies) to be its own power field.

While the idea of Paneuropa failed to generate a mass following, it drew the attention of several contemporary or future political leaders, including Georges Pompidou, Thomas Masaryk, Konrad Adenauer, Winston Churchill, and two French prime ministers, Edouard Herriot and Aristide Briand. Both Herriot and Briand saw economic cooperation as lying at the heart of prospects for European cooperation, and Herriot—disagreeing with the prevailing view in France that European cooperation was an impossible dream, and that the best hope for peace lay in French strength and German weakness[55]—was moved to call in 1924 for the creation of a United States of Europe, to grow out of the post-war cooperation promoted by the League of Nations. For his part, Briand called for a European confederation working within the League of Nations, and in May 1930 distributed a memorandum to governments outlining his ideas.[56] In it he wrote of the need for 'a permanent regime of solidarity based on international agreements for the rational organization of Europe'. He used such terms as 'common market' and 'European Union', and listed specific policy needs, such as the development of trans-European transport networks, and anticipated what would later become the regional and social policies of the EU. But all such idealistic notions were now swept aside by the gathering influence of fascism, which replaced the nineteenth-century idea of national self-determination with a newly aggressive assertion of German national interests.

While acknowledging that the nation was a myth, Mussolini—whose Fascists came to power in 1922—argued that it could be converted into a spirit or a passion around which Italians could unite. He used the symbols of ancient Rome, arguing that the spirit of Italy's greatness could be translated into making Italy a quantifiable force. In Spain, Franco's coup d'état in 1936 brought to power a nationalist government, but it was in Germany where nationalism was most clearly translated into aggression. On the basis of Germany's fall from greatness, and its considerable social and economic problems, Hitler was able to make the case for righting the wrongs of Versailles, for basing Germany's regeneration on the unity of the German people, and for creating a German 'living space'. Hitler was just the most vocal exponent of nationalism, but nationalist ideas had become popular in most European states, and when war finally broke out in 1939 it was to be fundamentally a conflict among nations, and yet another attempt by a dominant actor to expand control over as much of the continent as possible. The Third Reich would eventually spread to include Austria, Bohemia, Alsace-Lorraine, and most of Poland, and to occupy much of the rest of continental Europe.

The rise of Hitler was the inevitable outcome of a process of historical evolution that had seen power within Europe redistributed on the basis of religious priorities, territorial aggrandisement, aristocratic deal-making, self-determination, nationalism, and great power conflict—in short, on the basis of almost anything except the idea that there might exist a broader European interest or identity, or a set of norms and values that might unite Europeans rather than divide them. Initially, Europeans were defined by who they were not, rather than by who they were, and it was external pressures that formed the core of what little sense of association existed. Later, Europeans shared a common religion, but it became a source of divisions, and allegiance to lords and monarchs was the key calculation in the lives of ordinary peasants. With the Enlightenment, the French Revolution, and the industrial revolution, identity and association were reordered, and the earliest signs emerged of what might be defined as Europeanist values. But Europeans were to be diverted by the division of power among states, and then the power of states was challenged by nationalism. The latter was born as a cultural movement, and one that proposed self-determination but only in a way that recognized differences rather than using those differences to build aggressive or competitive postures. Nationalism later became politically based, and the end result was two European civil wars that destroyed the old order and paved the way for the most recent, and perhaps final, reordering of European affairs: the construction of a united Europe.

2

The Redefinition of Europe

Prior to the Second World War, the great European powers were dominant players on the global stage, their influence based primarily on the size and reach of their militaries.[1] The United States had begun its ascent to power in the late nineteenth century but was still only a supporting actor; its economy had overtaken that of Britain's by the Second World War, but domestic issues still mattered most to American leaders, and as late as 1939 the US military ranked only twentieth in the world in size, smaller even than that of the Netherlands.[2] China, meanwhile, was distracted by seismic internal convulsions, Japan was no more than a regional power, and India remained part of the British Empire. Europe's economies, empires, armies, and corporations were the world's largest, its political influence was global in scale, and its scientific and technological advantages were second to none. But the continent suffered a single, critical vulnerability: the nationalism that had already sparked repeated conflicts and that had culminated now in two European civil wars that evolved into global wars.

The end of the Second World War left Europe contemplating three hard new realities. First, developments in technology meant that the human and physical costs of waging war had risen dramatically. Conventional conflict could no longer be contained or localized, the advent of nuclear weapons raising the prospect of destruction at levels far beyond anything previously known. Second, the continent was divided into two hostile ideological camps, posing the most serious challenge yet to the concept of Europe. There had been divisions before the war, but their sources had always been internal; now the divisions had been imposed from outside, and the European states found themselves subject either to American or to Soviet hegemony. Finally, Europe was distracted by the need to rebuild economies, political systems, social relations, and infrastructure, while at the same time seeking protection from the threats posed by poverty, economic insecurity, and cold war division. Churchill expressed it most cogently when he reflected on the 'tragedy of Europe', and on the sight of a continent that had been the fountain of Christianity and of great achievements in culture, the arts, philosophy, and science, but that was now populated by 'a vast quivering mass of tormented, hungry, care-worn and bewildered human beings [gaping] at the ruins of their cities and their homes, and [scanning] the dark horizons for the approach of some new peril, tyranny or terror'.[3]

It was clear to many that western Europe had no choice but to rise above narrow state interests and to adopt a more inclusive view of the needs of the region and of its place in the international system. As the need for cooperation became clearer, western European leaders took the first steps along the path of political and economic integration that would lead to national and state identity being joined and to some extent superseded by a pan-European identity. Prior to the Second World War, identification with the nation or state had suffocated any prospects of identification with Europe. States were competing too much with each other to allow them to give much thought to pan-regional cooperation, there was little sense of a shared history and culture, and the great European powers were at odds with each other not only over regional influence but also in their management of global empires and in their attempts to win relative economic advantage. Now those great powers found themselves marginalized by the new assertion of American and Soviet global influence, and trapped within a dangerous web of economic and security threats. The sources of these threats were both internal and external, and the struggle to respond led to yet another restructuring of the old order in Europe. This in turn was to create an environment more conducive to the discovery of the meaning of Europeanism. Where Europeans had long defined their interests in national or state terms, they were now to become more conscious of their shared values, purposes, and goals.

Internal incentives: peace and prosperity

There were two overarching internal incentives for regional cooperation in Europe. The most important was the search for a lasting peace, which in turn meant addressing the historical causes of conflict. Violence, argues Heffernan, 'is integral to the European collective experience'. Even though Europe's wars are often still recalled by national governments and commemorated in national terms, they were often waged and justified in European terms.[4] 'The safety of the world', warned Winston Churchill in his March 1946 iron curtain speech, 'requires a new unity in Europe, from which no nation should be permanently outcast. It is from the quarrels of the strong parent races in Europe that the world wars we have witnessed, or which occurred in former times, have sprung'.[5]

Prime among the most recent causes of war were nationalism and struggles for the balance of European power, and more particularly the role in that struggle of Germany, which had been at the heart of three major conflicts in seventy years: the Franco-Prussian war of 1870–1, the First World War, and the Second World War. The last of these had dealt the latest and most severe blow to the political order in Europe, with relations among the European states reordered once again, and Europe's place in the world changed out of all recognition. Many now argued that peace in Europe was impossible unless Germany could be contained, reintegrated back into Europe in such a way as to remove any threat it might pose to European security, and its power diverted from destructive to constructive ends. In contrast to the race for revenge that dictated the terms of Versailles in 1919, the prevailing view now was that Germany had to be allowed to rebuild its economic base and its political system but in ways that were productive and cooperative rather than threatening; France was particularly eager to make sure this happened.[6]

The key to achieving this goal, argued Jean Monnet, was economic integration. There could be no peace in Europe, he argued, if states were to re-establish themselves 'on the basis of national sovereignty with all that this implies by way of prestige politics and economic protectionism'. European states should instead create a federation that would blend them into 'a single economic entity'.[7] War had discredited the state system, and nowhere more so than in the views of the wartime Resistance. This had brought together participants from multiple different states and varying ideological, political, economic, and social backgrounds, who idealistically believed that their differences could be set aside, that nationalism could be overcome, that state boundaries could be transcended, and that Europe could unite. However, economic integration demanded political support, which demanded in turn that Britain—leader of the fight against Nazism and still the dominating power in western Europe after the war—should provide leadership. But the new Atlee government was not interested, and western European governments instead became resigned to a new era of American leadership, while the east retreated into the shadows of Soviet domination.

But the cause of peace through unity was never forgotten, and as western European states built ties of political and economic cooperation, and as the expansive pre-war model of nationalism was replaced by a more benign reassertion of historical identities, peace prevailed. The long-term results were to be remarkable. In his speech accepting the Nobel peace prize in 1998, Northern Irish politician John Hume was to conclude that the European Union had become 'the best example in the history of the world of conflict resolution'.[8] The dynamic at work was explained by Coppeiters et al.: Europeanization can trigger critical political, security, economic, and societal developments in such a way as to positively change the interests of parties to a conflict, transforming notions of statehood and sovereignty, encouraging respect for the rule of law, reducing corruption, bringing civility to business and political relations, and all without impeding national self-determination.[9] Even eurosceptics have little choice but to acknowledge the role of integration in ending conflict in Europe.

If peace was the first priority of European regional cooperation, then prosperity was the second. There was no denying the urgent need for economic reconstruction: an estimated 36–40 million people had died during the war in Europe, which had left behind broad swathes of devastation. Cities lay in ruins, agricultural production was halved, infrastructure had been destroyed, and communications were disrupted. Denmark, France, and the Benelux countries had suffered heavily under occupation; Britain's national wealth was cut by 75 per cent and its exports by two-thirds; Germany and Italy were under Allied occupation, their economies devastated.[10] In all of Europe, only the neutral countries were relatively undamaged or unchanged.

Western Europe had moved quickly to begin the process of economic recovery, and by 1948 had almost reached the pre-war levels of industrial and agricultural production and of investment.[11] But there was a pressing balance of payments problem, and concerns about how quickly and widely the benefits of reconstruction would be felt. American leadership of the international economic system had been established at Bretton Woods in 1944, when a formula determined mainly by American preferences had been agreed: expanded trade; non-discrimination; convertible currencies; and stable rates of exchange built on the foundations of the dollar as the new international reserve currency and underpinned by the creation of the General Agreement on Tariffs and Trade (GATT), the International Monetary Fund (IMF), and the World Bank. So it was to the United States that Europe inevitably looked for assistance with reconstruction; the United States had already provided more than $10 billion in loans and aid, but by 1947—prompted by the slow pace of economic reconstruction and a political shift to the left—it was decided that something more ambitious and strategic was needed.[12] The response was the Marshall Plan, announced in June 1947, and under which an additional $13 billion in aid was made available to western Europe between 1948 and 1952.[13]

Opinion is divided on the long-term effects of the Marshall Plan investment, one school arguing its importance (particularly in providing investment and technical assistance); another downplaying its importance and arguing that recovery was already well under way by 1948; and a third arguing that its real value lay in altering the environment in which economic policy was made, encouraging support for market forces over support for government intervention.[14] But on one conclusion there is a high level of agreement: in addition to the funds spent and the political symbolism of the gesture made, we must appreciate the effects of the manner in which decisions were made about how the funds were to be dispersed. In the interests of achieving order and structure, the Organization for European Economic Cooperation (OEEC) was created in April 1948 at US insistence, with representatives from the sixteen states participating.

The goals of the OEEC included the reduction of restrictions on trade and payments, the reduction of tariffs and other barriers to trade, and an examination of the prospects for a free trade area or customs union among its members.[15] It was clearly founded, Milward notes, 'as the first stage in the attempt to build a United States of Europe',[16] and while it fell short of being a new supranational body, and had many structural and political limitations, it encouraged western European governments to work with one another, and obliged them to agree and establish joint decision-making procedures. These included a Council of Ministers that in some ways was to herald the Council of Ministers of the European Union, expert committees that were later reflected in those that lie at the heart of the European Commission, and a European Payments Union that foreshadowed the European Central Bank.

On the internal front, then, peace and prosperity were western Europe's overriding concerns. The achievement of a lasting peace had long been beyond the abilities of Europeans themselves, dragged as they had been over the centuries into one war after another. Matters were made worse now by economic devastation, which had weakened the foundations upon which such a peace might have been built, and by the ideological divisions of the cold war. Prior to the First World War, Europeans had always negotiated their own peace agreements and rebuilt their own economies, but now they were obliged to seek external assistance. External pressures had been critical to the meaning and purpose of Europe for centuries, but at no time more so than after 1945.

External incentives: the role of the United States

Charles de Gaulle is reputed once to have commented that it would not be a European statesman who would unite Europe, but the Chinese. He was wrong about the Chinese, but his implication that external forces would play a greater role in shaping European cooperation than domestic leadership was to prove correct. In the event, it was to be the Americans and the Soviets who were to play the leading roles in the unfolding drama. Their influence was to be expressed in part by deliberate policies: the economic investments, the security guarantees, the political support for cooperation provided by the Americans, and the threats to security and human rights posed by the Soviets. But much of that influence was to unfold unconsciously; in spite of the Atlantic alliance, western Europeans were to be dismayed by the US policies that posed a threat to European interests or ran counter to European preferences; eastern Europeans were to resent the stranglehold imposed by the Soviets; and the divisions of the cold war were to remind all Europeans of their weaknesses, their vulnerabilities, and their lost global influence.

There were three overlapping phases to the manner in which the external impulses evolved. The earliest and most immediately obvious was the military insecurity posed by Soviet power. This dominated western European calculations from the Berlin crisis of 1948–9, which confirmed Soviet geopolitical intentions, through to the late 1960s and early 1970s, when it became clear that cold war tensions were no longer focused mainly on Europe but were expanding to the global stage, with the result that western Europeans no longer had the undivided attention of American leaders and military planners. Worries about security did little to promote a sense of common European purpose; Europe was, after all, divided into eastern and western blocs, and security policy was defined less by Europeans themselves than by the priorities of the two regional hegemons. For the west, policy options were determined by the priorities of the North Atlantic Treaty Organization (NATO), which was dominated by the United States, and for the east they were limited by the priorities of the Warsaw Pact, which was dominated by the USSR. Europeans were (often unwilling) participants in an ideological confrontation between the two external actors; their role mattered only marginally, and their interests were subsumed to those of the Americans and the Soviets.

As the age of the remaining great European empires drew to a close in the 1940s and the 1950s, and the era of globalization began to loom in the 1960s, a second phase emerged in which military insecurity was joined on the agenda by economic insecurity. Before the war, Europe had dominated global markets, accounting for the lion's share of global gross domestic product and global trade. The pound sterling had been the primary reserve currency for much of the world since the early nineteenth century, Britain's trade dominance was underpinned by imperial preference, and European corporations were the world's largest and the most competitive. But the Second World War redefined western Europe's economic position: in addition to the need to rebuild economies and infrastructure devastated by war, the close of the imperial era removed critical economic advantages for Britain, France, Belgium, the Netherlands, and Italy, and the rise first of American and then of Japanese economic power meant new sources of competition. American economic influence in western Europe was felt less in terms of direct investment or leverage, argues Judt, than through a consumer revolution and the Americanization of popular culture.[17]

When the initial attempts to build a European common market helped return strong economic results, western European leaders became more particular about their assessments of the American leadership. By the 1960s, the European Economic Community had joined Japan as one of the new powers in the international system, and there was rising dissatisfaction with the privileged role in that system of the US dollar, particularly in light of the stresses created in the United States in 1965–70 by the combined costs of fighting the Vietnam War and paying for the Great Society social programmes. With the dollar overvalued, and US budget and trade deficits growing, the Nixon administration decided unilaterally in August 1971 to cut the link between the US dollar and gold, bringing to a close the Bretton Woods system of fixed exchange rates. Nixon's lack of reference to his European allies encouraged even the most pro-American among them to argue that this was clear proof of Europe's need to unite in order to protect its interests.[18] The energy crises of the 1970s further emphasized European economic vulnerability, as well as placing additional strain on transatlantic relations because of the differences between the United States and western Europe on how to deal with Israel and Arab oil producers. Then, as the US economy began to recover in the early 1980s, western Europe went into decline, prompting the coining of the term Eurosclerosis to describe the pattern of low job growth, high unemployment, and depressed economic growth that seemed to afflict much of the region.[19]

The third phase in the evolution of external pressures saw the agenda widening still further as military and economic impulses were joined by philosophical and ideological differences between western Europe and the United States. The Americans had played a critical role in the early stages of western European reconstruction, supporting economic initiatives through the Marshall Plan, and providing Europe with security reassurances through NATO. They also gave their political blessing to European integration, understanding that it played an important role in building European peace and stability, in building western European foundations as a marketplace for American exports, in reinforcing US abilities to resist and offset Soviet power, and in helping strengthen western Europe as a political and economic partner of the United States. It was President John F. Kennedy who in 1962 had announced that the United States looked on 'this vast new enterprise with hope and admiration', and viewed Europe not as a rival but as 'a partner with whom we can deal on a basis of full equality'.[20]

Early on, western European public opinion towards the United States was generally positive. Asked in polls in 1955 and 1961 to select among several terms that would describe their perceptions of the United States, interviewees in France, West Germany, Italy, and Britain opted for *democratic* (49 per cent), *peace-loving* (43 per cent), *cooperative* (39 per cent), and *trustworthy* (32 per cent) over *imperialistic* (29 per cent), *reckless* (12 per cent), and *aggressive* (8 per cent). But there were also clearly some doubts: in polls carried out between 1956 and 1959, half of West German respondents agreed that the United States treated West Germany as an equal partner in affairs that concerned both countries, but equal treatment for their countries was acknowledged by only 30 per cent of Britons, 25 per cent of Italians, and 9 per cent of the French. A significant majority (60 per cent on average) in all four countries felt that national foreign policy depended too much upon the United States, and the majority of those felt that their countries cooperated with the United States not because they wanted to but because they could not afford not to, for economic reasons more than for military reasons.[21]

The tensions within the Atlantic alliance began to build as the Americans and the western Europeans disagreed over policy. Alarm bells had begun to ring over Korea in 1950–3, when western Europeans had been initially encouraged by the US-led invasion to expel North Korean invaders, but reconsidered when US and South Korean forces crossed into the North, sparking an intervention by China, raising the prospect of Soviet hostility, and encouraging talk in American political and military circles of the possible use of nuclear weapons. Then came the Suez crisis of 1956, with its humiliations for Britain and France in the face of US opposition, and its revelations about transatlantic differences over the shape of the post-war international system. When construction began in 1961 of the Berlin Wall, western Europeans were disappointed that the Kennedy administration did little to discourage the Soviets. But then they began to worry that the Americans might be prepared to go *too* far: the October 1962 Cuban missile crisis took the world to the brink of a nuclear war, and was conducted by the Kennedy administration with little reference to the views of its European NATO partners.[22] Western Europeans needed the American security guarantees, but they worried about American motives and priorities, and there was new support for the idea of policy independence from the United States.

Transatlantic tensions continued to grow in the late 1960s following Lyndon Johnson's decision to escalate the US military action in Vietnam. No western European government was prepared to offer material assistance, but none was willing to go public with its reservations, conscious of the extent to which the region depended upon US security guarantees, and not wishing to hand a moral victory to the Soviets. But the European public felt no such reticence: large anti-war demonstrations were held in most major western cities, a 1967 poll found that 80 per cent of those questioned were critical of the war,[23] and criticisms of the American views on international affairs continued to harden. Then came the fallout over the end of Bretton Woods, followed quickly by transatlantic differences over relations with Israel during the Yom Kippur War, and by the 1973 energy crisis that grew out of both events. Many of the building doubts among western Europeans about US priorities coalesced during the Reagan administration, with its controversial policies on nuclear weapons, its support for right-wing rebellions and insurgencies in southern Africa and Central America, its association with religious conservatives, and its involvement in the Iran-Contra affair.

The underlying source of the transatlantic differences was philosophical. Americans took a more uncompromising view than western Europeans towards the management of the cold war, seeing the communist threat in everything from Soviet hegemony over eastern Europe to Soviet arms sales, Third-World nationalism, and fifth columnists wandering the hallways of Washington government departments and Hollywood film lots. US moral credibility was undermined first by McCarthyism and then by American willingness to support authoritarian regimes—the shah in Iran, the Duvaliers in Haiti, Batista in Cuba, Trujillo in the Dominican Republic, and Mobutu in Zaire, among others—so long as they were anti-communist. The prevailing view in American foreign policy circles—later given bald expression by the administration of George W. Bush—seemed to be that you were either with the Americans or you were not. But western Europeans saw the world in more nuanced terms, and—in part because they were on the frontlines—were more interested in engagement and détente than in confrontation and belligerence; hence, West Germany's overtures to East Germany in the late 1960s, and western Europe's ongoing bemusement over US policy on Cuba.

Perhaps nothing so clearly illustrated the transatlantic differences—and continues to do so today—as the question of Israel. Prior to the 1967 Six-Day War there was a prevailing view in western Europe that Israel was a welcome member of the international community. But as the occupation of the West Bank, the Gaza Strip, and the Golan Heights achieved a new permanence in the 1970s; as Jewish settlements were built outside Israel's borders; and as Israel adopted an increasingly uncompromising attitude towards the campaign for a Palestinian state, western European views on Israel parted company with those of the United States. While American administrations were unwilling to criticize Israeli policy except in the most general terms,[24] western European views on Israel became increasingly hostile. An early indication of the differences came during the Yom Kippur War, when most western European governments were reluctant to provide the United States with the means to deliver military support to Israel. This was followed by western European criticism of Israeli policy on Lebanon, and most persistently by its criticism of Israeli actions in the occupied territories. Israel has responded in kind by keeping Europe at a distance, and by occasionally dismissing European criticism as anti-Semitism. By 2003, nearly 60 per cent of Europeans were willing to consider Israel a greater threat to world peace than even Iran or North Korea (see later in this chapter).

Policy disputes such as these not only drew attention to the differences between western European and American values and priorities but they also made western Europeans more sensitive to their political and economic weaknesses, and to the extent to which their voice on the international stage was overwhelmed by the United States. This prompted redoubled efforts to build networks of cooperation aimed at both competing economically with the United States and ensuring that western European views were reflected in debates about critical international issues. It was competition from US corporations in the 1960s, for example, that helped western

Europeans realize how little progress they were making on preparing for the challenges of globalization, and it was the US decision to drop dollar convertibility with gold that led to the exchange rate volatility and inflation that helped concentrate European minds on the importance of monetary union. These, in turn, built the foundations of new thinking about the meaning of Europe and the qualities of Europeanism.

The end of the cold war in 1989–91 changed everything. It meant the removal of the most important project in which the Americans and the western Europeans had been jointly engaged, and thereby shed new light on just how shaky the edifice of the Atlantic alliance had become. It also set the wheels in motion for the rejoining of western and eastern Europe, which in turn encouraged Europeans to think of themselves less as victims of cold war crossfire than as a region bound by a common history and culture, and perhaps also by common views about the manner in which politics should be structured, economic systems managed, and social problems addressed. Europe before the First World War had been ambitious, confident, extroverted, and arrogant. During the cold war it was divided, handicapped, frustrated, and introverted. The stage was now set for its rediscovery of itself, the path to which had been prepared by the creation of the European Union.

The dawn of a new Europe

Support for the idea of regional cooperation after the war had been reflected in the creation or revitalization of several groups of pro-Europeanists, some of which traced their roots back to the inter-war years, and others of which were inspired by a new concern to finally remove the causes of war and to respond to growing US power. Among them were the United European Movement in Britain, the Europa-Bund in Germany, the Socialist Movement for the United States of Europe in France, and the European Union of Federalists. Several of these groups were involved in the organization in May 1948 of the Congress of Europe in The Hague, designed to draw attention to the cause of European unity, which led to the creation of the Council of Europe a year later, whose goal was to promote 'a closer unity between all the like-minded countries of Europe'. The Council fell short of being the kind of organization for which the more enthusiastic European federalists hoped, but it has gone on to play a key role in promoting Europeanist values on human rights (see Chapter 7).

A step in a different direction was taken with the signature of the Treaty of Paris in 1951, which created the European Coal and Steel Community (ECSC), a limited venture in the pooling of responsibility for two strategic industries. The argument made by its two main sponsors—French foreign minister Robert Schuman and French entrepreneur and bureaucrat Jean Monnet—was that only 'through concrete achievements which first create a de facto solidarity' could European unity be promoted.[25] But while membership of the ECSC was open to all European states, only six—France, West Germany, Italy, and the three Benelux countries—joined, the others staying away for reasons that reflected how much work would need to be done to build a common European agenda: Britain did not trust the French or the Germans and still had too many political and economic interests outside Europe; memories of the German occupation were still too fresh for Denmark and Norway; Austria, Finland, and Sweden valued their neutrality; Portugal and Spain were dictatorships with limited interest in international cooperation; and eastern Europe was under Soviet control.

Judt notes the limitations of the ECSC—it had little authority and it was the lowest expression of possibilities for western European unity—but it was 'a political vehicle in economic disguise',[26] and allowed western Europeans to take the first step on the road to regional integration. The next step was the signature in 1957 of the Treaty of Rome, designed to take cooperation to a new level by creating the European Economic Community (EEC). This would build the foundations for a European single market by removing all restrictions on internal trade; agreeing a common external tariff; developing common agricultural and transport policies; and eventually removing all barriers to the free movement of people, capital, goods, and services among EEC members. Only the six ECSC members initially joined the EEC, but there were already early signs that other western European states had begun to reconsider their positions.

Britain had taken part in plans for a looser European Free Trade Association (EFTA, created in 1960), but was monitoring developments on the continent with interest. Interestingly, and in spite of the reputation that Britain has developed as a reluctant European, a poll taken in October 1954 found that public opinion in support of efforts to unite western Europe was greater in Britain (78 per cent) than in France or Italy (63 per cent) and only slightly less than in West Germany (82 per cent).[27] As it decolonized, Britain's attachments to other parts of the world declined, and the dispute with the United States over Suez in 1956 had shaken the foundations of the special relationship. Just five years after the signature of the Treaty of Rome, and two years after joining EFTA, Britain applied for membership of the

EEC. Vetoes cast by a resentful and suspicious Charles de Gaulle prevented it from joining until 1973, but the tide was clearly turning. Denmark and Ireland joined in 1973; Greece in 1981; Portugal and Spain in 1986; and applications or expressions of interest were received from Austria, Cyprus, Malta, Norway, Sweden, Switzerland, and Turkey.

Economic change still lagged behind political will, however. Efforts to complete the single market were undermined by the persistence of non-tariff barriers to the single market, and by corporate and regulatory cultures that worked against the interests of multinational European corporations. While their American and Japanese counterparts were dynamic and egalitarian, and understood the needs and opportunities of the new global marketplace, western European corporations were complacent, nationalistic, and conservative, and more willing to merge or launch joint ventures with other companies within their own states than to reach across borders and take advantage of the growing European market; fewer than 10 per cent of corporate mergers in the period 1966–9 involved companies in different Community states.[28] Also clearly needed was a unified monetary policy, in which cause false starts were made in the 1970s and 1980s with attempts to stabilize exchange rates as a prelude to creating a single currency. But it was not until 1989 that a three-stage plan was agreed upon, resulting in the adoption of the euro in 1999.

The late 1980s also saw a plan to revitalize movement on the completion of the single market, which led to the signature of the Single European Act (SEA) in 1986, the first new treaty since Rome in 1957. The SEA outlined the steps needed to complete the single market by 1992, and although they were not all completed in time, the single market was all but in place by the deadline. More importantly, the SEA revived public interest in the Community, about which most western Europeans until then knew and cared little. It outlined a programme and targets with which even many of those who were lukewarm on integration could identify, and the idea of allowing free movement of people across borders was a critical psychological step in the process of helping ordinary Europeans identify with the European project.

It had been clear from the outset that European integration would always be handicapped so long as there were disparities among states in income, education, social mobility, and economic opportunity. The Community had created a European Regional Development Fund in 1973 to help direct investments at poorer parts of the Community, but it took the SEA to move economic cohesion to the heart of integration, and new prominence was given to (and new spending directed at) the Community's structural funds, aimed at helping achieve a more level economic playing field. A further boost to Community social policy was provided in 1989 by the Charter of Fundamental Social Rights for Workers (the Social Charter), focused on encouraging the free movement of workers, fair pay, better living and working conditions, freedom of association, and protection of children and adolescents.

Alongside these developments on the economic front, integration also brought changes in other areas of policy. The SEA gave the Community new responsibility over environmental policy, research and development, and regional policy; eased or lifted many internal passport and customs controls; made protectionism illegal; broke down monopolies on everything from the supply of electricity to telecommunications; and allowed banks and companies to do business and sell their products and services throughout the Community. And in order to make all of this more efficient, institutional changes took place: the European Parliament (which had been directly elected for the first time in 1979) was given more power relative to the Council of Ministers, and new powers were given to the European Court of Justice (whose workload was growing).

New attention was also paid to Community foreign policy. The transatlantic rift over Vietnam had emphasized the need for better western European foreign policy coordination, leading to the agreement on European Political Cooperation (EPC), which brought Community foreign ministers together regularly to coordinate policy. It achieved some modest early successes, including a joint EC policy declaration on the Middle East; the signing of the Yaoundé Conventions on aid to poorer countries; and collective European responses during the 1980s to the war in the Falklands, developments in Poland and Iran, and apartheid in South Africa.[29] However, it was always going to be limited by the extent to which the Community governments and their citizens could be encouraged to see national interests coalescing and aligning into a common European interest.

Another step down the road to European integration was taken in February 1992 with the signature of the Treaty on European Union in Maastricht. This created a timetable and conditions for a European currency; extended Community policy responsibilities into areas such as consumer protection, public health policy, immigration, asylum, transportation, education, and social policy; and created a new European Union of which the Community would be just one part. Perhaps most significantly for European identity, Maastricht created an ambiguous EU 'citizenship', which included the rights of citizens (with some limits) to live wherever they liked in the European Union and to stand and vote in local and European elections. Psychologically, this built on the effect of the replacement of national passports from 1985 with a standard burgundy-coloured passport bearing the name and coat of arms of each member state, and also bearing the legend 'European Community' (changed in 1997 to 'European Union'). Europeans now had another symbolic reminder of the European project, adding to the EU flag that was becoming increasingly visible throughout the Community. Although these developments may have been relatively trivial, they were more real to most Europeans than new treaties or grand policies.

In spite of all this progress, the early 1990s provided reminders of just how much work remained to be done to move Europeans in the same direction. First came the embarrassment of the Gulf crisis of 1990–1, which shed harsh light on Community divisions: Britain and France made large military commitments to the effort to expel Iraq from Kuwait, but Germany stayed on the sidelines; Belgium, Portugal, and Spain kept their distance; and Ireland protected its neutrality. Commission president Jacques Delors noted that while the member states had taken a firm line against Iraq on sanctions, once it became obvious that force was needed, the Community realized that it had neither the institutional machinery nor the military resources to allow it to act as one.[30] For Belgian foreign minister Mark Eyskens, Europe's response showed that the Community was 'an economic giant, a political dwarf, and a military worm'.[31]

Worse was to come on Europe's own front doorstep when the end of the cold war released ethnic, religious, and nationalist tensions in Yugoslavia. A unilateral declaration of independence in June 1991 by Croatia and Slovenia sparked a violent intervention by the Yugoslav federal army, which offered an opportunity for the Community to show that it could take an initiative without US prompting. When it arranged a peace conference, Luxembourg foreign minister Jacques Poos was prompted to boast that 'This is the hour of Europe, not of the United States'.[32] But the Community lost its credibility by recognizing Croatia and Slovenia in January 1992, war erupted in Bosnia in April, and it was eventually left to the United States to broker the 1995 Dayton peace accords. Further embarrassment came in 1997–8 when ethnic Albanians in Kosovo tried to break away from Yugoslavia and it fell to NATO—again under US leadership—to organize a bombing campaign against Serbia in 1999.

European integration had long focused on economic cooperation; what the serial failures in the Gulf and the Balkans had shown quite clearly was that more attention needed to be paid to foreign policy cooperation, and even to the building of a European military. Maastricht had included agreement on the development of a Common Foreign and Security Policy

(CFSP), but its goals were only loosely defined, with agreement to safeguard 'common values' and 'fundamental interests', to 'preserve peace and strengthen international security', and to 'promote international cooperation'—but little else. However, agreement and negotiation were becoming habit-forming, and EU foreign ministers were able to agree on a series of common strategies, joint actions, and common positions. More focus was also provided by institutional changes, including the creation of a High Representative for the CFSP in 1999, who was intended to be the European voice on foreign affairs.

If the end of the cold war was to find Europe unprepared to take the initiative on new foreign policy challenges, it also led to events that would have a critical impact on European integration and on the idea of Europeanism: after decades of being an exercise in western European integration, the collapse of Soviet hegemony meant that the European Community could now expand eastwards. East Germany was the first member of the former Soviet bloc to join (entering through the back door as a result of German reunification in 1990), just as most of its neighbours were making clear that they saw membership of the Community as a priority. When Austria, Finland, and Sweden joined in 1995, the European Union for the first time had a border with Russia, and by 2000 negotiations on membership had been opened with Bulgaria, Cyprus, the Czech Republic, Estonia, Hungary, Latvia, Lithuania, Malta, Poland, Romania, Slovakia, and Slovenia, all of which joined the European Union in 2004–7. After the forty-five-year interruption of the cold war years, Europe was no longer divided by ideology, and the east and west could start thinking again about what they had in common. The west influenced the east through the rediscovery of democracy and capitalism, but the east challenged the west to rethink the definition of Europe, and to abandon the assumptions that had emerged during the cold war. Even though several states remained (and continue to remain) outside the European Union, the way was now clear for Europeanism to develop more distinctive outlines.

One problem that had not gone away, however, was nationalism. In much of the west, it was old-style cultural nationalism, with groups such as the Welsh, the Catalans, the Sardinians, and the Bavarians demanding recognition of their separate identity, and in some cases autonomy. This nationalism spilled over into political pressure for independence in Scotland, Belgium, and Italy, and into political violence in Northern Ireland and the Basque country. But it was in the east that the pent-up demands for change were released with the most force in the wake of the end of Soviet hegemony: Czechoslovakia broke into two and Yugoslavia—following bitter civil wars—into seven new states. The map of Europe continued its almost constant process of change, and even today there are unresolved disputes over authority and cultural boundaries in about two dozen European states; among the few exceptions to the rule are Austria, Bulgaria, Iceland, Ireland, Luxembourg, and Malta.

The impact of Iraq

The 1990s, then, proved to be an active period of rediscovery and learning for Europeans. The cold war had ended, the European Union was embarking on critical new initiatives (completion of the single market, signature of the Maastricht treaty, new discussions about a single currency, further enlargement), and the ideological and political divisions between the east and west were fast disappearing. Eastern European states were casting off the restraints of state socialism, preparations were made for membership of the European Union, and the European Union was evolving into something more than an exercise in regional economic cooperation. All was not well, it is true, as reflected only too clearly in the Gulf and the Balkans, and in the resurgence of nationalism in the east. But it was now possible for the first time in two generations to ponder once again the meaning of Europe, to drop the labels *western* and *eastern*, and to consider European values and priorities without the shadows cast by American and Soviet hegemony. While the post-cold war rediscovery of Europe and Europeanism continued to be influenced by internal priorities, external pressures also continued to play their part, and once again the critical actor was the United States.

Clouds began to gather in the mid-1990s as the Americans and the Europeans fell out over trade issues. Whatever doubts there may have been about European progress on building a single market and making preparations for a single currency, the Common Commercial Policy had boosted the Community's standing as a trading power, which it had used to good effect in the meeting chambers of GATT.[33] The Community and the United States were each other's biggest trading partners and sources of foreign investment, and while the security relationship clearly favoured the United States, the trade relationship favoured the Europeans. If the Europeans had failed to achieve much unity on foreign policy, they had achieved a great deal with trade policy: once common positions were agreed, the European Commission represented and argued those positions on behalf of all the member states, and given that the European share of world trade was fast growing over that of the United States and Japan, the European voice in trade negotiations was the loudest.

When GATT was replaced in 1995 by the World Trade Organization with its powers of dispute resolution, the European Union was quick to send a message to the Americans that, on the trade front at least, it would no longer be business as usual. Conflicts broke out over agricultural exports, the steel industry, government subsidies, and US concerns over the rise of Europe as a unified trading bloc with external barriers working against US trade interests.[34] In the period 1995–2008, 13 per cent of all disputes taken to the WTO involved both the United States and the European Union, but in 63 per cent of those cases the European Union was the plaintiff, while in 37 per cent the United States was the plaintiff.[35]

More clouds built as the two sides parted company over the Gulf, the Balkans, trade with Cuba, the creation of the International Criminal Court, the response to climate change, the Arab–Israeli dispute, and relations with Iran. The storm that had been brewing perhaps as far back as Korea or Suez, or certainly Vietnam, finally broke in the eighteen months between the September 2001 terrorist attacks in New York and Washington, DC, and the March 2003 US-led invasion of Iraq, when transatlantic relations first achieved a new zenith of good will, and then plumbed new depths of disagreement. The 9/11 attacks generated an unparalleled outpouring of support and sympathy and a hope by European leaders that the war on terrorism might be a valuable opportunity for transatlantic cooperation, with an emphasis on multilateralism and diplomacy. There was agreement on the need to attack Afghanistan, a haven for terrorists, but relations soured when it became clear that the Bush administration planned a contentious and uncompromising response to terror ('You're either with us or against us in the fight against terror', Bush warned in a November 2001 press conference), and that it had its eyes on Iraq. When it began claiming that Saddam Hussein possessed weapons of mass destruction and posed a threat to neighbouring states and to US interests, and then prepared to invade in March 2003, the cracks in the transatlantic partnership widened.

European governments were famously divided in their response to Iraq: the British government predictably sided with the Americans, along with those of Denmark, Italy, the Netherlands, Spain, and many eastern European states, while the governments of France and Germany were quick and vocal in their opposition, along with those of Austria, Belgium, and Greece. Rather than learning from the criticism, however, and adjusting course, US defence secretary Donald Rumsfeld—during off-the-cuff remarks made at a January 2003 press conference—dismissed France and Germany as 'old

Europe', and argued that the centre of gravity in Europe was shifting to the east, where new NATO members supported US policy. The division between pro- and anti-war European governments was routinely touted by analysts and the media as yet another example of the failure of Europe to build common foreign policy positions. But almost universally overlooked in the analysis was the strength and unity of European public criticism of the invasion. Polls found majorities of between 60 and 90 per cent opposed to the US action in Iraq without UN backing policy in almost every country surveyed, including Britain, the Czech Republic, France, Germany, Hungary, Italy, Poland, and Spain.[36]

On 15 February 2003, a coordinated day of protests saw massive anti-invasion demonstrations in almost every European capital, including Berlin, Brussels, Budapest, Dublin, London, Madrid, Oslo, Paris, Rome, Warsaw, and Zagreb. Several pro-invasion governments—notably those in Britain and Spain—found their public support declining: in Spain, the conservative Popular Party was set to win a third term in office, but was already in trouble when—four days before the March 2004 general election—ten bombs set on trains coming into Madrid killed 191 people. The opposition socialists won the election and announced a month later that Spanish troops would be withdrawn from Iraq. In Britain, meanwhile, a clamour of questions was directed at Tony Blair, and although he won a third term in office in 2005, his administration was permanently tainted by Iraq and by charges of a misrepresentation of the intelligence used to justify the attack. As never before, questions were asked about the merits of the special relationship and about Britain's obligations to its EU partners. The British had often been challenged about their lukewarm views on Europe, but never more so than over the issue of Iraq.

But this was not just a dispute over Iraq. Western Europeans had chafed under US leadership through much of the cold war, the end of which had caught them unprepared; they had been focusing too much on economic cooperation, and had been spoiled by the luxury of being able to rely on US investment and security. They found themselves challenged during the 1990s by the need both to redefine the meaning of Europe as the iron curtain fell and to decide how that redefinition would translate into internal and external priorities. Now they found all the questions about what Europe represented demanding new attention. The long-term effects of Iraq have not yet worked themselves out, and it may be years before we have the benefit of enough hindsight to be sure about what the dispute represented. But there is no question that it provided vivid justification for the doubts that many Europeans had long held about US leadership in the world, and helped give Europeans a new awareness of the values and priorities that they had in common, and how their view of themselves and of Europe's place in the world was evolving. The many doubts that existed during the cold war about European values and norms were now dusted off, and Europeans from both sides of the old iron curtain were encouraged to think again about how they viewed themselves, and about how Europe was viewed by others. The prospects of using Europeanism as a legitimate and useful means of analysis had suddenly become more real.

Eurobarometer polls taken annually between 1993 and 2007 found two-thirds of Europeans consistently in favour of a common European foreign policy, and only about one-fifth opposed.[37] The underlying disquiet with the US lead was forcefully illustrated by the remarkable results of an October 2003 Eurobarometer survey carried out in the (then) fifteen member states of the European Union. When asked to name the countries they felt posed a threat to world peace (from, it must be said, a list provided by surveyors), 59 per cent chose Israel; 53 per cent chose Iran, North Korea, and the United States; and 52 per cent chose Iraq. It was only in Germany and Italy that the number of people who saw the United States as a threat was less than 50 per cent, but even in traditionally staunch US allies the numbers were high: 88 per cent in Greece, 64 per cent in the Netherlands, 60 per cent in Ireland, and 55 per cent in Britain. By contrast, China was seen as a threat by only 30 per cent of respondents, and Russia by only 21 per cent.[38]

The fact that Israel was at the top of the poll attracted more political and media attention than the high ranking of the United States; the Israelis were furious, Commission president Romano Prodi was moved to speak of 'the continued existence of a bias [against Israel] that must be condemned outright', and the Italian government (then holding the presidency of the European Union) dismissed the question as 'misleading' and the findings as sending a 'distorted message'. Pro-Israelis rolled out their routine charges of European anti-Semitism, failing to acknowledge that European criticism of Israeli policy towards the Palestinians might have been motivated by a genuine disagreement over policy. European discomfort with Israeli policy towards the Palestinians had long been known, and the result of the poll should not have been that surprising. Far more surprising was the lumping of the United States—the long-time ally, economic investor, and security guarantor of western Europe—together with the three members of George W. Bush's 'axis of evil'.

Evolving European sentiments were further reflected in Eurobarometer surveys that found 83 per cent of respondents in favour of the European Union having a common position in the event of an international crisis, 78–80 per cent in favour of an EU foreign policy independent of US policy, 68–78 per cent in favour of a common EU defence and security policy, 69 per cent in favour of the European Union having its own foreign minister who could speak on behalf of common EU positions, and 69 per cent in favour of the European Union having its own seat on the UN Security Council.[39] When asked to compare the global roles of the European Union and the United States, there has been majority support for the former over the latter: on 'peace in the world' about 60 per cent of Europeans (in round figures) favoured the European Union and 25 per cent the United States, on protection of the environment the ratio was 60:20, on the fight against terrorism it was 60:40, and on the fight against poverty it was 50:20.[40] And anyone who might have agreed with Rumsfeld's east–west divide, or who reasoned that eastern European states remembering the leadership of the United States during the cold war might take a more favourable view of US policy, was to be quickly disabused of this notion; support for a common defence and security policy was highest in eastern Europe with 76–86 in favour in 2007 compared to 50–75 per cent in favour in Britain, Spain, Italy, and the Scandinavian states.[41]

The idea that Europe might aspire to become a superpower and exert global influence is widely dismissed by scholars, pundits, and political leaders, and yet it seems to ring true with most ordinary Europeans. A 2002 survey in six European countries found 65 per cent of respondents in favour while just 14 per cent felt that the United States should remain the sole superpower.[42] They do not feel that the European Union should be a superpower so as to better compete with the United States, but rather that becoming a superpower would help the European Union 'cooperate more effectively with the United States in dealing with international problems'. Enthusiasm for the new role was more muted when respondents were asked if they would still support the idea if it meant greater military expenditure by their governments, but a majority was still in favour in most countries. Illustrating transatlantic differences on how to deal with international problems, and the existence of a clear Europeanist position, large majorities in all the countries surveyed saw economic power as more important than military power in determining a country's overall level of global influence.

The new possibilities of Europeanism

For an entity that has been with us—in one form or another—since the early 1950s, and that has had such a manifest and substantial impact on so many people, the European Union still continues to attract a remarkable amount of scepticism and doubt. It seems that no political disagreement among its leaders, no failed vote on a proposed new treaty, no breakdown in talks on a new policy initiative, and no hesitancy to take action on a new international problem is allowed to pass without declarations of imminent collapse. While occasionally conceding that the European Union might have made progress on some relatively minor policy front, academics and the media have mined the thesaurus for every possible synonym for 'crisis' to describe its failure to make progress, creating the impression that they fully expect it to fail. It has become typecast as a failure; the *Economist* noted in July 2007 that the role assigned to Europe in the previous decade was that 'of a sclerotic under-achiever: a slow-growing, work-shy and ageing continent that is destined to be left behind by the United States, China and India'.[43]

The sources of the doubt are many and varied. First there was Europe's cold war marginalization, when it was never really expected to play more than a supporting role as either a potential battlefield or a useful but not always essential source of moral or political support. Then there was the unmistakable size and reach of the American military, which was interpreted after the cold war as proof that nobody else—least of all the Europeans—could come close to challenging the hegemony of the United States, which went on to 'win' the cold war and by the late 1990s was reaping rewards as the lone superpower, and even possibly a new kind of hyperpower.[44] Then there was the difficulty that so many had wrapping their minds around the idea that twelve or fifteen or twenty-seven or even more sovereign states might set aside jealousies and tensions built over centuries to become part of a larger entity that might present a united front on matters of international concern. There is not even yet a satisfactory term to describe what the European Union has become, with terms such as 'actor' and 'sui generis' being bandied about in some frustration, and Commission president Jacques Delors once describing it as an 'unidentified political object'.

More recently, there have been doubts about just how much support European integration has had from Europeans themselves, amid criticisms of the EU's elitism and democratic deficit. Europe is out of touch, runs the conventional argument, its member states unwillingly giving up sovereignty and control to unelected bureaucrats in Brussels. And in addition to the problems with the EU's democratic credentials, there are all the broader economic and social indications that Europe is in decline: its population is shrinking, its people are working fewer hours, its levels of productivity are not keeping up with the competitors, and it is unable to assimilate its new immigrants. Under the circumstances, it is hardly surprising that assessments of the new international order should have skipped over the European Union and moved straight to the so-called BRIC countries: Brazil, Russia, India, and China.

And yet Europe is enjoying its longest uninterrupted spell of general peace in its recorded history. The European marketplace is the world's richest and most productive. When measured by all the usual standards of quality of life, including education and health care, Europeans are among the healthiest and most personally satisfied humans on earth. The core goals of European integration—peace and economic reconstruction—were long ago achieved, and Europe has moved on to address an expanding range of new interests and challenges. The end of the cold war division of Europe has accelerated the rediscovery of the meaning of Europe and the construction of a European consciousness that was always bubbling under the surface but had been prevented from breaking through by the narrow agendas of individual states. And it is not just the European Union that we must consider in all these calculations; making a distinction between the European Union and Europe has become increasingly meaningless, and Europeans both inside and outside the European Union are rediscovering what they have in common—or, at least, how they differ from others on their values and priorities.

Although polls find that about one-third of Europeans still feel that there is a distance among Europeans in regard to values, a slight majority of those surveyed in 2008 felt that the EU states were close to each other, and coming closer. Tellingly, younger Europeans agreed more strongly than their older counterparts, by a margin of 62 to 46 per cent. While 44 per cent of respondents agreed with the statement that there were no distinctive European values, only common Western values, 61 per cent agreed that common European values existed, and that these were different from those found in other parts of the world; only 22 per cent disagreed. When asked which values they thought best represented the European Union, the list was topped by human rights, peace, democracy, and the rule of law.[45]

During the cold war years, Europeans were diverted from their voyage of rediscovery by economic challenges, by political divisions, by the tensions of Soviet–American confrontation, and by their unwillingness or inability to press European perspectives and interests. But the end of the cold war offered them the opportunity both to bridge their political and ideological cleavages and to think more about what they had in common. Claims that the massive anti-war demonstrations of 15 February 2003 may have marked the birth of a new 'European nation' or a 'European public sphere' may have been more rhetorical than real, but the event was reflective of a debate that has been ongoing for decades about what Europe means, and that is only now becoming more clear.

For most of its recorded history, the term *Europe* was little more than a geographical expression, used to describe a territory in which political, economic, and social boundaries were in a constant state of change, and whose residents felt little or no sense of common identity. Since 1945, its meaning has changed. The region is still divided politically and culturally, but on the back of the economic cooperation encouraged by regional integration, there is now a clearer sense of superimposed identities, and of the prospect of Europe achieving a significance that continues to approach that of association with culture, nation, and state. The Roman Empire might have been no more than a 'single cultural complex', but the new Europe has travelled far along the road to becoming a single economic complex, with the prospects for becoming a single political complex waiting over the horizon. In the chapters that follow, the common political, economic, and social themes in the debate about Europe will be discussed in more depth, and the case made that Europeanism is both a real and a valuable analytical concept.

3

The State: Decline and Reinvention

The state lies at the heart of our attempts to understand and conceptualize politics and international relations. Realists argue that states are the primary actors in an anarchic international system and that security and material concerns dominate their agendas. Liberalists argue that there are more opportunities for cooperation than realists would admit, particularly on economic matters, but concede that state preferences are still the essential driving force in the international system. Constructivists place less emphasis on security or economics, arguing instead that ideas are the foundation of the international system, but again their primary assumptions are based on the actions of states. Functionalists—members of the school of theory most closely associated with the evolution of the European Union—may reject the realist idea of state self-interest, but they still focus on the shared interests of states.

And yet the state is under siege from numerous quarters, leading some to conclude that it is in decline or in retreat.[1] It is pressed by globalization; the rise of international institutions and law; changes in technology and communications; the power of multinational corporations; the growth of international markets and more complex trade regimes; new levels of personal mobility and new patterns of migration; global culture; and the need for multi-state responses to shared or common problems such as terrorism, transboundary pollution, illegal immigration, and the spread of disease. Czempiel concludes that it is time to give up on the state and its associated terminology because 'there are no "states" acting in the transitional world'.[2] Scholte argues that states are no longer sovereign in the traditional sense of the term.[3] Strange suggests that the state has become just one source of authority among several: 'the impersonal forces of world markets, integrated over the postwar period more by private enterprise in finance, industry and trade than by the cooperative decisions of governments, are now more powerful than the states to whom ultimate political authority over society and economy is supposed to belong'.[4]

Others come to the defence of the state, arguing that many of the developments offered as evidence of its declining authority, such as economic interdependence and international cooperation, are not as new as they seem. States still have a monopoly on the control and use of militaries; they are still the most powerful managers of economic production and of the forces that make globalization possible; the citizens of states still identify mainly with those states and have many of even their most fundamental choices determined by the rules of their state; and the capacity of states to respond to new challenges has grown because of technological innovation and the state's responsibility for regulation and surveillance. Rather than a decline of the state, it has been suggested, what we may instead be witnessing is a transformation, with globalization, trade, international law, changes in national identity, and modernization combining to alter the nature of state power, the relationship among states, and the relationship between states and citizens.[5]

Since Europe was the birthplace of the modern state system, perhaps it is fitting that it is also in Europe where the most compelling evidence of the retreat of the state has been found. European states have been buffeted not just by the forces more broadly at work in the international system but also by four additional and peculiar transformative influences:

- Regional integration has weakened or removed internal borders within the European Union, and laws and policies have been harmonized, reducing the authority of state governments over their citizens.

- Europeans have reconsidered their attachment to national identity, such that the assertive state-based nationalism of the nineteenth and early twentieth centuries has been replaced by a more benign community-based cultural nationalism focused on the rediscovery of historical identities within a broader sense of Europe, thereby weakening the link between authority and the state.

- The meaning of citizenship has been redefined, along with a concomitant reassessment of the targets and the character of patriotism. State citizenship may still be the norm in Europe, but only because the law offers no alternative.

- The influence of cosmopolitan ideas has been spreading as more Europeans adopt the view that local, European, and global concerns cannot be divorced.

As this transformation has occurred, new questions have been asked about the meaning of identity. While this is a much contested term, it is clear that most humans have (or seek) a group consciousness, allowing them to share with others a sense of belonging and a support for common values and norms. In Europe, argue Delanty and Rumford, 'it is no longer possible to say what is national and what is European'.[6] Similarly, it is no longer possible to say what can be identified with the state and what can be identified with Europe. Europeanism has meant not just the retreat of the state, and weakening links between authority and the state, but also new approaches to understanding the nation, citizenship, and patriotism, driven by the cosmopolitan idea that all humans belong to a single moral community that transcends state boundaries or national identities.

The changing character of the European state

Since the mid-1970s, the European Union has managed a People's Europe programme designed to make Europe closer and more real to its citizens. It has included the creation of a 'European citizenship', the extension of rights to EU citizens (including the right to vote and stand in municipal and European elections wherever they live), the replacement of national passports with a standardized European passport, wider use of the EU flag, the declaration of 9 May as Europe Day, and the adoption of Friedrich von Schiller's 'Ode to Joy' as the European anthem. The Maastricht treaty included a commitment by the European Union to 'contribute to the flowering of the culture of the Member States' by helping improve knowledge of the culture and history of Europe, conserving Europe's cultural heritage, and supporting and supplementing non-commercial cultural exchanges.

Some of the effects have been substantial, altering the legal relationship between Europeans and the states in which they live, and adding real entitlements to the abundant rhetoric of integration. Others have been more symbolic or psychological, offering little in the way of real change to the way Europeans relate to states, and amounting to little more than invented traditions. The latter are defined by Hobsbawm as 'a set of practices, normally governed by overtly or tacitly accepted rules and of a ritual or symbolic nature, which seek to inculcate certain values and norms of behaviour by repetition, which automatically implies continuity with the past'. He distinguishes between three types of invented tradition, each with a distinctive function: those establishing or symbolizing social cohesion and collective identities, those establishing or legitimizing institutions and social hierarchies, and those socializing individuals into particular social contexts. He also argues that invented traditions use references to the past both to cement group cohesion and to legitimize action, and that—to the extent that there exists reference to a historic past—continuity with that past is largely fictitious.[7]

Deliberate attempts by governments or bureaucrats to encourage a sense of common identity and purpose do occasionally succeed, but they open themselves to criticism for at best being artificial, and for at worst generating myths that serve to strengthen the control of elites rather than promote a genuine sense of belonging. In the European case, EU initiatives have courted the danger of overlaying national identity with a homogenized and sanitized version of European identity designed by committees. Shore notes that 'it is one thing to identify the contours and currents of Europe's shared cultural heritage, quite another to weave this into a new popular narrative for awakening European consciousness by interpolating the masses as "Europeans"'. History can be manipulated and even rewritten to suit the purposes of elites and to send a message that best fits with the prejudices and tastes of the era. He characterizes EU cultural policies as a programme to 'invent Europe', pointing to attempts by the Commission to introduce a 'European dimension' into European education, quoting suggestions by Commission staff that school textbooks be written from a 'European perspective', and noting the predilection of some historians to rewrite the history of Europe as 'a kind of moral success story'.[8]

But the 'tradition' of a unifying Europe, as symbolized most visibly by the EU flag, has only partly been the result of actions taken by European elites. They paved the way by agreeing and establishing the purposes of integration, signing cooperative treaties, and creating European institutions. However, far more telling as an explanation of how integration has diminished identity with states and engendered a sense of European identity has been the cumulative effect of shared experiences: the trials and errors of joint decision-making; the economic and social effects of the single market; the merging of knowledge and experience as patterns of migration within Europe have become more complex; the standardization of procedures and behaviour engendered by European law and policy; the new interest that Europeans have shown in events in their neighbouring states; the acknowledgement that European states share problems to which coordinated responses are the most effective; and the awareness that in dealing with international problems there is often a European perspective which may or may not coincide with the American, Russian, or Chinese perspectives.

Above all, there has been a new sense among Europeans that their interests are tied as much to those of Europe as to those of their home states.

In the broad sweep of history, states are a relatively new phenomenon. Their outlines first appeared in Europe in the Middle Ages, and—as noted earlier—were given firmer identity with the 1648 Peace of Westphalia. But there were still less than two dozen recognizable states in place worldwide by the end of the eighteenth century, and only forty-five more had been created by the outbreak of the Second World War. True, the powers and reach of the state expanded as governments launched welfare programmes, built national systems of taxation, education, transportation, energy supply, and food supply, expanded their regulatory authority, and sought to protect state interests. There was a further expansion in numbers after the Second World War, as the end of empire brought independence to more than ninety former colonies in Africa, Asia, the Pacific, and the Caribbean, and again after the end of the cold war, as more than two dozen new states emerged out of the break-up of the Soviet Union and Yugoslavia. But the grip of the state has always been variable at best, and in few places has its hold weakened more clearly than in post-war Europe.

European states could once take largely independent decisions on new laws and policies (although, of course, they were never entirely independent because they were obliged to react to events and pressures outside their borders). But since the 1950s there has been a clear shift of authority to the institutions of the European Union. The representatives of state governments still play their roles in the meeting chambers of the Council of Ministers and the European Council, but rather than working independently they must now negotiate and compromise. True, European institutions may only act in areas where they have competence (i.e. authority), but the number and the reach of those areas has been growing. Owing to Europeanization—defined by Graziano and Vink as 'the domestic adaptation to European regional integration', or the process by which integration 'feeds back' into national political systems[9]—laws and policies in the member states have been brought into alignment with EU law and policy. But Europeanization involves more than laws and policies. It can also help us understand new patterns of political association, the economic effects of the single market, the accordance of European values, the effects of the project of integrating Europe, and even the process by which integration has changed our understanding of the meaning of Europe.

The extent to which Europeanization has affected the abilities of European states to act independently is hotly debated. Risse et al. argue that, while Europeanization has led to distinct and identifiable changes in the domestic institutional structures of every EU member state (albeit through a process of adaptation rather than wholesale convergence), it has not weakened the state because there is still abundant evidence of interactions and linkages between state governments and European-level governance.[10] In reviewing the academic debate about the 'end of sovereignty', Sørensen argues that even though states consent to comply with supranational regulation, they are themselves the sources of that regulation, they consent in their own best interests, and the new arrangements give states new influence over other states and offer them new possibilities for controlling events outside their borders.[11]

The steps taken by European political leaders to bring down the economic barriers that for so long divided European states, and to build a shared body of law and a common set of policies, have been critical. However, the transformation of the European state and the new clarity of Europeanism can be ascribed just as much to the manner in which Europeans have exploited the new opportunities so created. Consider the impact of policy spillover in the process of building the single market. The Treaty of Rome declared that the Community 'shall have as its task, by establishing a common market and progressively approximating the economic policies of member states, to promote throughout the community a harmonious development of economic activities, a continuous and balanced expansion, an increase in stability, an accelerated raising of the standard of living and closer relations between the states belonging to it'. The authors no doubt had a fair idea what this might actually entail, but few could have anticipated with any assurance the numerous changes that have since come in the interests of ensuring the free movement of people, money, goods, and services:

- The development of common standards and regulations on environmental quality, which the European Union has expressed abroad through its participation in negotiations on matters such as climate change, trade in endangered species of wildlife, and energy use.

- The creation of numerous specialized agencies needed to bolster the work of the major EU institutions.

- The expansion of the EU's legal tools through decisions made by the European Court of Justice, including the principle of direct effect (EU law is directly and uniformly applicable in all member states), and the principle of the supremacy of EU law (EU law trumps national law in policy areas where the European Union has responsibility).

- The expansion of EU policy interests into justice and home affairs; the development of common visa, asylum, and immigration policies; and cooperation in dealing with organized crime, money laundering, drug trafficking, and terrorism.

- EU policies on regional development, designed to reduce the barriers to trade and economic opportunity created by differences in levels of wealth, employment, income, and investment,

- The Bologna Process, under which a European higher education area is being developed through comparable and transferable credits and qualifications, and uniform quality standards.

- Policies aimed at protecting consumer interests, including food and product safety, truth in advertising, unfair commercial practices, and animal health and welfare.

- The promotion of cultural diversity, including greater awareness of the shared heritage of Europe.

The cumulative result of these changes has been to make the European state weaker than its counterparts in any other part of the world. Other states are subject to the same limiting forces of globalization and international cooperation, but none are members of organizations with quite such demanding obligations as the European Union. States are still the critical actors in the EU decision-making process, but their decisions have had the effect of reducing state independence, of reducing the significance of internal borders and their value as a means of control, and of fundamentally redefining the role that the state plays in the lives of Europeans. The state continues to make its presence felt through regulation, but Europeanism has evolved on the back of a weakening in the role of the state in the lives and identities of Europeans. Accompanying these changes has been a redefinition of the meaning and role of the nation.

The changing face of European nationalism

In spite of the disrepute into which it fell as a result of the tensions leading to two world wars, nationalism is alive and well in most parts of the world. The end of the colonial era in Africa prompted a surge of nationalism (understood rather differently from its European equivalent) as leaders sought to assert their authority, to confirm political sovereignty, and to build state unity in the face of ethnic divisions. The struggles to build that unity continue today, sparking civil war and political conflict as minorities struggle to live together in states that often bear no relation to social or cultural realities. In eastern Europe and Russia, nationalism was contained during the cold war only by Soviet hegemony, and quickly re-emerged during the 1990s as minorities asserted their rights to self-determination. In much of Latin America, a reaction to US policy continues to underwrite both political and economic nationalism. And while the forces at work in the United States are usually described as patriotism, Pei describes the United States as 'one of the most nationalist countries in the world', its views based on a belief in the ideals of American democracy.[12] Lieven writes of an American Creed which espouses liberty, democracy, and egalitarianism, but has a dangerously 'messianic' element contained in the desire to extend 'American' values and democracy to the rest of the world.[13]

Europe, however, has become the exception to the general rule. Nationalism is still part of the European political landscape, but it has been redefined since the end of the Second World War. Prior to the nineteenth century, as we saw in Chapter 1, most Europeans were tied politically and economically to sovereigns, royal dynasties, and the church. Following the Peace of Westphalia, states began their inexorable rise to prominence, the picture being complicated after the French Revolution and the Napoleonic wars by the surging role of national identity. For Breuilly, nationalism was encouraged by elites, social groups, and foreign governments seeking to mobilize popular rejection of the state.[14] For many, the ideal political association was a state based on a single nation, but the reality more often was a state containing multiple national groups, some of them divided by state borders. Nationalism encouraged attempts to promote and uphold identity through political action, which was in turn the foundation of nineteenth-century competition for power and influence in Europe, and then of the two world wars. The Nazi abuse of nationalism brought it into disrepute, since when there has been a reformulation of allegiances in Europe: a Europe of the nations is emerging within the broader sweep of the rise of the European Union, and the state is being squeezed between the two.

State identity (usually wrongly described as national identity) is based on a complex blend of factors. The ability of an individual to identify with a state rises with citizenship, recognition of the legitimacy and authority of the state, comfort with its prevailing norms and values, a belief that the state provides economic and social opportunities, a sense of association with its history and culture, the ability to speak the dominant language, empathy with the myths and symbols of the state, trust in fellow citizens, confidence in the stability of the state, and a sense of pride and of the more nebulous idea of 'belonging'. These factors were all important during the era of states, but as the grip of states on European consciousness declined after 1945, the balance between the state and European identity changed. How and why this has happened is not entirely clear, but there are at least three key forces at work.

First, there has been the decline of state authority in the face of regional integration. Combined with the effects of privatization and devolution, this has resulted in the transfer of economic authority to private agencies, and of political authority to sub-state agencies. There are still many who cling to state identity in the face of European integration, and even in some cases support the idea of their state leaving the European Union. But regardless of how Europeans may feel about the implications of European integration, the political and economic role of the state in Europe has been permanently changed (see Chapter 4 for further discussion).

Second, there has been the recognition of the benefits of EU membership. We are constantly reminded by the media of the scepticism that is attached to that membership, and yet Eurobarometer polls reveal that since the early 1990s a plurality of Europeans feel that their country has benefited from EU membership, and that a majority has felt this way since 2004. When respondents were asked by Eurobarometer in 2007 what they considered to be the most positive result of European integration for their state, security was identified by 66 per cent of respondents, global influence by 65 per cent, the economy by 56 per cent, and the standard of living by 51 per cent.[15] The single market in particular has been a project that even the most sceptical of Europeans have mainly been able to support; indeed, for most eurosceptics it is one of the few acceptable results of integration. And when it comes to creating a sense of community among EU citizens, Europeans give the most credit to cultural and economic factors (followed by history, sports, and values).[16] Icons are an important element of promoting 'belonging', to be sure, and the EU flag, for example, has played a vital role in giving the European Union a personality that goes beyond the work of its bureaucrats. But the growth of the single market has been essential to the sense of a shared mission among Europeans, and the adoption of the euro has helped remove much of the 'foreignness' that was perpetuated by different currencies, and that reminded Europeans of their differences.

The final and most telling influence on the development of a European consciousness—and a critical part of the meaning of Europeanism—has been the repudiation of state-based nationalism. Best understood as a belief that multiple national groups can and should live together within a shared and independent political community, state-based nationalism is founded upon the construction of a collective identity and consciousness, using political action, myths, and shared history and culture. It holds that states can be the same as nations, and that the ultimate goal of nationalism is the creation of a nation state. As we have seen, however, nations must be invented, and political leaders have exploited nationalism to build the strength and unity of their communities by describing other nations or national groups as foreign, and have attempted to draw attention away from internal divisions and problems by portraying other nations as a threat. In some cases, state-based nationalism has spilled over into racism and ethnocentrism, and the view that the superior nation should work to protect itself against external influences, and perhaps even dominate other communities as a way of projecting the superior values of the dominant nation. In the most extreme cases, it has evolved into genocide and ethnic cleansing.

As we saw earlier, national interests were at the heart of competition among the great European powers in the nineteenth century, underpinning the growth of colonial empires and sparking the outbreak of both world wars. But the character of nationalism in Europe has changed profoundly since 1945, with a growing dissociation between nation and state that has been a stimulus for—and a result of—regional integration. So widespread has been the rejection of state-based nationalism that, in the broader sweep of history, it may one day come to be seen as no more than a brief interlude in the changing definition of Europe. These changing views about nation and nationalism have had at least three main effects.

First, the assertive and expansive state-based nationalism of the nineteenth and early twentieth centuries, based on a desire to impose control and protect national interests, has been largely replaced by a community-based cultural nationalism that focuses on the rediscovery of historical identities, and calls for greater political autonomy—a Europe of the nations, in other words. So instead of nationalism being used to promote the interests of one nation-state over others, it has instead come to mean recognition of—and respect for—the separate cultural identities of different national groups. A few national minorities have demanded independence, and some (such as the Basques and protagonists in the Northern Irish problem) have been prepared to use violence to achieve that goal, but nationalism in Europe today is driven more by the pressures for greater self-determination and for formal recognition of a separate identity.

In Britain, nationalism has been less about what Britain means externally than about its internal character; it has been part of a reassertion of Scottish and Welsh identity, leading in turn to questions about British state identity, and sparking something of a reactive English nationalism—if the Scots and the Welsh are going to question their British identity, many English seem to be saying, then so can we. In Belgium, tensions between Flemings and Walloons—dating back to the creation of Belgium in 1830—have grown, and a sizeable minority today favours partition. In Spain, there has been an assertion of the separate identities of Andalusia, Catalonia, and Galicia. In France, minority identity is an issue in Brittany, Corsica, and Occitania; in Italy there are separatist pressures from Sardinia; and in eastern Europe national identity has already led to the break-up of Czechoslovakia and Yugoslavia, while the separate identities of Moravia (in the Czech Republic) and Silesia (in Poland) remain.

Assertive nationalism has not entirely gone away, to be sure, and continues to fester on the margins of politics in several parts of Europe. But its goals and targets have changed. Where German Nazis believed in racial superiority, the need to defend themselves against a conspiracy to subvert, the promotion of a religious and cultural hierarchy, and the dangers of linguistic and ethnic diversity, assertive nationalists today concentrate instead on what they see as external threats to a white, Christian Europe. They promote populism, a return to 'traditional values', economic protectionism, stronger law enforcement, and a reduced role for the European Union. At the heart of their policies, though, is opposition to immigration, and particularly to non-white immigration from outside Europe. They have had their greatest impact in Austria, Belgium, France, and the Netherlands, but rather than heralding a resurgence of assertive nationalism, their actions have—for most Europeans—continued to help promote its bad name.

Second, the pre-war association between nations and states has been replaced with a broader European consciousness, and with what Europe collectively might represent, as distinct from what the individual states of Europe once represented. Europeanists existed before 1945, but they were a rare and marginalized breed: a few politicians, scholars, and philosophers who shared ideas among themselves but were rarely able to break out and reach a wider audience, or to much influence overwhelming public identification with the state. Since 1945, European consciousness has moved into the public sphere, and has become a matter of wider discussion.[17] Identity with Europe alone is still restricted to only a small number of Europeans, but identity with the state has declined, as has defence of the interests of the nation-state in the face of European integration and national self-determination. The poll data are reflective of the trends:

- A 2004 Eurobarometer poll asked respondents in the EU-15 how they would conceive of themselves in the near future in terms of identity. While 4 per cent said they would think of themselves as European only, 6 per cent answered European and their nationality, 46 per cent answered their nationality and European, and 41 per cent said nationality only. In other words, a sense of identification with Europe was apparent with 59 per cent of the population.[18]

- Another 2004 Eurobarometer poll taken in thirty states found high levels of pride in being European: 68 per cent of respondents in the EU-25 states expressed such pride, with majorities of more than 80 per cent in Hungary, Romania, Ireland, Slovakia, and Poland, and a low of 50 per cent (still a plurality) in Britain. Levels of pride were highest among younger respondents, and among those born in the European Union or who knew most about the European Union. The sense of attachment that respondents felt to their town, region, or state was higher than their sense of attachment to the European Union, but more than two-thirds still felt a sense of attachment to the European Union.[19] (The level of attachment to the European Union had fallen to 53 per cent by 2007,[20] presumably because the views of ten new eastern European and Mediterranean member states had entered into the equation.)

- A 2006 Eurobarometer poll found that 54 per cent of respondents often or sometimes thought of themselves as European in addition to their nationality, while 43 per cent never thought of themselves as European.[21]

- Polls have also found that while about 90 per cent of the residents of the European Union feel an attachment to their local community and to their state, about half of Europeans feel an attachment to the European Union, about half often or sometimes feel European, and about 60 per cent feel proud to be European.[22] The numbers would be higher were it not for lower levels of enthusiasm about the European Union in most eastern European member states (see Figure 3.1). Generally, however, more Europeans are coming to identify with Europe, if not in place of identity with their community and state then certainly alongside those associations.

Polls give us one indication of the changes, but Europeans are also voting with their feet. Although the official data on the number of Europeans who are resident in a European state other than their home state suggest that the number did not change much between the 1950s and 2000 (about 1.5 per

Figure 3.1 Identification with the European Union

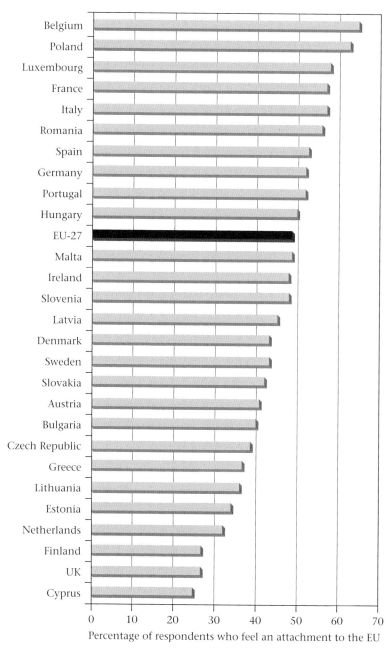

Source: European Commission, *Eurobarometer* 68, May 2008.

cent of the population), they are not entirely reliable. They do not account, for example, for people who have changed their citizenship; who have dual citizenship and may move back and forth between two states (and thus are not registered as foreign in either state); who are temporary residents (students, workers, people who have holiday homes in other states, or retirees who spend time in more than one state); or who simply fail to officially register their move.[23] If these groups are added, the total number of people living outside their home state will be much higher, and the picture of the ebbs and flows of migration will be more complex. By 2007, data indicated that foreigners legally resident in EU member states accounted for 6 per cent of the population (see Chapter 7 for details), the majority of them being citizens of other European states.

The decline of state-based nationalism has combined with the growth of European consciousness to prompt a redefinition of the meaning of being European. As Ash puts it, 'If I go to Warsaw, Berlin, Paris, or Madrid I am abroad. If I go to Warsaw, Berlin, Paris, or Madrid I am at home. This being at home abroad is the essence and wonder of Europe'.[24] The British may be the one notable exception to the rule, with the persistent belief among many of their number that 'Europe' is not just something physically separate from Britain, but also philosophically and historically separate. Otherwise, most Europeans have for long been of the view that their individual nations and states are part of the broader idea and project of Europe. The decline of both national and state identity can thus be considered core elements of Europeanism.

Redefining citizenship and patriotism

One of the core questions raised by the changing face of identity in Europe is how this might be translated into citizenship. Attempts to promote European citizenship have been under way as long as attempts to build European integration, but progress has been slow, compromised by the lack of agreement on what the term means in practical terms, and by the absence of a fuller understanding of its implications. The earliest initiatives were based on providing workers with the right to move freely within the single market, the discussion only widening in the 1970s as more consideration was given to social and political rights for the numerous workers who had taken advantage of free movement opportunities.[25]

The emphasis given in the 1975 People's Europe report (otherwise known by the name of its chair, Belgian Prime Minister Leo Tindemans) to bringing

Europe closer to its people generated further efforts to expand rights, which were in turn reflected in the concept of European citizenship introduced by the Maastricht treaty in 1992. This declared that 'Citizenship of the Union is hereby established. Every person holding the nationality of a Member State shall be a citizen of the Union. Citizenship of the Union shall complement and not replace national citizenship'. Hailed as one of the major accomplishments of Maastricht, the idea of European citizenship was described by the European Commission as a new stage in the process of creating an ever-closer union among the peoples of Europe. But few Europeans gave much thought to it until their new burgundy-coloured passports began arriving in the mail, and even then their lives were not made much different. Was it really an important new step in the definition of being European, or was it less than it seemed?

State identity is most commonly determined by citizenship. While this is a quality that would seem to be easily measured—a citizen of a state is a person who holds a passport of that state, or who has the right to claim such a passport, with all its attendant rights and responsibilities—it is philosophically more complex. Heater notes the distinction between two traditions of citizenship: the civic republican strain which stresses duties and the liberal strain which stresses rights. Although discussions of such duties as virtue, patriotism, upholding the republic, civic engagement, community-mindedness, and military service are still relevant to an understanding of citizenship, it is the liberal strain that has dominated debates for the last two centuries. Tracing its roots to the transition in Britain from a monarch–subject relationship to a state–citizen relationship, it includes the right to vote, the right to just treatment under the law, and the right to own property.[26]

The legal and scholarly debate over citizenship focuses on abstract concepts such as a belief that the people are the source of legitimate political power; that they have rights to participate in the life of a state; and that they have rights of political participation and legal protection, including equality before the law, freedom of speech, the right to own property, and the right to a minimum standard of economic and social welfare. But these are all rights which extend also to the legal residents of states who have not become citizens of those states. What truly differentiates citizens from non-citizens is a series of practical qualities; only citizens can typically vote and run for elective office in their home state, can serve on a jury in that state, are eligible to serve in its armed forces (although some countries allow non-citizens to serve), are protected against forcible removal from that state to another without the agreement of the governments involved, have the right to receive protection from the home state when outside its borders, are recognized as subjects of that state by other governments, and must usually obtain the permission of other governments to travel through or live in their territory.

Citizenship is conventionally associated with a legitimate state that has the power to confer citizenship, and thus statelessness equates with an absence of citizenship; hence non-Israeli Palestinians have no citizenship because they have no state, and residents of Hong Kong who had British passports without the right of abode in Britain became stateless after 1997. But there is no European state, so unless it is possible to be a citizen of a non-state, then it is not possible to be a citizen of Europe. Furthermore, the old bifurcation of the residents of states into citizens and foreigners has been complicated by the changing patterns of international migration, which have created at least three other core groups of state residents: legal aliens (who are granted almost all the same legal rights as citizens without formally becoming citizens), refugees (who typically have fewer rights than legal aliens but are often *de facto* and *de jure* permanent residents of the states in which they reside), and illegal aliens (who have no formal legal rights, but again are often long-term or permanent residents, and participate in almost every aspect of daily life in their state of residence).

Citizenship is usually acquired by inheritance (through parents), by birth (citizenship of the state in which one is born), or by application. The law of most democracies says that someone born in a state can claim citizenship of that state, even if one or both the parents are not citizens. The citizenship of EU member states is clearly established by law, and contains all the conventional rights and obligations associated with citizenship in any state. When Maastricht created a European citizenship, it was not the same as state citizenship, nor did it confer the same rights as those held by state citizens. Ward saw it as 'a pleasant touch, but of limited practical value', while Guild saw it (a little unfairly) as no more than 'some fancy words on a piece of paper' that failed to confer on the holder 'any rights which he or she did not already have'.[27] In fact it did confer additional rights, including the following:

- To move through and live in any of the EU member states (subject to some limitations).
- To vote and stand in municipal elections if legally living in an EU member state of which an individual is not a national.
- To vote and stand in European Parliament elections if legally living in an EU member state of which an individual is not a national.

- To be accorded help and protection by the diplomatic representatives of any member state if an individual is in need in a third country where their home state has no representation.

- To petition the European Parliament and appeal to the European Ombudsman.

- To be treated equally regardless of gender, race, ethnicity, religion, disability, age, or sexual preference.

What this European citizenship did not provide, however, was an alternative to state citizenship. In other words, it did not replace the legal obligations that bind citizens and state governments with legal obligations that would bind citizens and a European government. It did not provide the option of what Balibar has described as 'transnational citizenship'.[28] In practical terms, German or Danish or Bulgarian citizens cannot turn in their state passports and have them replaced with a European passport. The core problem is that there is no European state or government that would be responsible for protecting the rights of European citizens. As the powers of the state in Europe decline, however, as borders become more porous, and as migration patterns become more complex, we move closer to the day when Europeans might be given the option of either state citizenship or European citizenship. This certainly appears to be the view of the European Court of Justice, which—in a 2001 judgement on the right of a French student living in Belgium to receive Belgian social security—noted that 'Union citizenship is destined to be the fundamental status of nationals of the Member States, conferring on them, in the fields covered by Community law, equality of the law irrespective of their nationality'.[29]

As the fields covered by Community law expand, and as non-discrimination against citizens of EU member states who have exercised their free movement rights wins greater recognition, European Union and state citizenship will likely become more comparable. For Maas, the creation of a European citizenship reflects not just the growth of individual rights associated with integration but 'also signifies a move to a new form of supranational political membership'.[30] In spite of the rearguard action fought by the political right and eurosceptics, who see European citizenship as yet another expression of the threats faced by state identity, the tide is clearly turning. Free movement has allowed those Europeans whose state and national identity is weakest or least personally important the kind of personal mobility that is both the result and the clearest expression of the growing chorus of questions about identity.

If the creation of a European citizenship is one of those limited but well-meaning initiatives of European bureaucrats that has not had much impact on Europeanism, more telling has been the new thinking on the meaning of patriotism. Defined generally as love of country, patriotism can be value-based (driven by support for the merits and achievements of a country) or egocentric (driven rather less rationally by a personal association—a patriot loves his or her country simply because it is theirs).[31] It has far from disappeared in Europe: in France the tricolour is omnipresent and presidents repeatedly speak of the importance of national pride; in Britain almost any anniversary involving the monarch is an opportunity for an explosion of patriotic fervour; and international football contests such as the European Championship and the World Cup inevitably lead to much flag-waving in those countries whose teams have qualified, and despondency in those whose teams have not. There have also been repeated instances of economic patriotism as Europeans debate the sale of 'national' businesses and corporations to foreign buyers, and—particularly in the wake of the economic downturn of 2007–9—much evidence of the ambivalence that many Europeans feel about globalization.

But where patriotism as a cornerstone of culture has been largely unchallenged for generations in the United States, there are relatively few Europeans today who are willing to wear it on their sleeves. Patriotism has been sullied in Europe by its historical association with nationalism, and by its co-option in recent decades by assertive nationalists using national symbols to express their opposition to immigration. So far has this gone in Britain, for example, that the British Union Jack has—absurdly—come to be associated in the minds of some with racism, nationalism, and opposition to multiculturalism. More tellingly, however, patriotism has been weakened by the declining allegiance of Europeans with the states that have for so long been the cradles and the nurseries of patriotism.

Once again, polls reflect the distinctive views of Europeans. The World Values Survey in 2003–4 found that less than half the residents of most European states were 'very proud' of their nationality, compared to 79 per cent of Americans (see Figure 3.2). A 2004 Harris poll found that while 84 per cent of Americans expressed pride in their country, figures in Europe ranged from a high of 57 per cent in Spain to a low of 23 per cent in Germany.[32] When a Pew Global Attitudes survey presented the statement 'Our people are not perfect, but our culture is superior to others', 60 per cent of Americans agreed, but only 33–40 per cent of Germans, Britons, and French.[33] Not only are Americans more patriotic but they are more assertive with that patriotism: Americans repeatedly describe their country as the

Figure 3.2 Levels of patriotism

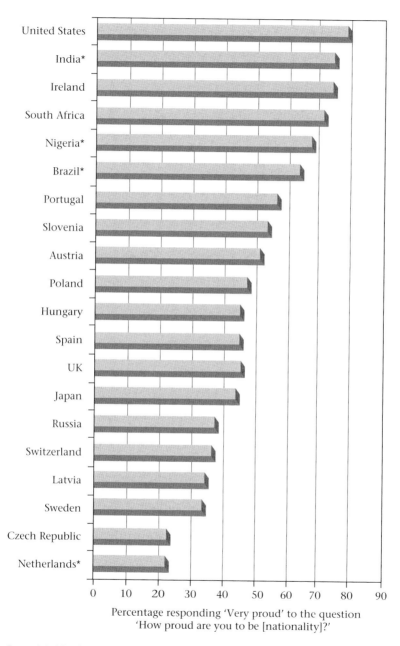

Percentage responding 'Very proud' to the question
'How proud are you to be [nationality]?'

Source: World Values Survey 2003–4, at http://www.worldvaluesurvey.org (retrieved June 2009).
*Data from 1995; all other data from 2003.

greatest on earth, the one most blessed by God, and the one where democracy and the free market allows ordinary people to achieve more with their lives than is possible anywhere else. It is this comparative and superlative element that is missing from the utterances of most Europeans—they are proud to be European, but they rarely claim that Europe (or Germany, or France, or Sweden, etc.) is superior, or offers its residents greater opportunities, or is more blessed by God.

The role of patriotism in American ideas has been such that it is routinely regarded as central to the American conception of democracy. But Johnston challenges this idea and argues instead that patriotism subverts democracy—this was evident, he notes, in the way that the Bush administration held that questioning the war in Iraq would undermine the morale of US troops and embolden the 'terrorists'.[34] Patriotism is also often criticized for being too parochial and for encouraging the promotion of state or national interests at the expense of broader and more universal interests. Europeans now not only debate patriotism but also debate the object of such patriotism. Against the background of a declining attachment to the state and a growing attachment to the nation, what are the prospects for a new European patriotism? The answer depends upon the extent to which Europeans can be convinced that they have enough in common and that their self-identity need not rest alone on association with states or nations.

One possible alternative to conventional state- or nation-based patriotism is constitutional patriotism, or the belief that the universal principles of the democratic constitutional state are the only acceptable basis for identification with a state.[35] This is a concept whose origins lie in a post-war West Germany looking to rediscover pride without reviving the kind of nationalism given such a bad name by Nazism. For West Germans, their new constitution was seen to embody the most important political values of the new state, and thus constitutional patriotism suggested that political attachment should centre on 'the norms, the values and, more indirectly, the procedures of a liberal democratic constitution'.[36] It began with the reflections of the philosopher Karl Jaspers on the notion of German guilt, and was developed by his student Dolf Sternberger, who argued that it had a tradition dating back to Aristotle, and that until the rise of nineteenth-century nationalism, all patriotism had been based on a love of laws and common liberties. It was further refined in the 1980s as Jürgen Habermas reflected on how German political identity and history might be reconciled, while casting a worried eye at the racial and ethnic intolerance that has so often been a product of identity with nation-states. (Continuing German worries about state- or nation-based patriotism were reflected in the coining of a new phrase in 2006—'positive patriotism'—to describe the pride that Germany felt in hosting the football World Cup.)

The idea of constitutional patriotism should not be taken too literally—it is not so much about pride in a constitution as about pride in the ideas upon which liberal constitutions are based, and which they help protect and promote. Constitutional patriotism has been dismissed by critics as being too conceptual and sterile, and as an idea that works better in theory than in practice. (Müller quotes the journalist Joachim Fest describing it as a typical academic idea invented by a professor, discussed with other professors, then dismissed as 'a beautiful idea [that] doesn't work because people don't feel that way'.[37]) Matthias Kumm is particularly sceptical: how can identity focused on universal ideas help build identity focused on European ideas, he asks, and how can abstract principles—rather than blood, sweat, and tears collectively shed—unite a political community? He also argues that 'rights, democracy and the rule of law cannot serve as focal points for [European] identity as long as there is no European consensus on what they mean', and that the identities of citizens cannot be shaped by constitutional texts unless those texts 'have been the focal point of political and legal contestation and deliberation meaningfully connected to the citizens' collective political action'.[38]

However, identification with ideas does not seem to have discouraged Americans, whose core political texts—the Declaration of Independence and the US Constitution—were drafted by a handful of well-educated white men and confirmed only by a small part of the adult population, and for whom patriotism is tied closely to undefined assumptions about the meaning of life, liberty, and the pursuit of happiness. The problem for Europeans is not so much the lack of common values as a failure always to acknowledge and understand those values. Furthermore, patriotism is conventionally tied to the state or the nation, and the history of that link in Europe has not been a happy one. One of the core purposes of European integration has been to encourage Europeans to think more about what unites them than what divides them. Finally, constitutional patriotism is not so far removed from the core underlying precepts of conventional patriotism: a pride in values and a sense of personal association. True, there is no European fatherland, no European nation, and no European state; so Europeans experience few of the sparks that ignite and sustain conventional state- or nation-based patriotism. But this should not prevent them from taking pride in ideas, an attempt at which has been made in the treaties that form the foundation of the European Union: there is no reference in these documents to a common history or culture, but Europe is described as being based on the principles of liberty, democracy, human rights, and the rule of law.[39] Few 'constitutional' documents have failed to elicit pride so effectively as these treaties, but they have a philosophical base with which few Europeans would take much exception.

Kumm argues that Europeans are unlikely to embrace constitutional patriotism, not because of anything inherently implausible in the idea but because the institutional features of European politics make it improbable. Without meaningful electoral politics at the heart of the European political process, he argues, a robust European identity is unlikely to develop, and the attitude of the citizenry towards the European Union is 'likely to continue wavering between fickle support and a lack of interest in European political life, on the one hand, and a stubborn nationalism on the other'.[40] But this conclusion assumes that institutions and political processes are more likely to instil a sense of pride and belonging than identification with values and principles. As Europeans give more consideration to what they have in common and how they differ with non-Europeans, the idea of constitutional patriotism might have more appeal. Given the Europeanist rejection of conventional patriotism, it has more relevance to European thinking than has to date been allowed or admitted.

Cosmopolitan Europe

Identity with a state or nation means identity with a discrete legal or cultural community, usually defined by territory, and with the laws, history, culture, and traditions that bind that community. But broader affinities may also be possible: why not association with the world, with universal ideas, and with the belief that that all humans belong to a single moral community that transcends state boundaries or national identities? When Diogenes declared that he was a citizen of the world (*kosmopolitês*), he voiced an opinion that still rings true more than 2,000 years later to idealists uncomfortable with more parochial associations.

The idea of cosmopolitanism has been revitalized since the mid-1990s as one of a multitude of explanations for contemporary society, taking its place alongside (and overlapping with) such concepts as globalization, multiculturalism, post-modernism, post-industrialism, and late capitalism.[41] Although the academic debate about the EU's cosmopolitan qualities has begun to expand in recent years,[42] much still remains to be done to give it clarity. Archibugi describes the European Union as the 'the first international model which begins to resemble the cosmopolitan model', Roche claims that Europe is 'leading the world in the construction of a globally relevant regional international and trans-national order and governance system', and Delanty argues that to be European is less about culture and politics and more about an orientation to the world that fits with the cosmopolitan spirit.[43] But cosmopolitanism is a concept rarely mentioned or even implied by EU leaders, and it is almost entirely overlooked by Europeans, in spite of how much it offers to our understanding of changing European perceptions about the state, and of the qualities of Europeanism.[44]

Cosmopolites hold that all humans belong to a single community in which they are subject to the same moral standards and have a responsibility for other humans. Local and global concerns cannot be separated or divorced, and rather than the world being separate from the community or state in which each of us lives, it is in fact the only community that matters. Cosmopolites accept the foreign hospitably, argue that all humans should be treated equally, and emphasize the importance of drawing on different traditions and cultures, and of remaining open to other ways of life.[45] As Beck puts it, if nationalism is based on the principle of 'either/or', then cosmopolitanism is based on the principle of 'both/and'.[46] David Held defines it as a 'moral and political outlook which builds on the strength of the liberal multilateral order, particularly its commitment to universal standards, human rights and democratic values, and which seeks to specify general principles on which all could act' and that could serve as 'the guiding ethical basis of global social democracy'.[47] For Beck, it is about issues of global concern becoming part of the everyday local experiences of ordinary people.[48]

Cosmopolitanism has conventionally been portrayed as little more than an ideal, compelling in theory (to some) but essentially impractical and impracticable (to others). And yet it has fired the imagination of many since Diogenes. The Stoics argued that all humans belonged to two communities: the community of their birth and 'the community of human argument and aspiration'. All humans, argued Hierocles, live within concentric circles, ranging from the self through family, neighbours, citizens, countrymen, and humanity, and their task should be to 'draw the circles somehow towards the centre'.[49] Cicero wrote of the notion of a community of mankind and of the duties that humans have to all other humans. Cosmopolitan ideas have been traced through the Renaissance and the Enlightenment, and are reflected in the work of Voltaire, Bentham, and Hume. Immanuel Kant gave them an international dimension by arguing that all rational humans were members of a single moral community, and argued in *Perpetual Peace* in favour of a league of states without military power, and of a cosmopolitan law under which individuals had rights as citizens of the earth rather than of states, as well as affirming the universal right to 'hospitality'. Marx and Engels too were cosmopolites, who wrote of an international proletariat and of the prospects of the state withering away following the revolution.

But with the rise of nineteenth-century nationalism, cosmopolitan ideas were marginalized and were to remain largely dormant until the second half of the twentieth century, when they were given new life by the cumulative effects of the two world wars and the subsequent threat of nuclear and environmental destruction.[50] Cosmopolitan principles were at the heart of the Universal Declaration of Human Rights and its focus on rights as the entitlement of all, regardless of race, gender, religion, national or social origin, or the political, jurisdictional, or international status of the country or territory to which people belong. They also underlay the concept of crimes against humanity, whose origins are conventionally traced through the 1907 Hague Convention to the post-war Nuremburg and Tokyo trials.

The end of the cold war and the widening awareness of the effects of globalization have brought cosmopolitanism to a wider audience, although it is a concept still debated more by philosophers and sociologists than by political scientists or economists. It has been associated with a belief in global political institutions, but this idea of world government is controversial; rather than implying the surrender of sovereignty or security, cosmopolitanism instead expects world citizens to place the welfare of human society above the more narrow pursuit of national interests. In terms of international relations theory, it stands in clear distinction to realism, which emphasizes power in the international system and the importance of states pursuing their own interests. It is based on what Caney describes as a 'society of states' approach, which 'maintains that a just global order is one in which there are states and the states accept that they have moral duties to other states'.[51]

That Europe is not yet more routinely discussed in cosmopolitan terms is probably due to a combination of two key factors. First, there are the unresolved questions over the identity and meaning of Europe and over the character and personality of the European Union. The conventional perception of Europe as a community of states, combined with the many doubts pertaining to the achievements of European integration, has diverted the focus of the debate away from the prospects for the kind of supra-European society that cosmopolitanism implies. Second, the bulk of academic debate so far about the meaning of cosmopolitanism is heavily theoretical, consisting mainly of attempts to clarify its meaning with little effort made to apply it to real-world situations.[52] Firth makes an attempt to see how cosmopolitan principles are reflected in gender issues in the European Union, which leads him to the modest conclusion that the issue of gender equality 'offers further evidence that cosmopolitan democracy should not be dismissed as simply utopian dreaming'.[53] But few others have applied cosmopolitan principles to an understanding of EU policy action.

And yet among the debates about nationalism, citizenship, and patriotism it is not difficult to identify the cosmopolitan ethos in Europe. Even if Europeans are not necessarily cosmopolites on a global scale, they are becoming cosmopolites on a regional scale. Increasingly, they believe that local, state, and regional European concerns cannot be separated or divorced, and that Europe is as important for their political and economic welfare as the communities or states in which Europeans live, or the nations with which they identify. As the hold of the European state declines, as the meaning of nationalism is redefined, and as the focus of citizenship and patriotism changes, the loyalty of Europeans is shifting away from an exclusive focus on the state or the nation, and is moving towards identity with the ideas and values that Europeans have in common. Even if only a small minority could be called true cosmopolites today, most Europeans take a cosmopolitan view of how Europe should be organized.

And even if it is not explicitly described as such, much of the assessment of Europe's new place in the world is implicitly cosmopolitan. Rifkin, for example, argues that what he calls the European Dream has begun to advance the cause of universal morality, and that with its emphasis on inclusion, peace, diversity, quality of life, sustainability, universal human rights, and the rights of nature, it is 'increasingly attractive to a generation anxious to be globally connected and at the same time locally embedded'.[54] John Hume also acknowledged Europe's cosmopolitan qualities in his 1998 speech accepting the Nobel peace prize, when he noted that all conflict was about difference; that European visionaries had decided that difference was not a threat, but was in fact the essence of humanity; and that respect for diversity was the most fundamental principle of peace.[55]

Cosmopolitanism is clearly at the foundation of European positions on human rights, the environment, capital punishment, and conflict resolution, and can also help us better understand European perceptions about the place of Europe in the international system, and the way that Europe conducts its collective foreign policy. While nobody could claim that

Europeans are innocent of bigotry, discrimination, or narrow-mindedness, or that they always know or much care about what goes on in the rest of the world, their world-view is broader and more inclusive than that of most other societies. By living for so long so closely to other cultures with other languages and histories, and by having learned so expensively the costs of nationalism, they—perhaps more than the peoples of any other societies—have been obliged to learn how to cooperate and to respect differences.

The implications are not just European, but perhaps global. Kaldor suggests that we may be in the midst of a historical transformation akin to that which produced nation-states; because globalization implies that territorial sovereignty is no longer viable, the way in which we classify humans will no longer be identified with territory. She believes there will be a growing cultural dissonance between the cosmopolites who see themselves as part of an international network and those who cling to or who have found new types of territorially-based identities. While the latter may take the form of traditional nationalism, it is often transnational in character because it reaches beyond territory to include members of the global diaspora of different groups. This new nationalism, she argues, is primarily a European phenomenon, and mainly eastern European at that.[56] But the European case may just be the most advanced indicator of what is already under way throughout the world, with fundamental implications for the way in which we understand political associations and global networks.

4

Politics: The Parliamentary Model

The study of national politics and government in Europe has a long and creative history, to which has been added, in recent decades, an expanding literature on the qualities and character of the politics and governance of the European Union and its impact on government in the member states.[1] But far less attention has been paid by scholars to the shared features and principles of government and politics across Europe. Social scientists have offered us at least two different European economic models (see Chapter 5), at least three different European welfare models (Chapter 5 again), and a European social model (see Chapter 6), but have been relatively inactive in considering the question of whether there might also be a European political model.

Much has been written and said about European support for democracy in its broadest sense, including political equality, freedom, the rule of law, representative government, pluralism, free and fair elections, respect for human rights and civil liberties, privacy, civic duty, popular sovereignty, and freedom of expression. But in spite of their philosophical roots in Europe, these are not European values so much as democratic values. What, rather, of the principles, habits, norms, or traditions of political Europeanism? Just as there are common and distinctive themes in the way that Europeans approach social and economic questions, are there common and distinctive themes in the way that Europeans relate to politics and government, in the way that European political institutions and processes are structured, and in the positions that Europeans hold on key political and policy questions? Is there, in other words, a European political model that is distinct from the national models within which most political activity in the region takes place?

In those few instances where reference is made to a latent European political model, it is typically applied as shorthand or code for regional integration or the construction of a European superstate. Thus eurosceptics might argue that the 'European political model' is not one they wish to see imposed on their home state; in other words, they do not want to see additional integration. For their part, sociologists might point to the post-national quality of politics in the European Union,[2] arguing that if there is a European model then it is one in which the role of the state has declined and a new relationship has evolved between nations, states, and Europe. Finally, scholars of international relations might point to how the European model—by which they once again mean the European Union—is impacting the nature of the global system. But none of these analyses shed much light on the political qualities of Europeanism.

The logical starting point in the search for any such qualities would be a consideration of political culture, if understood—along the lines proposed first by Durkheim, and then developed by Almond and Verba[3]—as the collective norms, values, and attitudes that govern the expectations of society about politics and government. Put another way, are there common themes in the way that Europeans believe that government should be conducted, in the role they feel that government should play in their lives, in the role they see themselves playing in the political process, in their views regarding the core purposes of government, and in their views regarding the political goals and ideals of society? Pinning down such attitudes at the national or state level has proved challenging enough, but identifying the common views of a multinational community—particularly one as diverse as Europe—is a problem of a different order. Studies of political culture incorporate psychological, sociological, hypothetical, and even linguistic factors, and must take account of geography, history, religion, ethnicity, and external relations. Combining all these factors in order to construct a model of politics and government in Europe presents considerable difficulties.

Undeterred, this chapter attempts to offer at least a preliminary assessment of the norms and principles that give political Europeanism its particular character. It moves beyond a general association with the principles of democracy, which are both clear and highly evolved in Europe, and instead looks at the cultural, institutional, and procedural qualities that make European politics—that is, politics in Europe, not politics at the level of Europe—distinctive. It first identifies the particular qualities of European political culture as they relate to questions over the relative responsibilities of the state and the individual, and then assesses communitarianism as a concept that sheds light on Europeanist views towards the nature and responsibility of government. It ends with a discussion of the impact of the parliamentary model—created and most highly evolved in Europe—before offering some concluding thoughts on the nature of the European political space.

Is there a European political culture?

Little attention has been paid by scholars of Europe to the possibility that there might be a pan-European political culture. Assuming that political culture is a useful analytical tool (and not all agree even on this), the critical difficulty in the European case has been to identify themes common to societies that have often had quite different political histories. Consider, for example, the distinction between the republican and revolutionary heritage of politics in France and the monarchical and evolutionary heritage of British government, or the attempts to build or rediscover democratic traditions in eastern European states not long removed from Soviet-style one-party government. Consider also the unusually unstable character of government in Italy, where the office of prime minister changed hands thirty-eight times between 1945 and 2008, while the chancellorship of Germany changed hands just eight times over the same period. Consider also the often different national responses to European integration, whether in regard to its very purpose and its implications for state sovereignty, or in regard to the functional details of the manner in which integration has evolved. 'The tension at the core of the European project', concludes Athanassopoulou, 'may be seen as a consequence, partly, of the reality that modern Europe has never developed a shared political culture'.[4]

An additional layer of complexity is added by the volatility of political culture. In studies of the nature and character of politics in individual European states, the political science literature is replete with such terms as *realignment*, *decline*, *crisis*, and *revival*, and bulges with lengthy philosophical and theoretical debates about the reordering of values and attitudes, with analyses and studies of changes in the relative powers of executives and legislatures, of changes in party support and voting behaviour, the rise and fall of interest groups and social movements, the realignment and dealignment of ideological politics, the emergence of altered forms of political behaviour and association (often prefixed with terms such as *new* and *post*), and the replacement of old styles and orders with new. There is nothing consistent about politics in Europe, it seems, except change.

These analyses almost entirely focus on politics at the state level, rarely moving into the pan-European realm. And in those rare cases where European political culture has been examined, it is typically done so in the context of how it might relate to European integration.[5] Little evidence has so far been produced to support the argument that there may be a core of shared European political cultural features, but this is probably less an indication that such a core does not exist than a reflection of the limited perspective of most social scientists. For comparativists, Europe is still largely seen as a collection of sovereign states, and the topic of 'European politics' focuses either on national politics in Europe or on the politics of the European Union, with relatively little attention paid to the idea that there might be a European political space separate from—or in addition to—those of the European Union or its individual member states. For their part, that scholars of international relations have long dominated studies of the character and quality of the European Union means that it is often assessed as an international organization writ large, overlooking the possibility that the European Union might be seen as a political system in its own right. So instead of a common political culture, what most students of Europe see is a constellation of national political cultures. And yet we know that Europeans support the qualities that we associate with democracy, so why should they not also share other elements of political culture?

Girvin points out that within the shared pattern of beliefs that constitute a political culture 'there may be many subcultures but a common source of values which inform those beliefs. The presence of subcultures means that a political culture is not homogeneous in the sense that diversity does not exist, but it does mean that there is an irreducible core to which most, if not all, make reference'. Since early in the nineteenth century, he argues, this 'irreducible core' in liberal democracies has been a strong sense of state identity, which—as a focus for loyalty—has underpinned the continuity of political culture, and has allowed conflict to occur without threatening the system.[6] However, as we saw in Chapter 3, the value of state identity as a point of reference has been in decline, with the result that Europeans are now located within some combination of national, state, and European identity. Thus the frame of reference has changed, and instead of state identity being the main source of values, Europe itself may be taking on the role of the 'irreducible core'. But how we understand the role of Europe depends on how we understand the dynamics of political culture, and here we are faced with at least three options.

First, has there been a top-down dynamic at work, by which the process of European integration has had an homogenizing effect on political culture, institutions, and processes across Europe? Has there, in other words, been a Europeanization of political culture? Relatively little effort has been made until recently to understand what impact European integration has had on government, politics, and policy in the member states,[7] and in the expanding debate about the meaning and application of Europeanization it is notable how little it has been applied to norms rather than to institutions and processes.[8] And even in the case of institutions, most of the discussions so far have been inconclusive at best. Consider the conclusions offered by three studies of parties, executives, and courts:

- Mair looks at the impact of Europe on national party systems (restricted by his own admission to its direct rather than its indirect impact) and concludes that there is little evidence that Europe has much changed or influenced those systems, and that its impact is likely to remain limited so long as there are no elections for a European-level executive.[9]

- An analysis by Goetz of the impact of Europe on national executives describes it as a cause in search of an effect, noting the doubts about the explanatory power of European integration as a force driving domestic executive change, and concluding that not enough research has been directed at trying to understand the relative role of Europeanization compared to other explanations of change.[10]

- In her study of the impact of the European Court of Justice on national courts, Conant is able to conclude only that the transformation of domestic judicial structures remains incomplete and that there is still much national institutional variation.[11]

Second, has there been a bottom-up dynamic at work, with the political culture of the European Union being driven by an accumulation of the cultures of the member states? Since the structure of EU institutions and processes has evolved via a process in which member states have worked to achieve a consensus, it might be reasonable to conclude that European political culture has been influenced by the manner in which competing national norms and values have been exported upwards. But the EU institutions, and the manner in which they function, are more a reflection of the political compromises that have been made along the road of integration, rather than a reflection of national political cultures. This is true even of the European Parliament, the one institution with the most direct links to European voters. It has many of the features of a conventional national legislature but still lacks some of its powers (such as a monopoly over the adoption of new laws), it lacks the conventional relationship with an executive found in national legislatures, and its party groups have a role within the EP that is quite different from the role of parties in national legislatures. And in the case of the European Court of Justice, its structure is more a reflection of the French precedent than of a melange of the arrangements at work in the six founding members of the EEC. Laterally, though, we can see political culture in some EU states being exported to others via the process of integration. Hence that process has been a critical motive force behind the spread of democratic ideals to those member states—such as Portugal, Spain, and some of the eastern European states—that became members of the European Union not long after being freed from the confines of authoritarianism.

Finally, to what extent has European political culture been driven and formed by a wider set of pressures common to all member states? These pressures might have grown out of the process of integration, or out of the broader political and economic changes that have come with modernization, or out of the external pressures that have helped bring Europeans together, or out of the place of liberal democracies within the new environment of globalization. In other words, it has not been a top-down or a bottom-up process that has been at work, but rather a phenomenon within which all European states—members and non-members of the European Union alike—have been carried along on a wave of change that has impacted the entire region. But the challenge here is to determine the dynamics of those pressures and to distinguish them from other influences on the formation of the norms and values that constitute political culture.

Almond et al. argue that political culture can be understood at three levels: system (views about the political community and the values and organizations that hold the political system together), process (what citizens expect of the political process, and how they should relate to that process), and policy (what citizens expect governments to achieve).[12] At the system level, patriotism and national identity play a critical role, but we saw in Chapter 3 how attitudes towards the state, citizenship, and patriotism have changed in Europe, leaving most Europeans once again reviewing their attitudes towards the system. Another critical systemic quality—support for welfarism and for government management of the economy—is addressed in Chapter 5, yet another—the distant relationship between church and state—is addressed in Chapter 7, and we have already noted that the support of Europeans for democratic values is clear and uncontested. What, then, of the underlying features that make European political culture distinctive? There are at least five of note.

First, while Europeanism reflects all the conventional liberal democratic attitudes regarding human rights and democracy, Europeans have a singularly pragmatic view of the nature, purposes, and possibilities of democracy, driven by their historical experiences and by their views about the nature of both civil society and the mechanics of today's relationships between and among European states. European pragmatism stands in notable contrast to American idealism, which has long emphasized the achievement of goals, even if those goals have occasionally seemed to be just beyond reach. There is considerable cynicism towards elected officials in the United States, as reflected in polls in recent decades about public attitudes towards Congress and members of Congress; but there is also considerable faith in the political system, and in its abilities to change and to emerge from crisis. Words such as *hope*, *dream*, and *vision* routinely appear in the rhetoric of elected officials (nowhere more so than in the speeches of Barack Obama as he ran for office and then dealt with the global economic crisis), and there is also a persistent belief that almost all problems are capable of resolution.

For their part, Europeans are more restrained in how much they believe can be achieved without the necessary combination of time, effort, political will, and good fortune. This might be described as pessimism, but it might also be regarded as realism or pragmatism given the limitations of achieving change within complex political and social arrangements. The views of Europeans are reflected in the extent to which they place a premium on results over rules, while Americans tend to take the opposite view. Americans feel that the primary purpose of a government is to guarantee fair processes, and that it is up to individuals to make the most of the opportunities offered by those processes, while Europeans are more focused on ensuring that the results are as equal as possible. While Americans are more inclined to believe that if the process is fair the results will also be fair, Europeans are unwilling to place as much faith in the possibilities of the rules.

Second, patterns of political participation in Europe have been changing, with a drift away from the conventional and towards the unconventional. The data show that participation in the electoral process has been declining through much of Europe, with fewer people engaging in campaign activities, and turnout at national elections either falling or remaining static (see Figure 4.1). The most common explanation for this has been a growing sense of political alienation, and yet there is evidence from multiple European states that more people are rejecting indirect participation in politics through their elected officials—in whom they generally have declining trust and faith—in favour of more direct influence through joining interest groups, demanding and voting in referendums (which

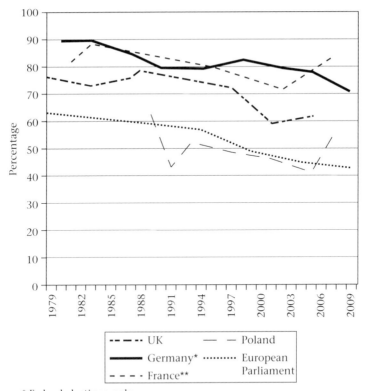

Figure 4.1 Trends in voter turnout

* Federal elections only

** Presidential elections only

are now a significant feature of decision-making on EU matters), signing petitions, or taking part in direct political action. There has, in other words, been something of a shift from representative democracy to participatory democracy in Europe.[13] This is a trend that stands in contrast to the American experience, where turnout at elections has recently been rising (up from a low of 49.1 per cent in 1996 to 55.3 per cent in 2004 and 56.8 per cent in 2008) at the same time as worried commentaries have been written about the extent to which Americans are disengaging from politics and their communities.[14] Americans still join groups in greater numbers than Europeans, and civil society is less organized in Europe,[15] but membership of a group does not necessarily mean engagement with its work, just as a lack of membership does not mean that Europeans do not network informally.

Third, political culture in most European societies reflects a high degree of fragmentation and heterogeneity, even in those states where there are relatively few social or economic divisions, such as Finland, Norway, and Sweden. The sources of these qualities are multiple and various, lying in a combination of class differentiations, elite versus mass tensions, secular versus religious tensions, disputes over the goals of the welfare state, national identities, ideological variation, and the relatively new contribution of racial and religious diversity. Attitudes towards the state have never been entirely stable, and the matter of loyalty to Europe has now been added to the nineteenth- and early twentieth-century competition for loyalty between states and nations, and to the divisions among those who support the achievements of integration, those who oppose or criticize, and those who do not care much either way. These multiple cleavages influence the manner in which Europeans relate to national political systems and their elected governments, and also the manner in which they relate to one another and define their political priorities. They also help explain the sometimes high levels of political alienation and distrust, and the inclination of many Europeans to move to unconventional means of engaging with government.

Fourth, government in Europe is attuned to the needs and procedures of international (actually, inter-state) decision-making. While this is generally true of all governments that engage in the work of international organizations, that ratify international treaties, and that take seriously their obligations under international law, with Europeans this phenomenon has evolved further. The obvious explanation can be found in the patterns of cooperation and consensus that have been required under EU decision-making, where the independence of national governments has been reduced in favour of broader European interests. Less obvious, however, has been the impact of changing views about the role of the nation and the state, and the growing hold of cosmopolitanism on the Europeanist political imagination. While much is made of the difficulties that European governments have experienced in finding common ground on numerous issues, the existence of a substantial body of European law and policy attests to the extent to which a consensus has been achieved. It also illustrates the extent to which national interests have been combined with and often subsumed under European interests, and the extent to which the European governing style combines local, national, state, and European interests.

Finally, political culture in Europe is notable for its distrust of—or perhaps simply its failure to understand—federalism. Logically, it might seem that federalism should fall quite naturally into Europeanist calculations: a European federation would reflect many of the new realities of the relationship between Europe and its states and nations. But while most Europeans are exposed to federalist ideas, they tend to distrust them. This is partly because few Europeans have experienced federalism in practice: of the forty European states, only Austria, Belgium, and Germany are formally federal; Spain and Britain have some federal qualities; and Bosnia and Switzerland are confederal. The remaining states are unitary, which means that most Europeans have been socialized to work within political systems in which most power is focused in the hands of a relatively strong state government, while the local government has little or no independent authority.[16]

This view has been exploited by eurosceptics, who have employed federalism as code for the loss of national sovereignty and the move towards a United States of Europe. The actual and potential reach of the European Union is often expressed in federalist terms, and federalism has been at the core of the debate about European integration since the beginning, generating a lively and wide-ranging academic literature. But while interest groups such the Union of European Federalists, the European Movement, and the Young European Federalists have been active in promoting federalist ideas, and while federalism comes in many forms, with the debate over its nature, quality, and effects suffering significant theoretical confusion,[17] this matters little to most Europeans. This is unfortunate, because the debate about federalism has much to offer in the way of shedding useful light on the nature of European integration.

Communitarian Europe

Individual rights are central to notions of democracy, but so is the question of how the rights and interests of individuals relate to those of the community. The emphasis on the individual is clear in the United States, where most Americans would argue that the primary purpose of a government is to promote the freedom of the individual and that individuals are ultimately responsible for their own welfare and opportunities. Individualism and self-interest predominate in American calculations, a point made by de Tocqueville almost 200 years ago,[18] and for which much evidence continues to exist today. Europeanism represents a rather different view, arguing that there has been too much emphasis on individual liberty and too little on the community, and that there should be more of a balance between individualism and social responsibility.[19] Most Europeans would argue that too much emphasis on individual rights runs the danger of the interests of the community beginning to suffer, and that government has a primary responsibility for protecting and promoting the interests of both the individual and the community. As Tony Blair put it in a 1998 speech, the view in Britain—contrasting with the 'crude individualism' of the 1980s—was that challenges had to be met collectively, that 'the best route to individual advancement and happiness lies in a thriving society of others', and the view that 'It's up to me' was being replaced by 'It's up to us'.[20]

Europeanism is closely affiliated with communitarianism, perhaps the most quintessential of European political values, but a concept with which (like cosmopolitanism) few Europeans are familiar. Selznick defines it as 'any doctrine that prizes collective goods or ideals and limits claims to individual independence and self-realization'.[21] Etzioni sees it as a concern with 'the balance between social forces and the person, between community and autonomy, between the common good and liberty, between individual rights and social responsibilities'. Communitarians, he argues, are not majoritarians, but instead seek a 'strong democracy' in which activity goes beyond occasional political participation, and government is instead responsive to all its members. Each member of the community owes something to all others, and the community owes something to each of its members.[22] On the economic front, communitarians argue that the debate between supporters of the private sector and the public sector has overlooked the needs of society.

Tracing its philosophical heritage back to the mid-nineteenth-century notion of communalism, which argued that the interests of individuals were best served through promoting the interests of the communities to which they belonged, communitarianism is based on two core principles:

• The idea of positive rights, meaning rights which oblige or permit action, or provide for the availability of a service by—for example—the state. These are distinct from negative rights, which oblige inaction, or provide against actions by others. Examples of positive rights include public education, health care, housing, social security, and government programmes to ensure a clean environment and a minimum quality of life—all objectives that are central to Europeanist values. Negative rights include civil and political rights such as freedom of speech, religion, assembly, and the press, and the right to life, liberty, security, and equality before the law.

- The idea of social capital, described by Putnam as the connections among individuals and the networks that arise from them, as distinct from physical capital (physical objects) or human capital (the properties of individuals).[23] Societies where social capital is strong will have healthy and active social networks, both formal (organized group activity) and informal (family and personal ties), which will result in higher levels of interpersonal trust and of trust in institutions, greater participation in civil society, and stronger evidence of shared norms and values. The greater the interaction among people, the greater the sense of community spirit and shared interests. While Europeans are voting less, express low levels of trust in political institutions, and are the subject of numerous worried debates about isolation and social fragmentation, they are participating more in other forms of political activity, their informal social ties generally remain strong, and they have not yet been as impacted as Americans by the rise of suburban life, the decline of group membership and participation, or the increased use of courts to resolve disputes (see Chapter 6).

Because it rejects the notion that people 'should be left to follow their own conception of the good in most matters of social conduct',[24] communitarianism has been described by its critics as 'anti-individual'[25], and some of its principles have been associated with those of communism and even totalitarianism. Its critics may quote Abraham Lincoln's argument that prohibition runs the danger of making a crime out of something that is not a crime, or Hitler's argument in *Mein Kampf* that communities can only be conserved by the readiness of individuals to subordinate personal interests. But this rather misses the point regarding the way it is approached by Europeans, who are more likely to argue—like Tony Blair—that a decent society is based less on rights than on duties and that for the opportunities provided by society, individual responsibility is demanded. Communitarianism underpins attitudes towards social welfare in Europe, but it is also a defining part of the manner in which Europeans approach government: they would argue—unlike many Americans—that society can be a better judge of what is good for individuals rather than vice versa, and that the state has a role in restricting individual rights for the greater good of the community. In other words, while they support negative rights, they are more willing to allow the state to take action on individual issues in the interests of the community.

The emphasis here is on the state rather than on government, in which Europeans have low levels of faith and trust (but no lower than those in

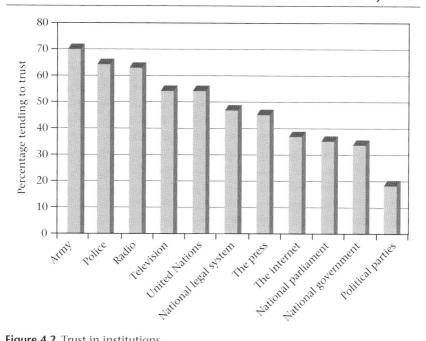

Figure 4.2 Trust in institutions

Source: European Commission, *Eurobarometer* 69, November 2008.

other liberal democracies).[26] Polls in the European Union indicate that levels of trust in the army, the police, and the media are significantly higher than those in government institutions and political parties (see Figure 4.2). Few believe that national administrative institutions are transparent (68 per cent believe they are not very transparent or not transparent at all, compared to 24 per cent who believe they are very transparent or transparent), and in spite of doubts about integration there is a greater level of faith in the direction being taken by the European Union (42 per cent right direction, 25 per cent wrong direction) than in the direction being taken by the country in which they live (32 per cent right direction, 45 per cent wrong direction).[27] Polls also indicate higher levels of trust in voluntary organizations, reflecting the extent to which Europeans are willing to replace political engagement with civic engagement.

Sometimes the question of whether or not motorcyclists should be required by law to wear crash-helmets is used to illustrate the issues at stake in the relative balance of individual and community interests. Many would argue that motorcyclists should have the freedom not to wear helmets, and that punishing them for going without helmets creates the kind of victimless crime that is so often a result of communitarian law. But what happens if a motorcyclist has an accident and sustains injuries that might have been prevented by a helmet? The medical attention they will need will take time and resources away from other patients, if they receive public health care the costs will have to be met by taxpayers, and if they receive private health care the costs will impact insurance premiums. How do the individual rights of motorcyclists weigh up against the collective rights of those who pay the costs of providing health care?

Another case in point, and one where the contrasts between Americans and Europeans are particularly clear, is the issue of gun control. In the United States, this is a headline political matter, the argument by the gun lobby being that the right to bear arms is protected by the constitution (in itself a debatable issue, reliant upon how the Second Amendment to the US Constitution is read and understood) and that the rights of individuals relative to the government can only be guaranteed if citizens are allowed to be armed. A 2008 poll found that 73 per cent of Americans believe that the US Constitution guarantees the right to own guns, and revealed that support for stricter gun control laws had fallen slightly since 2002, from 54 per cent to 49 per cent.[28] Another poll found that support for legislation to ban handguns has been falling steadily in the United States, from about 60 per cent in 1959 to about 30 per cent in 2007.[29]

In Europe, the view is quite different: there is no general expectation of a right to own weapons, and there is a prevailing view that on this particular issue the collective good outweighs most arguments about individual rights. Gun control is rarely debated except in the wake of massacres such as those in Scotland in 1996, in Germany in 2002, and in Finland in 2007 and 2008, all of which led to shifts in public opinion and encouraged the government in each case to tighten gun control laws. Even in Switzerland—where a reliance on a militia defence system has meant liberal gun owner-ship laws—there has recently been talk of a national referendum on the tightening of gun controls. Critics of gun control laws in Britain have argued that crime rates have grown there since the government banned handguns in 1996, while crime rates in the United States have decreased in the wake of the liberalization of gun laws, particularly those allowing individuals to carry concealed weapons. But supporters of gun control point to Europe's significantly lower overall homicide rates as evidence that gun control laws show how the collective good can be protected by the curbing of individual rights.

Europe's homicide rates are indeed notably low, and among the lowest in the world (see Figure 4.3). Compared to highs of 69 deaths per 100,000 people in South Africa, 61 in Colombia, and 30–1 in Russia and Brazil, its

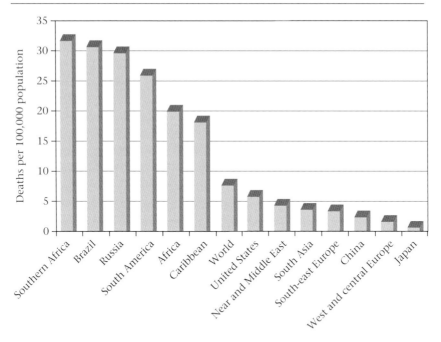

Figure 4.3 Homicide rates

Source: Estimates by UN Office on Drugs and Crime, at http://www.unodc.org (retrieved August 2009). Figures are for 2004.

overall rate of 8.1 makes Europe look remarkably peaceful, and national rates appear even more so: 2.2 in the Czech Republic and Hungary, 1.6 in Britain and France, 1.0 in Germany and Greece, and 0.8 in Austria and Norway. Only the three Baltic republics, with rates of 9–10, are significantly outside the general European range. As regards homicides committed with guns, compared to an estimated global figure of 60 per cent and a rate of 59 per cent in North America, the figure of 19 per cent in west and central Europe is notably low. Various explanations have been offered for the European situation, including better policing, improved systems of criminal justice, higher levels of urbanization, and improved education. But critical among these are changing attitudes towards violence, which are in turn a reflection of the extent—relatively speaking—to which Europeans place the interests of the community above the interests of the individual.

Critics of communitarianism argue that the nanny state can sometimes go too far in its attempts to protect or change the behaviour of society. While many conservative Americans bemoan the extent to which their government is prepared to coddle them and influence social behaviour, protective policies are more apparent in Europe, reflected in everything from extensive consumer protection regulations to the spreading presence of closed-circuit TV (CCTV) cameras in public places. While these trends are debated among Europeans, they are not always resisted. On the question of CCTV, for example, polls find that while there are concerns about their implications for privacy, their role in crime prevention is widely understood and appreciated (even if the hard evidence of their role in crime prevention is sometimes ambiguous).[30] And if the proliferation of conspiracy theories and web sites warning against the role of government as an Orwellian Big Brother is any indication, there is notably more concern about government regulation and surveillance in the United States than in Europe.

Communitarianism has much in common with cosmopolitanism in that it is a concept better known to academic audiences than to the general populace, and much of the debate about its qualities and merits has been theoretical rather than practical. And yet it offers much to an understanding of what drives Europeanist ideas. There is a clear emphasis in European calculations on positive rights, whether measured by expectations of the state or by the more limited emphasis on negative rights, and there has been little evidence of a substantial decline of social capital in Europe. While levels of social capital seem to vary across Europe, studies have suggested that the differences are driven more by the varied determinants of that capital, with some countries emphasizing formal networks while others emphasize informal networks.[31]

Institutions: the effects of parliamentary government

Are political institutions a reflection of the society in which they are embedded, or are societies a reflection of the character of their governing political institutions? In other words, to what extent do the structural principles of institutions reflect or shape the political cultures of the societies in which they function? The evidence suggests that there is a symbiotic relationship at work, with both elements shaping and being shaped by the other. Of one principle we can be sure: the relationship is never static, and new challenges, needs, and opportunities bring constant change in the internal organization of institutions; in their relationship to one another; and in their place within the political system.[32] A few attempts have been made to discern the outlines of political models in Europe; among them is the two-way distinction made by Schmidt:

- Statist polities such as France, Britain, and Italy, which are more closed to interest influence in policy formulation, more administrative than regulatory in policy implementation, and more conflictual in culture, with decisions generally taken at the top.

- Corporatist polities such as Germany, which tend to be open only to certain privileged interests in policy formulation, more corporative than regulatory because they work with those interests in applying the rules, and more consensual in culture, with decisions rarely taken at the top.[33]

But the one relative constant in the European case—and the nucleus of political Europeanism—has been the durability of the parliamentary model, which was born and bred in Europe, and is today used in one form or another in every European state. It has been exported outside Europe, to be sure, and has fared well (with local variations) in Japan, Israel, most of Britain's non-African former colonies and dominions, and some of France's former African colonies; but it is almost unknown in the Americas, in the Middle East, and in much of Africa. We may not be able to claim that the parliamentary model is any longer uniquely European, but nowhere does it dominate national government to the same extent, or provide politics and government with quite so strong an institutional identity or quite so distinctive a procedural character, as it does in Europe. The region remains—in the view of Müller et al.—'the heartland of parliamentarianism'.[34]

The parliamentary model has four core elements:

- The coexistence of a political head of government and a neutral or symbolic head of state.

- The fusion of executive and legislature; the former comes out of the latter, and the two have mutual sets of responsibilities to—and powers over—the other.

- Collective decision-making through a cabinet or council of ministers.

- The division of parliament into governing and opposition parties or coalitions.

A variation on this theme is found in the semi-presidential or dual executive model, in which executive presidents and prime ministers coexist. Both variations are quite distinct from American-style presidential republics, in which executive presidents are elected separately from legislatures, govern with independent powers, and combine the roles of head of state and head of government. Only two European states (Belarus and Cyprus) use an executive presidential system, while eight (Bosnia and Herzegovina,

Table 4.1. European political systems

Executive presidencies (2)
Belarus, Cyprus

Semi-presidential systems with elected executive presidents (3)
France, Romania, Serbia

Semi-presidential systems with elected semi-executive presidents (5)
Bosnia and Herzegovina, Finland, Lithuania, Poland, Ukraine

Parliamentary systems with elected non-executive presidents (21)
Albania, Austria, Bulgaria, Croatia, Czech Republic, Estonia, Germany, Greece, Hungary, Iceland, Ireland, Italy, Kosovo, Latvia, Macedonia, Malta, Moldova, Montenegro, Portugal, Slovakia, Slovenia

Parliamentary systems with hereditary monarchs (8)
Belgium, Denmark, Luxembourg, Netherlands, Norway, Spain, Sweden, UK

Direct democracies (1)
Switzerland

Finland, France, Lithuania, Poland, Romania, Serbia, and Ukraine) use variations on the theme of semi-presidential systems, and Switzerland has its own uniquely collective executive structure. In all remaining twenty-nine European states, publics live under non-executive heads of state (whether monarchs or presidents), and their heads of government are mainly prime ministers or chancellors who are members of the legislature and whose power is almost entirely determined by the balance of party representation in the national legislature (see Table 4.1). There are four main effects of this political arrangement.

First, the coexistence of heads of state and heads of government encourages the view that allegiance to the state is not necessarily the same as allegiance to the government, and vice versa. Heads of government come and go, their position and power dependent upon changing levels of public support and approval, but the head of state remains as the embodiment of the values of the state, largely untouched (except in semi-presidential executives) by ideological partisanship. The situation in Europe stands in contrast to that found in executive presidential systems such as the United States, Mexico, Brazil, or Argentina, where the combination of political and state responsibilities in a single office blurs the distinction between allegiance to state and allegiance to government. Presidents may be the only government officials elected in a nationwide vote, but they are often accorded semi-monarchical status, the implication in more extreme cases being that criticism of the president verges on criticism of the state, and thus may be somehow unpatriotic.

Monarchies and non-executive presidents offer Europeans several advantages: they provide an institution that functions above politics and around which the citizenry can rally in times of trouble, they can arbitrate the formation of a new government should there be no party or coalition in clear control of a legislature, they can act as a moral constraint on elected political leaders attempting to extend their powers, and they can act as politically neutral symbols of the state. Legitimation can be provided by constitutions and courts, it is true, but the process of judicial review is often politically charged, and judges will often have their own political agendas. This is rarely the case with monarchs or non-executive presidents in the European model. At the same time, however, non-executive heads of state are often criticized for being expensive symbols, and monarchs in particular are rejected by republicans as a throwback to the feudal era, as perpetuators of the class system, and as dividers rather than uniters. In today's increasingly egalitarian Europe, however, where monarchs are expected to show the common touch, the socially divisive nature of monarchs and their attendant aristocracies has declined.

There are some forty monarchies left in the world today, of which nine are either absolute monarchies or systems in which monarchs have significant political powers. The remainder (of which fifteen are in states that were former colonies or dominions of Britain) are constitutional, meaning that there are limits to their political powers, which are typically outlined in a constitution. Most of these—including Bhutan, Japan, Lesotho, Morocco, and Thailand—are non-European, but the tradition of constitutional monarchies comes mainly out of European precedent: most European states had monarchies at one time or another, limits began to be placed on the powers of the British monarch by the Glorious Revolution of 1688 and the Bill of Rights of 1689, and the spread of republicanism in the wake of the French Revolution ensured that monarchical powers declined throughout the nineteenth century. Today, there are just seven remaining monarchies in Europe (Belgium, Denmark, the Netherlands, Norway, Spain, Sweden, and the United Kingdom) and one grand duchy (Luxembourg), but the spirit of a constitutional monarchy lives on in the twenty-one European states that have non-executive presidents, who are either directly elected by the people or appointed by legislatures. Furthermore, governments in many other parts of the world are characterized by a deliberate rejection of monarchy and support for republicanism, giving further support to the idea that the symbolism attached to non-executive heads of state is primarily a European phenomenon.

The second effect of the parliamentary model is that while a presidential republic along US or Latin American lines distinguishes executive authority and legislative authority (thus presidents and members of the cabinet cannot be members of the legislature, and presidents do not come to office as a result of the balance of party representation in the legislature), the European parliamentary model fuses executive and legislative functions. The prime minister is normally the leader of the biggest political party in the legislature, or the individual most acceptable to the parties joined in a coalition government. Thus the executive is closely identified with the balance of parties in the legislature, and prime ministers are themselves members of the legislature; there is typically no separate election for a prime minister. Prime ministers have extensive powers of appointment, and are rarely required to have their appointments confirmed by another body. They also have strategic advantages tied to their control of the party or coalition, and to their ability to decide the date of national elections. Decision-making within the cabinet is collective, but the prime minister coordinates, sets the agenda, and expects the support of cabinet colleagues. Governments with strong majorities in the legislature can also normally expect party unity, meaning strong influence over the legislative programme. The effect of this is to make the lines of policy responsibility relatively clear.

By contrast, an executive or semi-executive president may have to govern in conjunction with a hostile legislature, particularly when the opposition has a majority, but even in some cases when the president's own party has a majority. In the parliamentary system, partisanship is normal, party discipline is relatively tight, and lines of responsibility are more clear. In a presidential republic or a semi-presidential system, the links between the executive and the legislature are not as strong, mainly because the president does not control key appointments within the legislature. As a result, partisan lines are more blurred, and there is less association between voters and parties. There is also more opportunity for legislatures to block the policy programme of the executive (an event that would potentially set off a crisis or even a fall of the government in a parliamentary system), and for the executive to blame a hostile legislature for its own failures. Hence the lines of responsibility are often less clear.

The fusion of executive and legislature also influences the place of individual leaders in the political system, and the role of personality in a government. In presidential executives, presidents are typically the only members of government elected through a national vote, and thus are the only members of government (other than more senior or prominent members of the cabinet) who develop a truly national reputation. As a result, much about the character of government depends upon the character and personal preferences of the incumbent, who—in spite of the limitations imposed by constitutional rules, political realities, and the separation of powers—will often be able to make a distinctive mark on government, leading the country in a different direction from that taken by his or her predecessor. In parliamentary systems, by contrast, prime ministers are more often regarded as part of the collective government, senior members of the cabinet are often well-known national figures who may have aspirations to win the top office, and—except in the case of strong personalities such as a Margaret Thatcher or a Helmut Kohl—personality government will often be subsumed to collective cabinet government. Bryce long ago expressed this phenomenon rather differently by arguing that the presidential system 'leaves more to chance' than the parliamentary system, where prime ministers will be influenced and balanced by cabinet members; in the case of presidents the character of the individual comes more to the fore.[35]

The fusion of executive and legislature also speeds up the decision-making process. Where presidents must balance their influence and power with those of a legislature, and cannot be sure that even a large legislative majority for their own party will mean support for the president's policies, prime ministers are usually assured of strong support from their parliamentary base, the level of strength depending upon the size and stability of the majority held by the governing party or coalition and upon the unity of that party or coalition. (Thus Italian prime ministers are relatively weak because their coalitions are typically fragile, while British prime ministers are relatively strong because they almost always have majority party support.)

The third effect of the parliamentary model is that cabinet government is at the heart of the European political process.[36] Together with governing collectively and being the foundation of the power and influence of the prime minister, cabinets (or councils of ministers) are also testing grounds for future contenders for the prime ministership, and a vital link between the bureaucracy, the government, interest groups, and voters. Members of the cabinet are usually members of the legislature, and the cabinet as a whole is politically responsible to the legislature, which has the power of oversight over ministers and their departments and can compel the cabinet to resign. Cabinet government is by no means unique to Europe, and is found in some form in parts of Africa and Asia, but nowhere is it so generalized or so much a feature of the process of government as in Europe. In the United States, the cabinet is considered more a part of the bureaucracy than of the executive, it rarely meets as a whole, its membership is separate from that of the legislature, and cabinet experience is rarely an opportunity for political advancement.

Finally, the dynamics of the European parliamentary model are based fundamentally on the centrality of political parties to the political process. The prime minister and cabinet rely on the majority party or coalition as the base of their support and power, and for security of their tenure. In majoritarian systems[37] where large parties dominate, such as those in Britain, Ireland, France, and Greece, the executive can wield considerable powers and is almost guaranteed that its policies will be confirmed by the legislature. But this is relatively rare. More typically in Europe, there are multiple parties representing the entire political spectrum, from communists and socialists on the left through greens, social democrats, centrists, and liberals to Christian Democrats, conservatives, and fascists on the right. The result is that coalitions have become the norm, particularly in the Benelux countries, Scandinavia, Germany, Italy, and Switzerland. Whether these are coalitions of the centre–left or the centre–right, the number and variety of their membership results in a system in which parties are typically obliged to cooperate and compromise in order for business to be done.

Another quality of party politics in Europe is the critical role played by parties in defining and mobilizing opposition. In executive presidential systems, parties do not always typically function as the formal opposition, mainly because they do not have leaders in place who would take over the presidency were the party to win a majority at an election. In authoritarian systems such as China or many African states, opposition parties are either not permitted or are controlled and manipulated. But in Europe, opposition parties are a central and formal part of the political process, help clarify the political options for voters, and play a critical role in determining the structure and longevity of governments.

There has been much debate over the last few decades about the decline of European party systems, and even about periodic crises in that system. But while it is clear that parties may not always have as much power as they think they do, and that party systems constantly evolve, they continue to persist, and it is hard to imagine what would replace them.[38] Furthermore, while legislatures and courts in particular have lost some of their powers as a result of the twin effects of European integration and regional devolution, the same cannot be said for parties. Integration has been slow to impact national parties,[39] but the creation of a growing number of pan-European party confederations in recent years promises to bring national parties closer together and encourage them to run pan-European campaigns for elections to the European Parliament, giving them a more prominent role in pan-European politics. Meanwhile, rising support for devolution and national self-determination has injected new vitality into national party systems by both encouraging the creation of new regionalist parties and obliging national parties to develop policies on regionalism.

The European political space

Understanding government is only partly a matter of understanding institutions and processes. Another critical but more often overlooked part of the equation concerns the outputs or actions of government, or the public policies pursued by executives and legislatures. Where once the problems that faced government were defined mainly at the state level in Europe, and the responses were fashioned as a result of national priorities, national political realities, and national budgets, the process of integration has made this decreasingly true; problems are now defined and addressed increasingly at the European level. To the local and national agendas with which we are all familiar has been added a European agenda within which the broader interests of Europe have in several areas come to take priority over those of states and nations. Just how far the balance has changed is uncertain, with estimates—for example—that in areas where policy competence has shifted from the member states of the European Union to EU institutions, anything between 60 and 80 per cent of new laws are now developed at the European rather than at the state level. And non-EU states are impacted as well, given that most do the bulk of their trade with the European Union, have a variety of agreements with the European Union, and usually have aspirations eventually to join the European Union.

Mény et al. argue that the extension of the EU agenda does not necessarily mean that there is a European consensus on how to deal with policy problems, but rather that 'Europe is ever more the site of debate, the place where issues are formulated, where different interpretations confront one another, and where different actors engage in conflict or negotiation and where solutions are defined'.[40] Eurosceptics have offered much resistance to this trend, to be sure, and the debates over the meaning of Europe are still more often couched in terms of how individual states relate to Europe than in terms of how public opinion is evolving across the region. However, it has become all but impossible in practical terms for any European state to isolate itself from pan-European debates on issues as varied as agriculture, the environment, social policy, immigration, regional development, consumer protection, employment, culture, and foreign and defence policy.

Only in areas such as education, crime, and health care is the policy debate still mainly one pursued at the state or local level. And the debates are not limited to the member states of the European Union but spill over into non-EU states as well, enveloped as they have been in the web of economic and political pressures that have reduced state independence in the interests of the collective agenda of Europe. Even, in an extreme example, if a country was to leave the European Union, it would find itself continuing to be impacted both directly and indirectly by European rules, standards, and requirements.

Where once the individual states of Europe had discrete political identities, whose values often coincided but more often did not, today there is an homogenizing effect at work by virtue of which all states (European Union and non-European Union) are moving toward a common set of political values, institutions, and priorities. The distinctions between authoritarian and democratic systems are declining, the distinctions between eastern and western political cultures are declining, many of the old national stereotypes are now of little more than historical interest, and the political systems of all European states are becoming more similar in terms of their structures and priorities. There is still no clearly discernible European political model as such, and sceptics are likely to argue that there may never be—politics is never a static process, and even in a country like the United States, formally united for more than two centuries, it is still possible to identify regional political cultures, and to find that while the institutions of the fifty state governments are approximately the same, they are often managed differently and approached differently by their constituent citizens. However, the political cultures and institutions of European states are becoming increasingly similar, and there has been the steady construction of a European political space within which business is conducted that is influenced by the competing priorities of Europe's states and in turn results in those priorities moving closer together.

The dimensions, qualities, and meaning of that space are still not fully understood or appreciated, and debates over European political matters are still couched very much in state terms. Thus, for example, in all the analysis that was attached to negative votes on new European treaties in Denmark, Ireland, France, and the Netherlands, it was often forgotten that the results of those votes were at least as much a reflection of domestic political thinking as of public opinion about the content of the treaties; many voters were not so much voting on the treaties as taking the opportunity to express a critical opinion about their incumbent national governments. Similarly, the debate over the outcome of European Parliament elections is often driven more by what the results say about the standing of national governments and political parties than what they say about the state of Europe. This became abundantly clear at the time of the 2009 elections, for example, when media coverage of the results in several countries focused on gains made by anti-European, far-right, and xenophobic parties, and on what the results said about the health of incumbent national governments. Little, meanwhile, was said about the meaning of the results for the European Union.

As noted earlier in this chapter, there has been much analysis of the qualities and character of politics and government in the individual states of Europe, and an expanding literature on the qualities and character of the politics and governance of the European Union and its impact on government in the member states. But little attention has so far been paid to the shared features and principles of government and politics across Europe. This has been mainly a reflection of the interests and biases of the specialists in the two sub-fields of political science most active on European matters: comparativists prefer to focus on politics at the state level, while scholars of international relations prefer to focus on how the dynamic of Europe is impacted by relations between and among its states. That the European Union might be seen as a political system in its own right is an idea that has only begun to gain traction since the early 1990s, but the focus still remains on the qualities of EU institutions rather than on Europe as a political space, sharing common institutional structures, common values, and common processes. This chapter has noted several aspects of political culture that might be seen as pan-European, along with several qualities of the institutional nature of politics in the region. But much remains to be done if we are to better understand the possibilities and parameters of a European political model.

5

Economics: Sharing the Wealth

During the closing stages of the 2008 US presidential election, the then-candidate Barack Obama—in discussing his plans to alter the balance of the tax burden between the wealthiest Americans and the middle class—commented on the importance of Americans 'sharing the wealth'. His Republican opponent John McCain responded by accusing Obama of being a socialist, and conservative columnists and bloggers were quick to suggest that Obama seemed to be planning to make the United States into a 'European-style' social democracy. If the latter is understood to mean support for a democratic welfare state and a mixed economy, then clearly all European states meet the definition of social democracy to one degree or another. But so also do the United States, Canada, Japan, Australia, and New Zealand. Social democracy may trace its roots to nineteenth-century European socialism, and social democratic parties may play a more vital and visible role in contemporary European politics than is the case in the United States; but on the core principles of social democracy it is clear that the European economic model is not much different from that in all other capitalist liberal democracies. Nor do Europeans differ much from others on their support for the general merits of the free market and private enterprise.

Where Europe is distinctive—and where the principles of Europeanism are most clear—is in the extent to which social democratic principles have become embedded in foundational assumptions about economic management, and in the extent to which dirigisme and welfarism have the advantage over laissez-faire and self-reliance. Polls reflect European concerns that the state intervenes too much in the marketplace, but they also indicate European acceptance of a higher degree of such intervention than is the case in other liberal democracies. In particular, there is wide support for the core goals and purposes of welfarism, for which the provisions found in

Europe are broader and deeper than those found elsewhere in the world; Europeanism equates with strong support for the idea that government should provide basic services such as education and health care (albeit alongside private alternatives), and that the costs should be met through a progressive system of taxation. This view has become so fundamental to Europeans that it sits at the heart of their conception of political rights. Hutton argues that while the American liberal definition of rights limits itself to political matters, the European definition extends to economic and social matters as well, encapsulating free health care, free education, the right to employment insurance, and so on.[1]

We do not hear as much talk of a European economic model as we do of a European social model (see Chapter 6), and much has been made of the distinctions between a more interventionist continental style and a more hands-off Anglo-Saxon style. But while distinctions can be made among approaches to economic management in individual European states, or clusters of these states, when Europe as a whole is compared with the United States, the distinctions become less visible. And of course the European economic model is quite distinct from those found in Russia, China, India, or the developing world.

This chapter will focus on four particular aspects of Europeanist approaches to economic management. First, it is clear that while the state as a territorial, legal, or psychological entity is on the decline in Europe, there is still strong support for the collective over the private delivery of key services, such as education and health care. Second, welfarism is alive and well in Europe, where there is support for the idea that those who are less fortunate are not necessarily the victims of their own bad judgement, and emphasis is placed on equality of results over equality of opportunity. Third, where military spending was once at the heart of European economic priorities, since 1945 there has been the construction of a civilian–industrial complex with a new emphasis on non-military priorities. Finally, Europeanism has led the way on the injection of the principle of sustainable development into the setting of economic priorities. Indeed, sustainability has become one of the defining mantras of European approaches to economic and social management.

The role of the state: collective preferences

As suggested in Chapter 3, the independence and territorial authority of the European state has been declining as Europeans have reviewed and reassessed their sense of identification with states, nations, and the broader European project. And yet the role of the European state as an economic manager and as a guarantor of societal welfare remains strong. While privatization has been popular in recent decades, Europeans still rely on the state as the regulator of much economic activity, and it has even been suggested that the 2005 votes against the draft European Constitution in France and the Netherlands were motivated at least in part by concerns that it gave too much precedence to competition and the open market, and by worries about 'the return of the primacy of economics over the social aims of public intervention'.[2] Europeans have also pointed with a notable degree of moral superiority to the role of soft regulation, untrammelled credit, minimal savings, and corporate greed in the United States in setting off the 2007–9 global economic crisis. The explanation for Europeanist preferences lies in the practice of European social democracy.

In an essay written in 1906, the German social scientist Werner Sombart asked why there was no socialism in the United States. His answer was fourfold: American workers had a favourable attitude towards capitalism and the American system of government, and were not excluded by the kind of class system that existed in Europe; the American two-party system made it difficult to form a successful socialist party; the potential radicalism of American workers was cancelled out by the material rewards provided by American capitalism; and the American worker had greater opportunities for upward social mobility.[3] Presumably, then, something like the opposite of each of these points could be assumed to hold true in the European case, or at least they did so in 1906: support for socialism was both widespread and growing due to the class system, which often encouraged unfavourable attitudes among workers towards capitalism, socialist parties found fertile soil in the European parliamentary environment, and worker access to material rewards was limited, as was social mobility.

More than a century later, however, the social and economic divisions that once made socialism more attractive to Europeans have weakened, and in some cases have disappeared: in particular, European workers have become wealthier, more politically empowered, more socially mobile, and the class system has declined. Using Sombart's logic, then, the attractions of socialism should have become as weak in Europe as they have been in the United States. But they have not. While old-style redistributive and interventionist socialism of the class warfare variety has certainly been marginalized, the hold of social democracy in Europe remains strong, and nowhere more so than in expectations regarding the advantages of government regulation of the business sector and the public delivery of social services.

In spite of widespread privatization, the expectation that the institutions of the state will guarantee the delivery of goods and services is stronger in Europe than in any other part of the world outside what little is left of the communist world. Where the majority of Americans feel that it is more important for government to provide them with the freedom to pursue other goals, for example, the majority of Europeans feel that it is more important for government to guarantee that no one is in need.

Europe was the birthplace of modern capitalism, and dominated the international economic system during the imperial era; by 1900 it had the greatest share of world gross domestic product, manufacturing output, and trade, and its corporations were the world's largest and were the progenitors both of globalization and of the dominating role played today in the international economy by multinationals. But as wealth grew, so did the obvious maldistribution of that wealth, sparking social and political demands for a redistribution of opportunity and resources. The foundations of the modern welfare state were laid in Germany and Britain in the nineteenth and early twentieth centuries and built upon in the Netherlands and the Nordic countries in the mid-war years. Following the Great Depression and the Second World War, welfarism came to be seen as an alternative to communism and capitalism, and the post-war settlement saw western European states moving from the selective provision of social services to a more comprehensive programme covering education, health care, unemployment, and social security.

The era of Keynesianism also meant support for regulation of the economy, which at first seemed to bring growth and prosperity: the new post-war sense of abundance was encapsulated in the comment by British Prime Minister Harold Macmillan in 1957 that Britain was enjoying 'a state of prosperity such as we have never had in my lifetime—nor indeed in the history of this country', and that 'most of our people have never had it so good'. But a combination of two world wars, the end of empire, and rising competition first from the United States and then from Japan reduced Europe's global economic power and forced a reassessment of priorities. Thatcherism in Britain and Reaganomics in the United States meant a change in direction; both were based on a rejection of Keynesianism and a turn instead to the classical liberal and free market philosophies of Friedrich von Hayek and the monetarist arguments of Milton Friedman and the Chicago School. Thatcher and Reagan spearheaded radical pro-market assessments in the 1980s, which brought particular change to the British economy as labour unions lost their political influence and the state retreated from the marketplace.

The effects of Thatcherism helped draw new attention to the extent to which attempts to open up the European marketplace had become bogged down, with too little progress on the principal goals of the single market programme: the removal of non-tariff barriers to the free movement of people, money, goods, and services. The dark days of Eurosclerosis—when low job growth, high unemployment, and depressed economic growth afflicted much of the region—forced a reappraisal of priorities and a relaunch in 1986 of the single-market programme. This happened just as a new era of globalization was beginning to dawn, and while even eurosceptics could agree that the single market was a worthwhile endeavour, opinion on the implications and effects of globalization was mixed. One school welcomed the new opportunities provided, while another held on grimly to the principle of economic nationalism that had been so much a part of the European landscape for so long.

This difference of opinion has generated the view that there are now two distinctive European economic models. The first is the 'continental' or 'Rhenish' model, found throughout continental Europe (even, increasingly so, in eastern Europe as it makes the transition to capitalism) and even perhaps in Japan. The term was popularized by Michel Albert in 1993,[4] and describes a belief that the state should intervene actively in the marketplace in order to redistribute wealth, offer corporations and workers needed protection (particularly from the pressures of globalization), and work against economic inequality and poverty. In other words, deliberate attempts are made to combine economic growth and social cohesion. Albert contrasts this with the 'Anglo-Saxon' model, so called because it is associated with English-speaking countries such as Britain, Ireland, the United States, and Canada. This emphasizes lower levels of tax and regulation, a greater reliance on the private sector to provide key services, a greater level of market freedom, and fewer guarantees of job security for workers. Pontusson makes the same basic distinctions but with different labels: he refers to the 'liberal market economies' of the English-speaking world and the 'social market economies' of continental Europe. The latter are distinguished from the former by the extensive public provision of social welfare and employment protection, strong labour unions, institutionalized collective bargaining systems, and densely organized business communities.[5]

On the more particular question of welfare, the European picture is more complex. In 1990, Esping-Andersen identified three different welfare state regime-types: the liberal Anglo-Saxon model (strict entitlement rules, modest benefits provided mainly to low-income and usually working-class state dependents, and subsidies for private welfare schemes); the corporatist continental European model (shaped by the church, strongly committed to the preservation of families, and encouraging parenthood); and the social democratic or Scandinavian model aimed at promoting equality at the highest level rather than limiting itself to minimal needs.[6] These divisions are reflected in Sapir's distinction between four social models: the Anglo-Saxon system (with more limited collective provision of social protection intended to cushion the impact of events that would lead to poverty); the Nordic (with high levels of social protection and taxation, and extensive intervention in the labour market); the Mediterranean (high legal employment protection, lower levels of unemployment benefits, spending concentrated on pensions); and the Continental (provision of social assistance through public insurance-based systems, and a limited role for the market in the provision of social assistance).[7] To both of these can be added the post-communist models of eastern Europe, whose qualities further complicate the overall picture.

Whatever academic research may conclude about policies, however, it is not clear how far ordinary Europeans go along with the distinctions. A 2008 Eurobarometer survey found that 58 per cent of residents of the European Union believed that the state intervened too much in the marketplace, and that 61 per cent believed that the free market was the best guarantor of economic prosperity. Interestingly, it found majority support for the merits of free competition in the two major Rhenish states (68 per cent in Germany and 54 per cent in France) as well as in the two Anglo-Saxon states (65 per cent in Ireland and 58 per cent in Britain); and, it also found—contrary to what the models would suggest—that the British were more inclined to think there was too much state intervention (73 per cent) than the Germans or the French (63 and 57 per cent, respectively).[8]

More questions about the Rhenish–Anglo-Saxon dichotomy were raised by responses to the 2007–9 global economic crisis, when in spite of rhetorical differences among political leaders, the responses pursued by most European governments were not that different from one another in the fundamentals, and stood in contrast to American responses. The latter focused on bailouts and loans to large companies facing bankruptcy, the quasi-nationalization of several of those companies, job creation, tax cuts, spending on public works programmes and infrastructure, and aid to the most troubled states. Meanwhile, Europeans initially derived some pleasure from American woes, pointing to the perils of American profligacy and risk-taking, to the US emphasis on profits and its disdain for regulation, and to the willingness of banks and credit institutions to lend without due concern for the ability of creditors to meet their financial obligations. European leaders liked to argue that the crisis was ultimately the fault of under-regulation in the United States, that it was an American problem that did not call for an American-style rescue plan in Europe, and that the correct response was not to spend more but to put in place a stronger system of regulation that would ensure transparency and accountability, and thus prevent similar crises emerging in future.

The long tradition of using crises to illustrate the end of Europe was dusted off once again as disagreements broke out among European governments, and optimism fizzled that the crisis might provide an opportunity for Europe to show its unity and capacity for leadership. 'European efforts to contain the growing crisis degenerated into an embarrassing spectacle of every country for itself', noted one commentator, 'and erased whatever was left of the mirage that the EU is anything resembling a single country'.[9] Finnish foreign minister Alexander Stubb expressed his concerns about 'the EU's institutional chaos' and mused that never before in the EU's history had there been 'a period like this, with so many cliques'.[10] Critics mused on the recurring absence of European leadership, arguing that decision-making was too decentralized, and that more leadership was needed from Brussels. There was disagreement over whether to spend more or to adjust financial regulations, and speculation not only that there would be a rift between the euro and non-euro states but also between the western and eastern states, undoing much of the progress made since the end of the cold war in bringing the two parts of Europe back together again. While the European economy had been healthy, ran the arguments, progress had been made on regional integration, but once the crisis broke EU governments found that they had neither the institutions nor the processes nor the political agreement to respond.

And yet the critics were largely wrong. European governments initially chose to bail out banks and other financial institutions, working to recapitalize the banking system (including the purchase of bank shares) and to protect savers' deposits. Fears arose of a new climate of protectionism, with particular concerns for the economic fortunes of eastern European states. And yet a study of the behaviour of EU leaders reveals that there was in fact significant cooperation, with agreement to raise the minimum guarantee for individual bank deposits and not to allow any bank whose failure might pose systemic risks to the EU financial system to fail. The European Commission issued guidelines on bank recapitalization and announced a stimulus package to which EU leaders quickly agreed. Assistance was offered to the non-euro eastern European states and to any eurozone state facing a balance of payments crisis.

More broadly, the crisis was illustrative of a fundamental difference between European and American economic cultures: while the former emphasized the importance of living within financial means, the latter was more tolerant of living on credit. The crisis also emphasized contrasting attitudes towards risk, to which Europeans were clearly more averse than Americans. Presciently, the *Economist* in 2006—while looking at election results and at welfare and labour policies in Europe—had concluded that risk aversion had become 'the defining feature' of continental Europe's largest countries, and that while the American system rewarded risk taking, Europeans thought it better to be safe than to be sorry.[11] The global economic crisis offered vivid confirmation of this.

It is too early to say what the long-term effects of the crisis will be on European attitudes to the role of the state in the economy, but several possibilities suggest themselves:

- That the crisis should have emerged out of the United States and that there should be a link between the crisis and charges of under-regulation and risk-taking are likely to strengthen the hand of Europeanist arguments that governments should exert more control over the marketplace in order to prevent similar problems emerging again in the future.

- The distinctions between the Rhenish and Anglo-Saxon models are likely to decline as Britain realizes that many of the misplaced policy priorities that undermined the American economy also hurt British economic prospects, and that being outside the eurozone was of little help. At the same time, for Ireland (the other 'Anglo-Saxon' economy) it was clear that being within the eurozone was one of the main factors that saved it from the kind of economic collapse that afflicted Iceland.

- European leaders were taken by surprise, just as they had been with foreign policy crises in the 1990s, and the economic crisis will undoubtedly encourage them to pay even greater attention to economic policy cooperation, thereby further reducing the distinctions between the Rhenish and Anglo-Saxon models.

The distinction between the competing models also rather overlooks the homogenization of the structure of European economies that has taken place as a result of the single market, increased intra-European trade and investment, corporate mergers and acquisitions, and common policies on competition. Economic policy in Europe (European Union and non-European Union) is now made less as a result of national policy than as a result of European policy, and in spite of the residual sense of parochialism and nationalism that can still be found in many European states, the European economy today is heavily integrated and cosmopolitan, and economic styles and priorities are inevitably losing their distinctions. The diffusion of policy-making authority remains a problem in many regards, particularly in the realm of fiscal policy, but Europeanism means a greater emphasis on consensus and a greater emphasis on the role of the state.

The welfare state: equality of results

Nothing is more fundamental to Europeanist notions of economic management than the idea that while individual endeavour is to be welcomed, applauded, and rewarded, the community—via the state—has a high degree of responsibility for working to ensure that the playing field is as level as possible, and that opportunity and wealth are as equitably distributed as possible. Europeans, in other words, are champions of what Gelissen describes as 'a system of institutionalised solidarity'.[12] They are more ready than the citizens of other liberal democracies or of emerging democracies to pool resources—through higher taxes—in order to ensure that all are provided with access to education and health care and that a safety net is available to meet the immediate needs of those unable to provide adequately for themselves.

The welfare state (if we define it as one that makes provision through the law for those in need) was born in Europe, where it has since evolved furthest. Elements of welfarism are found in all other liberal democracies, to be sure, but only in Europe has welfarism become so much a part of the fabric of society, and on few matters related to economic and social management are the distinctions between the United States and Europe quite so marked:

- While Americans emphasize self-reliance and individual welfare, Europeans emphasize communal responsibilities and public welfare.

- While Americans place more emphasis on providing individuals with opportunities to accumulate and keep their wealth, Europeans are more ready to criticize capitalism as the source of many social ills, and to obviate some of those ills through the redistribution of resources and opportunity. Europeans complain about the abuse and mismanagement of welfare and about the failures of public programmes always to deliver services efficiently and effectively, but they would not deny the core benefits of having such programmes nor would they argue that they fundamentally stifle progress and innovation (as do many Americans).

- While Americans define citizenship mainly in political terms and as a question of the political rights and responsibilities of the individual, for Europeans the notion extends to social questions, meaning a belief that all should enjoy basic rights to education, health care, and social security. Only in Europe, furthermore, does citizenship include economic citizenship, meaning a belief in the rights of workers to a safe and healthy workplace, to having their views represented, to be protected against unfair dismissal, to having their work hours limited and regulated, and to being provided with extended parental leave (see Chapter 6).

While Europeans are as interested in the exploitation of economic opportunities as Americans, they have a rather different way of approaching that exploitation. As Prestowitz puts it, while 'Americans emphasize equality of opportunity, Europeans focus more on equality of results'.[13] The American philosophy is reflected in the much-quoted but typically misunderstood notion of the American Dream, which claims that all Americans should be allowed to pursue their goals in life through hard work and free choice, regardless of race, gender, age, religion, or class. The coining of the phrase is usually attributed to the historian James Truslow Adams, in whose 1931 book *The Epic of America* it is described as the dream 'of a land in which life should be better and richer and fuller for every man, with opportunity for each according to his ability or achievement'. It was not just a dream of materialism and wealth, he argued, 'but a dream of social order in which each man and each woman shall be able to attain to the fullest stature of which they are innately capable, and be recognized by others for what they are, regardless of the fortuitous circumstances of birth or position'.[14] This is a theme in American discourse whose lineage can be traced back to the idea within the Declaration of Independence that all Americans have the right to 'life, liberty and the Pursuit of Happiness'.

The definition offered by Adams clearly reflects the prevailing belief that Europeans were too diverted by class and privilege to allow for equal opportunity, and grew out of the view that many had left for the United States in search of opportunity and social freedom. But while political, economic, social, and religious inequalities were abundantly clear in Europe at the time that Adams was writing, so were they in the United States; women had only just been given the right to vote, and although blacks also had the franchise, many were prevented from voting; segregation was still a fact of life, and employment opportunities and compensation levels for women and ethnic minorities were less than those for white men. The American Dream, then, was built at least in part on a fallacy, which continues to be perpetuated by American political leaders who claim that it is only in America that individuals can truly live out their potential, an argument that rather overlooks the many political, economic, and social barriers they still face. There was a particular chorus of such claims following the election to the presidency of Barack Obama; while the United States thus became proudly the first predominantly white country with a black leader, it should not be forgotten that the United States has not yet had a female leader, while several European countries have.

If there is such a thing as a European Dream, most Europeans would probably say that it contains many of the same core goals and aspirations as those contained in the American model. But it is also about more than equality of opportunity; hard work and free choice are respected and admired, but Europeanism looks also at outcomes and supports the view—in word even if not entirely in deed—that equality should be encouraged at all points on the economic and social scale. Rifkin argues that while the American Dream is centred more on personal material advancement than on concern with broader human welfare, the European Dream emphasizes 'quality of life over the accumulation of wealth', along with 'community relationships over individual autonomy, cultural diversity over assimilation, ... sustainable development over unlimited material growth, deep play over unrelenting toil, universal human rights and the rights of nature over property rights, and global cooperation over the unilateral exercise of power'.[15] He concludes that the European Union has been developing a new social and political model better suited to the needs of the globalizing world of the new century, and that the European Dream is—as a result—eclipsing the American Dream.

The polling data are clear on the distinctive views of Europeans regarding welfare:

• When asked in national polls in 2002 if government should be responsible for making sure that nobody lived in poverty, 83–93 per cent agreed in Britain, France, Italy, and Spain, and 77 per cent in Germany, compared to 60 per cent in the United States. When asked if government should be responsible for making sure that older people had enough income to maintain their standard of living in retirement, 81 per cent agreed in Spain; 57–64 per cent in Britain, France, Germany, and Italy; and only 44 per cent in the United States. When asked if parents should be responsible for providing food, clothing, and shelter for their children aged under eighteen, 82 per cent agreed in the United States, compared to 66 per cent in France and 50–9 per cent in Britain, Germany, Italy, and Spain.[16]

- When asked in a 2003 Pew Global Attitudes poll to choose between the power of the state to guarantee that nobody was in need and the freedom of individuals to pursue their goals without state interference, the preference of Europeans for the former was clear (see Figure 5.1). When asked in the same poll about their views on the merits of the state playing an active role in society in order to guarantee that nobody was in need, two-thirds of Europeans were supportive of such a role compared to just one-third of Americans.[17]

- There is slightly more agreement between Europeans and Americans on the matter of the extent to which the state should take care of those at the poorest end of the economic scale, who cannot help themselves: 87–95 per cent of Britons, Poles, Germans, Italians, and French agree, along with 73 per cent of Americans.[18] But when it comes to success in life, two-thirds of Germans and Italians believe that it is determined by forces

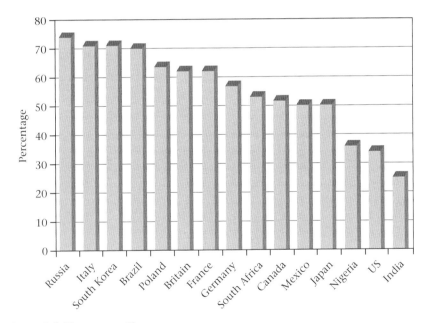

Figure 5.1 Views on welfare

Source: Pew Global Attitudes Project, 'Views of a Changing World', June 2003, at http://people-press.org/reports/pdf/185.pdf (retrieved March 2009). Percentage believing that it is more important for government to ensure that no one is in need than it is for individuals to be free to pursue goals without government interference.

outside their control, along with half of Britons and the French, but only one-third of Americans.[19]

The Europeanist emphasis on the role of the state is also reflected in the data on public social spending: while it accounted (before the global economic crisis) for between 20 and 30 per cent of GDP in most European states, it accounted for only 16–18 per cent in non-European, English-speaking OECD states (see Figure 5.2). Spending in Europe is highest in the northern states and lowest in the Mediterranean and eastern states. In spite of the numbers, however, the results do not show that life for all Europeans is necessarily improving. Europeans have not yet been able to address the problems of persistent poverty and widespread unemployment, and while they have been taxing more and spending more on social benefits (they spend three times as much on family policies as they did in the early 1980s), the gap between rich and poor in most European states is growing: the rich are becoming richer, incomes for those closer to retirement have grown, and poverty rates among the retired have fallen; but unemployment rates are rising among low-skilled and under-educated workers, the rising number of single-person or single-parent households has contributed to falling income rates, the number of people living below

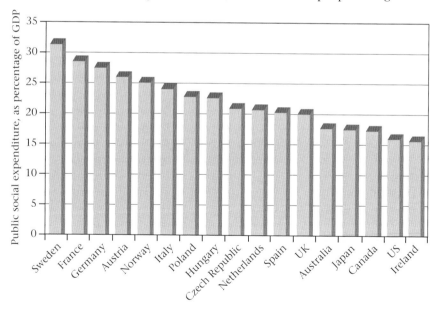

Figure 5.2 Public social spending

Source: OECD Society at a Glance, http://www.oecd.org/dataoecd (retrieved January 2009). Figures are for 2003.

the poverty line has grown, and the incidence of child poverty has grown.[20] All the more reason, then, why we might suppose that support for welfarism continues to be so strong; the welfare state has helped remove many inequalities, but much work remains to be done.

How is the Europeanist support for welfarism explained? Hutton traces the roots of these ideas to the feudal Catholic notion that wealth and property 'were associated with profound reciprocal social obligations', and that this ethical view was behind socialist ideas about common ownership of the means of production and the rights of workers.[21] Part of the answer may also be found in the historical contrasts between the European emphasis on communalism and the American emphasis on individualism. Europeans have long lived with strong states, a strong church, and strong class systems, and have had to build capitalism in the face of resistance to personal independence. For Americans, by contrast, entrepreneurial opportunities have long been available to a wider public, with fewer limitations imposed by class prejudices, and leading an independent life has historically been essential to expressions of individual freedom from political control. Americans have also long been resistant to centralized control and to the paying of taxes to support public social programmes.[22]

Alesina and Glaeser methodically review three different competing sets of explanations[23]:

- They look first at economic explanations, arguing that if democracies desire equality, then higher levels of inequality should encourage more aggressive redistribution. But the United States has higher levels of income inequality than Europe. As regards the notion that higher levels of inequality can be offset by higher levels of social mobility (the poor can more easily escape from poverty in the United States), they find few transatlantic differences in levels of mobility.

- They then look at the extent to which differences in the degree of redistribution might reflect differences in political structure: electoral systems in Europe make it easier for left-wing parties to achieve influence, and checks and balances in the United States have deterred large-scale changes in policy—a reflection of the extent to which American institutions were designed by eighteenth-century men of property determined to limit state expropriation of their wealth.

- They find the most convincing set of explanations in racial and cultural factors. Race is an issue, they argue, because individuals are more generous towards members of their own racial or ethnic group, and thus redistributive policies are stronger in less fragmented European societies.

> Cultural matters are reflected in survey evidence suggesting that while Europeans tend to think that the poor are unfortunate, more Americans tend to think that they are lazy; the more people who think that poverty is the result of lack of effort, the less support there is for redistribution.

In short, then, the explanation for Europeanist views toward welfare lies in a combination of a greater sense of communal responsibility, a greater suspicion towards the accumulation of wealth, a broader conception of the idea of individual rights, a more widely held belief that individuals are not wholly responsible for their lot in life, and a longer tradition of racial homogeneity. It remains to be seen what effect the growing racial and religious diversity of Europe and the widening gap between the rich and the poor will have on these views. At the same time, values developed over centuries of social construction will not be dislodged or fundamentally altered overnight.

Europe's civilian–industrial complex

Military power has long played a central role not just in conceptions of national identity but also in the setting of economic priorities. The assembly and maintenance of large armies, navies, and later air forces was a core driving force in the economic dominance of the great nineteenth-century European powers, and the subsequent reduction in the size of their military establishments was reflective of their declining global influence. It was only its enormous military power that gave the Soviet Union true claims to superpower status during the cold war; its international economic influence was far less than that of the United States, in part because so much of its economic development was directed at the maintenance of a large military; few states in history (if any) have been quite so clearly built upon the priorities of the military–economic nexus. Conversely, however, no great power in history has been quite so clearly built upon a civilian–economic nexus as the European Union.

In his farewell address in January 1961, President Eisenhower famously noted how war had left the United States with both 'a permanent armaments industry of vast proportions . . . [and] an immense military establishment', and warned that the country had now to 'guard against the acquisition of unwarranted influence . . . by the military-industrial complex'. He was pointing to the emergence of a symbiotic relationship between the government, the military, and defence contractors. The latter had become major clients for the federal government and its burgeoning defence budget, and as such were not only playing a greater role in setting the priorities of economic policy in the United States but were also exerting new political influence. This was a prospective danger that had been noted even by George Washington, who had argued that 'over-grown military establishments' were 'inauspicious to liberty'. Few heeded Eisenhower's warnings, however, and the United States today is a country in which military spending and the priorities of the military are critical to national economic calculations[24]:

- Considering only core Department of Defence spending, the US defence budget currently runs at about 4 per cent of GDP. Adding this to spending outside the Department of Defence takes the figure closer to 6 per cent. While this is less than the more than 9 per cent of GDP spent at the height of the Vietnam War, it is considerably higher than the 2.6 per cent of GDP today spent in Britain (the lowest as a percentage of GDP since the 1930s), the 2.4 per cent in France, and the 1.3 per cent in Germany. European states as a whole spend less on the military as a percentage of GDP than any of the other major powers (the US, China, India, and Russia), and less also than most Middle Eastern states.

- In fiscal year 2008, US defence spending accounted for 20 per cent of the US federal government budget, making it the eleventh straight year in which military spending had increased. The growth in defence spending during the Bush administration helped nearly double the US national debt to a record high in 2009 of more than $10 trillion. In the fiscal 2008, the United States spent $623 billion on defence, accounting for approximately 56 per cent of global spending on defence, and amounting to more than twice the combined defence budgets of all the twenty-seven EU member states. In Britain, defence spending accounts for just over 6 per cent of the government budget, and in France it accounts for about 5 per cent of national spending.

- US arms sales in 2006 amounted to more than $200 billion, or nearly two-thirds of the global total, more than twice the European total, and thirty-two times the Russian total. Military aid is a core part of American official development assistance: of the total assistance provided by the United States in the period 1997–2006, one-fifth was in the form of military aid, and in 2006 the proportion had risen to 30 per cent.[25] Although individual European states provide military aid to others, the European Union does not; and the issue of providing military aid has been assiduously avoided in policy debates.

European states too had had their own military–industrial complexes before the Second World War, forming an iron triangle between government, the military, and industry. But military spending declined dramatically after the Second World War for several reasons: most European states could no longer afford to maintain large militaries, economic and social reconstruction took priority, there was general social revulsion against war and conflict, European states no longer faced the threat of invasion by their neighbours (except as part of the broader cold war dynamic), and the role of regional military competitors and guarantors shifted to the United States and the Soviet Union. For western Europeans, now enjoying the luxury of being able to rely on the United States for their security, the result was the replacement of their old military–industrial complexes with new civilian–industrial complexes in which considerably more time and investment was to be expended upon meeting the needs of the consumer market than on military production, and in which the political role of non-military corporations was to become notably greater than was the case in the United States. Europe is today a region in which—as we will see in Chapter 8—there is a preference for the use of civilian over military power, in which threats and challenges are defined more in economic than in security terms, and, as a result, in which civilian interests have come to far exceed military interests in economic calculations.

The nature of the European civilian–industrial complex is reflected in the limited size and reach of defence corporations. While it is true that mergers and acquisitions since the early 1990s have created a substantial European defence and aerospace industry based around BAE Systems–Marconi in Britain and EADS on the continent,[26] the American defence industry is both far bigger and more politically influential. Where the *Fortune* Global 500 list of the world's biggest corporations in 2008 included such American giants as Boeing, Lockheed Martin, Honeywell, Northrop Grumman, General Dynamics, and Raytheon, it included only four relatively small European defence companies (EADS, BAE Systems, Finmeccanica, and Thales).[27] And where several of the US corporations rely mainly or almost entirely on government contracts for their business, most European arms manufacturers are more active in the civilian market. Excluding Boeing and EADS, many of whose profits come from the sale of civilian aircraft, the revenues of the three biggest American companies were two-thirds greater than those of the three biggest European companies. Of the world's 100 biggest defence companies in 2007 (by revenue), forty-five were American (including six of the ten biggest) and only twenty-five were European.[28] (See Table 5.1.)

European defence corporations also have a relatively limited impact on government policy, and vice versa. The restructuring of the European defence industry has been largely a private sector concern, with little

Table 5.1. The world's biggest arms manufacturers

Rank	Company	Country	Arms sales (billion US$)	Arms sales as % of total sales	Employees
1	Boeing	USA	30.7	50	154,000
2	Lockheed Martin	USA	28.1	71	140,000
3	BAE Systems	UK	24.1	95	88,600
4	Northrup Grumman	USA	23.7	78	122,200
5	Raytheon	USA	19.5	96	80,000
6	General Dynamics	USA	18.8	78	81,000
7	EADS	Europe	12.6	25	116,810
8	L-3 Communications	USA	10.0	80	63,700
9	Finmeccanica	Italy	8.8	57	58,060
10	Thales	France	8.2	64	52,160
11	United Technologies	USA	7.7	16	214,500
12	Halliburton	USA	6.6	29	104,000
13	Computer Sciences	USA	6.3	42	79,000
14	SAIC	USA	5.8	70	44,000
15	Honeywell	USA	4.4	14	118,000

Source: Stockholm International Peace Research Institute, *SIPRI Yearbook 2008: Armaments, Disarmament, and International Security* (Oxford: Oxford University Press, 2008), 281. Figures are for 2006, and exclude China.

government input other than through contracts.[29] Furthermore, the bulk of revenues for European defence corporations come from exports, and much of their recent growth has come from new demand in the United States. Thus BAE Systems saw its profits triple in 2006 and almost double again in 2008, due in large part to its acquisitions of US weapons manufacturers, and its sales to the United States, Saudi Arabia, and India, all of which more than compensated for a drop in sales in Britain and other parts of Europe. So important has the US market become for BAE that in 2006 it sold its 20 per cent stake in EADS (and Airbus) and used the proceeds to strengthen its market position in the United States, where by 2007 it had become the largest land systems defence contractor. Meanwhile, Finmeccanica has also seen its profits growing in recent years as it has followed the lead of BAE Systems by buying up US defence contractors and engaging in joint ventures aimed at developing aircraft for export markets.

If the voracious American market is the source of most new opportunities for European corporations, it is of course of great importance to US defence corporations, which are additionally politically influential as a result of the millions they contribute to the election funds of candidates for office through political action committees (PACs). It is telling that in all the debate over bailouts to corporations in the wake of the global economic crisis, no American defence contractor sought assistance from the government, while financial institutions and automobile manufacturers were first in line. The civilian business sector may have suffered greatly in the crisis, but the military business sector continued to be assured of great profits from government spending.

Europe's civilian economic priorities are also reflected in the extent to which its technology is driven by civilian rather than military applications. Two of the most important developments in new technology in recent decades—the internet and global positioning satellites (GPS)—grew mainly out of military priorities in the United States. The creation of what eventually became the internet was sparked by concerns in the late 1950s that the Soviets had an advantage in the development of space technology, and was encouraged and supported by the US Department of Defence and the US Air Force. GPS too was a military project, so much so that the Europeans were prompted in 2003 to agree to the Galileo global navigation satellite system as a civilian alternative that would be independent of the American and Russian systems, which can be manipulated and even (theoretically) blocked by their controllers. Although couched in technological terms, the justification for the development of Galileo is clearly political, and an expression of European independence. While it has been beset by delays and cost overruns, its supporters argue that it will have important and profitable economic applications.

Where once European states had economies that were deeply affected by war and the preparation for war, they have since 1945 enjoyed peace to some extent. While for western Europeans this was at least initially made possible by the provision of a security shield by the United States, the limited role played by investments in defence has become a habit, underpinned by the generalized peace that has come to prevail in Europe and by a belief that disputes are better addressed by diplomacy than by the rattling of sabres. The European Union has been busy trying to develop a common security and defence policy, and has had to make provision for the commitment of troops to trouble spots in the Middle East and Africa, but military calculations and expenditures—relative to what they once were—are today quite marginal to an understanding of European economic priorities.

The environment: sustainable development

The environment is an issue that crosses multiple jurisdictional boundaries, with implications for politics, public health, resource management, ethics, morality, and science. At heart, however, and in spite of the reservations of many environmentalists, most of the calculations that we bring to bear on the manner in which we consider our relationship with the natural and built environment are economic. In short, we look at the costs and benefits of the choices we face regarding the manner in which we exploit and manage resources such as air, water, land, and forests, and at the investments we are willing to make in order to ensure that demand does not exceed supply. Most of the responses to environmental problems are primarily economic, and failures to meet targets are often the result of the machinations of the free market. At the heart of contemporary Europeanist thinking is the concept of sustainable development, which is probably more central to European calculations than to those in most other parts of the world and certainly in rapidly industrializing societies such as China, India, Russia, Brazil, Mexico, and Indonesia. Usually defined as development that 'meets the needs of the present without compromising the ability of future generations to meet their own needs',[30] sustainable development is reflected both in the public choices that determine economic policy and in the personal choices that drive the parameters of consumerism.

The concept traces its origins back to the principle of conservation (managed exploitation) that was a driving force in late-nineteenth- and early-twentieth-century American resource planning.[31] It was reflected in the notions of harmonious development and balanced expansion contained in the Treaty of Rome, but has only moved to the heart of EU environmental policy since the 1986 Single European Act. This required 'a prudent and rational utilisation of resources', an idea that was given more clarity by the Treaty of Amsterdam, which made 'balanced and sustainable development of economic activities' a core objective of the European Union. The Single European Act also provided that 'environmental protection requirements' should be a component of all EU policies, making environmental calculations one of only four general sets of principles that must be reflected in all EU public policies (the others being consumer protection, culture, and health).

The Europeanist emphasis on public and personal sustainability stands in contrast to American consumerism, the former based at least in part on a greater awareness about the limitations on natural resources, and the latter on a traditional belief in bountiful supply. In almost every core respect, Europeans have shown a willingness and an ability to consume less, to more actively manage and protect, and to control the production of pollution and waste. If we look at per capita energy consumption, for example, we find that it is 40–50 per cent less in Britain, France, and Germany than in the United States, carbon dioxide emissions are 50–70 per cent less, municipal waste production is 10–30 per cent less, and water consumption is 70–90 per cent less.[32] Not all is good news, however: the threats posed to biodiversity in Europe remain unresolved, may be worsening, and have been likened to climate change in the extent of their seriousness.[33] But threats to biodiversity are not unique to Europe; humanity at large has not yet absorbed the importance of the links between the health of nature and the health of humans.

If broad trends are any indication, Europeans have wrested the initiative from the Americans. The United States long had a reputation of being an international policy leader on environmental issues, hence the popular quip often heard in the 1980s that first California would take the initiative on a new problem, then the rest of the United States would follow, and the rest of the industrialized world would later catch up. Many of the philosophical foundations of modern environmentalism were based on American thinking, including the writings of Henry David Thoreau, Edward Abbey, and Aldo Leopold. Whether dealing with air pollution, water pollution, species protection, or land management, the United States was long in the vanguard with original responses: its legislative initiatives between 1970 and 1976 on clean air, clean water, safe drinking water, and toxic waste were among the first such pieces of legislation in the world to take a comprehensive approach to the problem of pollution; it was a leader in institutional development (creating in 1970 the world's first national environmental regulatory body, the US Environmental Protection Agency); and a key player in the development and agreement of international environmental treaties.

But this is no longer so. On international or global problems in particular, the United States has become a follower rather than a leader, particularly on issues such as climate change, chemicals policy, and genetic modification.[34] Increasingly, the role of policy leader has fallen to the European Union, where a combination of political pressures and changing consumer expectations has led to a fundamental review of approaches to the environment that has changed policy throughout Europe. The dynamics behind the change are complex, and lie in several different sources:

- On a personal level, Europeans have been encouraged to make new choices by virtue of the tensions between supply and demand. They live in a relatively densely populated region of the world where public transport is widely available, where respite from urban stresses is highly valued, where the pollutive consequences of being the origin of the industrial revolution are still felt, where awareness of the dependence on imported energy is acute, where pressures on wildlife and nature are substantial, and where the problem of waste disposal is not easily resolved. As growing numbers of middle-class consumers seek to defend the improvements they have seen in the quality of their lives, they work harder to address the threats posed to the environment.

- Differences in environmental standards were identified early as a barrier to the development of the European single market, wherein economic pressures also allowed 'leader' states within the European Union (mainly Germany, the Netherlands, and the Scandinavians) to set the pace and to compel 'laggard' states to catch up, and ultimately oblige non-European states to respond. Europe has also become a leader in the development of new understandings regarding the mechanics of cross-border environmental problems, and in the development of creative new responses to those problems.[35]

- Europeans have been guided by cosmopolitan and multilateralist views (see elsewhere in this book) in their attitudes towards international agreements on the environment. Their heightened understanding of the cross-border nature of many environmental problems within Europe has encouraged them to take a more active approach to regional and international cooperation on problems such as air and water pollution, waste management, biodiversity, and climate change.

It is not that Europeans have significantly different views from those of Americans on environmental management. When asked in a 2003 survey if people should be willing to pay higher prices in order to protect the environment, more Americans (70 per cent) agreed than Europeans (53–60 per cent in Germany, Britain, France, and Italy), and Europeans and Americans were in approximate agreement with the view that 'protecting the environment should be given priority even if it causes slower economic growth and some loss of jobs' (78–82 per cent support in Italy, Britain, and Germany; 69 per cent support in the United States; and 66 per cent support in France).[36] But Europeans are prepared to support these positions through their patterns of consumption. They also take a broader and more holistic view of environmental problems, so that when asked in 2007 if they saw these problems as a key global threat, there was 66 per cent agreement in Sweden; 45–52 per cent agreement in Germany, Britain, France, and Italy; and only 37 per cent agreement in the United States.[37]

Europeanist thinking is reflected in support for green policies, if not necessarily in support for green political parties. While the latter have emerged in almost all industrialized countries, as well as in some developing countries (such as Egypt and Mexico), the green philosophy is fundamentally European in origin, and green parties have had their widest social and economic impact and their greatest electoral successes in Europe; in Belgium, Finland, France, Germany, Italy, and Latvia they have been members of governing coalitions. Green thinking emphasizes ecological wisdom, social justice, participatory democracy, non-violence, sustainability, and respect for diversity, all views that have worked their way into European consciousness and have become hallmarks—or, at least, aspirations—of the way that Europeans view economics, politics, social relations, and environmental management. Green philosophy developed in large part out of seminal works produced by European scientists, economists, and philosophers, including Jim Lovelock (British author of the Gaia hypothesis which argues that life on earth functions as a single organism), E. F. Schumacher (the German-born author of *Small is Beautiful*, which argued that economies, political units, society, and industry had become too large and had lost their human scale), and Arne Naess (the Norwegian philosopher who in 1972 coined the term 'deep ecology' to emphasize a deeper concern for ecological principles).

The issue of climate change is illustrative of the underlying goals and values (and also some of the limitations) of Europeanist approaches to the environment. The science of climate change has been understood for decades, but coordinated pressure for action only began with the 1979 World Climate Conference, which encouraged more research that in turn contributed to the creation of the Intergovernmental Panel on Climate Change in 1988. A Framework Convention on Climate Change was then negotiated and opened for signature in 1992, its purpose being to reduce the emissions of carbon dioxide (CO_2) implicated in climate change.[38] Although the convention was signed by 175 countries and came into force in 1994, there have always been two dominating actors in the negotiations: the United States, which is the source of about 22 per cent of global CO_2 emissions, and the European Union, which is the source of about 15 per cent of emissions (figures for 2006). Progress on climate change negotiations has since been heavily influenced by the dynamics of the US–EU relationship, which has in turn emphasized the quite different qualities and goals of the European and American views.

Under the 1992 convention, there was a commitment only to voluntary reductions in emissions, the details of which were to be worked out by subsequent meetings of convention parties. A meeting in Berlin in 1995 produced the Berlin Mandate, which held that industrialized countries should accept a greater share of the burden to reduce greenhouse gases, while helping developing countries, which were in turn excluded from any specific reductions in emissions of CO_2 and other greenhouse gases. Then came the critical meeting in 1997 in Kyoto, Japan, where an attempt was made to agree to a protocol containing specific reductions in emissions by 2008–12. While the European Union favoured a 15 per cent reduction by 2010 (on 1990 levels), the Clinton administration appeared to turn its back on the Berlin Mandate by objecting to the fact that China and India were to be exempted, and was prepared to accept only a return to 1990 levels by 2010. The final agreement at Kyoto was a compromise, allowing different reductions for different countries, including 8 per cent for the European Union and 7 per cent for the United States.[39]

While this marked some limited progress, these percentage reductions were too small to stabilize atmospheric concentrations of greenhouse gases, and when discussions among parties to the convention continued at The Hague in 2000, there was disagreement over implementation. The United States demanded more credit for the agricultural land and forests that act as a 'sink' for CO_2, but Europeans characterized this as an opt-out that would allow the United States to expend less time and fewer resources on developing emission reduction technology and changing its energy consumption habits. The transatlantic difference became abundantly clear in 2001 when the Bush administration announced its opposition to the Kyoto protocol, citing concerns about potential damage to the US economy and repeating American qualms about the lack of obligations on China and India. The Bush administration adopted this position even in the face of polls showing that a majority of Americans believed that climate change was a problem, and that the United States should have ratified and abided by Kyoto.

To be sure, European governments have not been united on climate change, and resistance has come in particular from four countries for different reasons: Poland is concerned because it is a relatively under-industrialized country that has the world's second-highest dependence on coal after South Africa; Italy is concerned because of the implications for its glass, ceramics, and paper industries (prompting prime minister Silvio Berlusconi at one point to threaten to block a deal); Hungary is concerned about the potential impact of emission caps on its industrial development plans; and in Germany there is opposition from key sectors of the energy supply and vehicle industries. Nonetheless, the European Union at the end of 2008 reached an agreement on the 20–20–20 plan: to cut greenhouse emissions by 20 per cent, to generate 20 per cent of energy from renewable sources, and to achieve a 20 per cent improvement in energy efficiency, all by 2020.

While the plan was hailed by European leaders as the world's broadest and most stringent agreement to date for dealing with climate change, and far more ambitious than the Kyoto goals, the European record so far on actually reducing emissions has been mixed: emissions in the EU-27 were down 7.7 per cent in 2006 from the 1990 baseline, which meant that the European Union was on target to meet neither its Kyoto commitment of an 8 per cent reduction nor its own 20–20–20 target. Furthermore, much of the change in 2005–6 was a result of warmer weather, which meant less need for central heating, and reductions in the west were offset by increases in solid fuel use in Poland and by increases in the volume of road transport in several eastern and western states.[40] But while Europeans may not have met their own ideals, they were not far short, and their record stood in notable contrast to that of the United States, where energy-related CO_2 emissions in 2006 were at an all-time high, and rather than falling by 8 per cent as agreed at Kyoto, emissions had actually grown by more than 17 per cent over the 1990 baseline.[41] Growth in emissions from electricity generation and transportation were the main causes.

Whatever the political disagreements, polls find consistent public views on the issue of climate change across the European Union. In a 2008 Eurobarometer poll, 62 per cent of respondents ranked climate change as the second-most serious problem facing the world, behind poverty (68 per cent) but ahead of international terrorism (53 per cent), armed conflicts (38 per cent), a major global economic downturn (24 per cent), the spread of infectious disease (23 per cent), and the proliferation of nuclear weapons (23 per cent). The numbers considering climate change as a serious problem ranged from a high of 90–2 per cent in Greece and Cyprus to a middle range of 71–4 per cent in Hungary, Germany, Denmark, Finland, and Sweden; and to a low of 45–7 per cent in Italy, Portugal, and the Czech Republic. A majority of the respondents in all the EU states were optimistic that action could be taken to reverse climate change; they felt that addressing the problem would have a positive effect on the economy, that not enough was being done, and that they had taken some kind of personal action already to contribute.[42]

6
Society: Quality Over Quantity

There has been much debate in academic circles in recent decades about the nature, problems, and possibilities of the European Social Model (ESM). There are disagreements about whether or not it exists, about its key indicators and features, about how the model emerged and where it is headed, and about just how many of its features are truly distinctive. Questions are asked about whether we should be referring to a European Social Model (a set of values and norms) or a European Model of Society (the shared economic, political, and social space that might grow out of integration). Should the European Social Model be portrayed in broad terms that pay obeisance to history, culture, the economy, capitalism, and social justice, or should it be more narrowly defined as a set of values limited to societal obligations, and focused on issues such as social welfare, education, workers' rights, and employment?[1] And, finally, should it be associated with the European Union alone, or are there broader similarities and commonalities than can be identified across Europe as a whole?

The European Social Model is a useful analytical tool, to be sure, but it is based as much on economic considerations as on social factors. Furthermore, it has excited more attention among policy-makers than among ordinary Europeans, which raises troubling questions about its elitist nature; the defining qualities of a society, after all, are to be found less in the statements of political leaders than in the behaviour of individuals. Society is best understood in terms of patterns of human relationships, as distinct from political or economic relationships, the focus usually being on networks, organizations, or hierarchies. But a key part of that understanding is to be found in shared beliefs, customs, and goals, and this is where the focus of this chapter will lie. It will examine the social trends and qualities that are most indicative of the broader features of Europeanism, with an emphasis on four in particular.

First, it will look at demographic trends in Europe, the only region of the world where population numbers are generally moving downwards. Population decline has been met with deep concern by political leaders and analysts, and yet the case can also be made that it might provide Europe with unique opportunities. These include wealth and redistribution, a rethinking of spending priorities, and a more sustainable use of resources. Second, it will examine the changing definition of the European family: fewer Europeans are marrying, fewer are having children, more of those children are born outside marriage, and the size of European households is shrinking. Third, it will assess the changing European work ethic, as Europeans work fewer hours, take more holidays, enjoy a greater variety of benefits than is the case anywhere else in the world, and are more inclined to work to live rather than to live to work. Finally, in responding to crime, it will examine Europeanist preferences for dignity, and for mildness over harshness, negotiation over confrontation, and addressing causes rather than effects. The picture that emerges from these cases is one in which quality trumps quantity, and in which there is less emphasis on growth, accumulation, and consumption, and more emphasis on manageable distribution, personal choice, and individual rights.

The European Social Model

The European Social Model is not much discussed or considered by most ordinary Europeans, who are generally unaware of its existence. Rather, it seems to hold greater fascination for policy-makers and academics, it is usually associated with the European Union specifically (as opposed to Europe more generally), and—in policy terms—it emphasizes the links between welfarism, social security, and employment policies. Put another way, it is based on the idea that the EU can and should work simultaneously to promote sustainable economic growth and social cohesion. For Giddens, it has four main features:

- Support for a developed and interventionist state (when measured in terms of the level of GDP taken up by taxation).
- A robust welfare system that provides effective social protection for all citizens, but especially for those most in need.
- The containment of economic and other forms of inequality.
- A key role for unions and other agencies promoting the rights of workers.

Each of these traits must be underpinned by expanding overall economic prosperity and job creation, and they are determined by five core values: a willingness to share risk widely across society; a belief in containing the inequalities that might threaten social solidarity; protecting the most vulnerable members of society through active social intervention; encouraging consultation rather than confrontation in industry; and providing a framework of social and economic citizenship rights for the population as a whole.[2]

The features and possibilities of the European Social Model were summarized in comments made in 2003 by Anna Diamantopolou, then European Commissioner for Employment and Social Affairs. The word *model*, she argued, encapsulated 'a progressive real convergence of views' among its member states on the employment and social policy goals of the European Union. The European Social Model was not limited to welfare and pensions, but included employment policy, worker training, and rules and policies on labour markets, equality, and benefits. It was not limited to goals and values but included institutional change and rules, such as consultation with management and labour. It has also reached outside Europe through the European Union's interest in building incentives into trade and aid agreements for third parties to respect International Labour Organization norms on issues such as child labour and forced labour, and its interest in encouraging sustainable development through corporate social responsibility. The European Social Model, she concluded, was 'a pragmatic, down-to-earth, joint attempt to make headway on reforms which are necessary if we are to adapt to a changing economic and social environment, both in Europe and beyond'.[3]

The European Trade Union Confederation (ETUC) offers another perspective, defining the European Social Model as 'a vision of society that combines sustainable economic growth with ever-improving living and working conditions,... [implying] full employment, good quality jobs, equal opportunities, social protection for all, social inclusion, and involving citizens in the decisions that affect them'. The ETUC then goes on rather cynically to argue that Europe's understanding on 'social dialogue, collective bargaining and workers' protection are crucial factors in promoting innovation, productivity and competitiveness' is what distinguishes Europe from the United States, 'where small numbers of individuals have benefited at the expense of the majority'.[4]

Social issues have been part of the agenda of European integration from the start, hence the references made in the Treaty of Rome to such principles as the 'harmonious development of economic activities, a continuous and balanced expansion, [and] . . . an accelerated raising of the standard of living'. The treaty also made provision for a European Social Fund designed to 'improve the possibilities of employment for workers and to contribute to the raising of their standard of living', and emphasized the need for cross-state collaboration on employment, labour legislation and working conditions, occupational training, social security, and trade union law. European social policy has since been driven by the argument that without equal pay, equal working conditions, gender equality, worker training, and comparable standards on workers' rights, the construction of the single market would be handicapped. Poorer European states would suffer from competition posed by wealthier neighbours, while those with less progressive employment laws would lose jobs to those offering better working conditions.

But the Treaty of Rome was based on the idealistic assumption that the benefits of the single market would improve life for all European workers, and while this proved true to the extent that economic integration helped increase wages, market forces failed to resolve problems such as gender and age discrimination, wage disparities, different levels of unemployment, and safety and health needs in the workplace. It was only with enlargement in 1973 that the problem of economic disparities among the Community's member states moved up the political agenda. Community leaders responded by creating the European Social Fund in 1974 and launching the first in a series of Social Action Programmes aimed at moving the EEC further along the road to full employment, improved living and working conditions, and gender equality.

Social policy came to the fore again in the late 1980s as debates over the Single European Act raised questions about worker mobility and social dumping. In 1987 the suggestion was made for a charter of basic social rights, supported by countries with socialist governments but resisted by those without. The resulting Charter of Fundamental Social Rights of Workers (or the Social Charter) was adopted at the 1989 Strasbourg Summit, with all member states but Britain initially in support. The Charter noted the right to freedom of movement, to fair remuneration for employment, to social protection (including a minimum income for those unable to find employment), to freedom of association and collective bargaining, to equal treatment, to health, safety, and protection in the workplace, and to a retirement income that allows a reasonable standard of living. It was eventually incorporated into the EU treaties by the Treaty of Amsterdam.

Where once the debate was about 'social Europe', the focus had changed in the 1980s to the 'European Social Model', whose qualities were addressed in a 1994 European Commission White Paper on social policy. This began by quoting Article 2 of the Maastricht Treaty, defining the social goals of the European Union as promoting 'a high degree of convergence of economic performance, a high level of employment and of social protection, the raising of the standard of living and quality of life, and economic and social cohesion and solidarity among Member States'. While agreeing that Europe had not yet been able to provide all these benefits, the White Paper argued that it could be 'fairly claimed' that nowhere else in the world had so much progress been made in that direction. Specifically, the core objectives to which the European Union should aspire were social and economic integration, competitiveness and social progress, a respect for diversity, and a level playing field of common minimum standards.[5]

While the rhetoric on social policy was substantial, it long failed to be reflected in progress on the ground, sparking a new debate in the 1990s about the possible responses to Europe's ongoing problems. As a result of calls for a new focus on modernizing the European economy, the Lisbon European Council in March 2000 set the goal of making the changes needed to finally complete the single market and to create the most competitive and dynamic knowledge-based economy in the world, a goal that included modernizing the European Social Model by investing in education and training, and combating social exclusion. The objective was to bring the European Union up to the levels of competitiveness and dynamism that were features of the US economy. It soon became clear that numerous structural problems remained: there was too little investment in research and development, Europeans had good ideas but were often unable to translate them into commercial innovation, there was too little investment in information technology, barriers to the final achievement of the single market remained in place, Europe still lacked a dynamic and entrepreneurial business culture, and too many workers lacked adequate education or necessary skills.[6]

Critics of the European Social Model—or, at least, those who question its meaning and prospects—are easier to find than champions. The doubters argue that in spite of social spending, the European Social Model has been unable to stand up to the challenges posed by globalization, and that Europe suffers high public debt, an aging population, persistent high unemployment, low productivity, and high rates of poverty.[7] They assert that the European Social Model is unsustainable because expanded social policies have expanded public debt, and the recipients of today's welfare and social security benefits are being paid by future generations. In a more competitive global environment, they suggest, Europe can no longer afford the 'luxury' of strong welfare measures, and if it is to compete with emerging economies like China and India, it must cut spending on social protection and ease regulation for business. Particular criticism is reserved for Europe's ongoing difficulties with unemployment, the charge being that regional integration has been unable to generate enough jobs for Europeans. And yet in the summer of 2008—before the worst effects of the global economic crisis had begun to be felt—the numbers in Europe were not that different from those found in other advanced economies. Unemployment in the euro area was running at 7.5 per cent, a respectable figure when compared to the United States (6.3 per cent), Canada (6.1 per cent), Russia (5.3 per cent), and Japan (4.2 per cent).[8] A year later, the differentials were roughly the same: 9.5 per cent in the euro area, 9.4 per cent in the United States, 8.6 per cent in Canada, 8.3 per cent in Russia, and 5.7 per cent in Japan.[9]

But whatever the qualities of debate over the European Social Model, it is clear that there have been a number of distinctive social trends at work in Europe that have emerged in spite of the actions and aspirations of planners and governments. Because of the unique combination of opportunities they face and the values they pursue, Europeans have adopted distinctive approaches to the manner in which they manage their own lives and their relationships with others. Not just must economic growth be sustainable, but material growth and wealth are no longer seen as the core measures of progress, and Europeanism places greater emphasis on enjoying the rewards of prosperity. Of course not everyone enjoys those benefits equally, and European society—like societies everywhere—is blighted by crime, economic deprivation, social dysfunction, and environmental decay. But Europe is quite distinctive in the way in which it chooses to deal with many of these problems.

The population implosion

Those who doubt the prospects for Europe's future sooner or later turn their attention to what is routinely regarded as the region's demographic Achilles heel: its shrinking and aging population. Because Europe's birth rate is falling, and because Europeans are living longer and working less, the number of workers relative to the number of retirees is declining, and workers will need to bear a growing share of the health care and welfare costs of the retired. The result, runs the conventional view, is that Europe's competitive edge will decline, that it cannot hope to be a world power without maintaining a large population (the best hope for which now apparently lies in increased immigration), and that its share of global economic output—and ultimately of political influence in the world—will inevitably decline. Europe as we know it is slowly going out of business, declares *Washington Post* columnist Robert Samuelson.[10] Europe's demographic decline is 'a crisis of civilizational morale', concludes American political activist George Weigel.[11] The shrinking European population will condemn the European Union to reduced international influence, argues historian Niall Ferguson, leaving Europeans with the choice of either opening their borders to more immigration or transforming the European Union into a 'fortified retirement community'.[12]

But there are curious inconsistencies at work here. Europe is charged with having too low a population growth, and yet it is also charged with a failure to provide enough jobs for its existing population, and a failure to deal effectively with poverty. And how is it to achieve its core goal of sustainable economic growth if it is also expected to expand the size of its population? How do the worries about there being too little immigration to make up the shortfall fit with the debate over the challenges posed by immigration to European identity and multiculturalism? Furthermore, while immigration is often touted as the demographic advantage that the United States enjoys over Europe, it has been a topic of heated debate in the United States, with concerns about the effect social and cultural changes are likely to have on American identity. Rather than Europe being threatened by population decline, is it not possible that the European population model may in fact contain important opportunities? With fewer people, societies might be more content, better supplied, and more cohesive, and with a reduced struggle to keep up with demand, Europeans might instead balance better supply and demand, more quickly meet the goal of sustainable growth, and more effectively address threats to the environment.

The data bear out the unusual position of Europe. While populations in much of the rest of the world are growing, those in Europe will—according to UN projections—fall from a peak of 734 million in 2015 to 691 million in 2050, a decline of six per cent. While once there was worried talk of the dangers of a worldwide population explosion, the concern in Europe today is of a population implosion (see Fig. 6.1). Numbers are expected to grow in several of Europe's smaller states—such as Denmark, Ireland, the Netherlands, Norway, and Switzerland—but they are already falling or are expected to fall in almost all the bigger states. The populations of Ukraine and Poland are already down from their respective 1990 and 1995 peaks of 51.5 million and 38.6 million, as is that of Germany from its 2005 peak of 82.1 million. The population of Italy is expected to start falling after 2020, and that of France to start levelling out after 2045. Alone, among

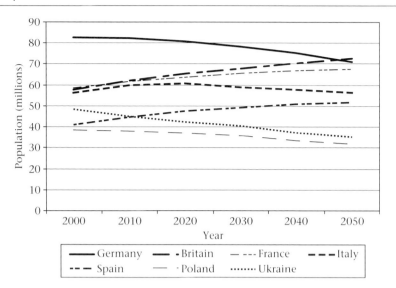

Figure 6.1 Europe's population implosion

Source: United Nations Population Division, http://esa.un.org/unpp (retrieved September 2009).

major European states, Britain's population is expected to grow, rising by 20 per cent between 2005 and 2050, thanks mainly to immigration. Meanwhile, the population of China is expected to grow between 2015 and 2035 by 5 per cent (to just under 1.5 billion) before starting to fall, that of the United States by 22 per cent between 2015 and 2050 (to 404 million), that of Brazil over the same period by 8 per cent (to 219 million), and that of India by 25 per cent (to 1.6 billion). That of Russia, however, will fall by 15 per cent.

But projections are based on current assumptions, the UN revised them considerably in 2009 (more growth in Europe, less in China and Brazil), and we can only guess as to the impact of changing future patterns of behaviour. Thus, for example, if there is enough immigration into Europe, and if European life expectancy continues to grow, due to improvements in health care and quality of life, then the decline may not happen as soon as is expected, and may indeed never happen—there may rather be a stabilization of population numbers. Much depends on fertility rates, the decline of which is the core explanation behind the UN projections. Rates in the European Union fell by 45 per cent between 1960 and 2004,[13] and today rest at 1.49 children per mother, well below the replacement level of 2.1. No EU states have a rate higher than 1.7, and in Austria, western

Germany, Italy, and Spain the rate is as low as 1.2–1.4. While natural increase in the 1960s accounted for almost all population growth in Europe, that growth is now almost entirely generated by net immigration, but this has not been big enough to make up the difference. So worried have some governments become about current trends that they have adopted policies aimed at encouraging their citizens to have more children, including increased job security, extended parental leave, expanded child care and after-school programmes, and flexible work schedules.

Immigration may help make up some of the falling numbers, but it of course offers its own problems, because many of the newcomers are Arabs, Africans, and/or Muslims. If Europeans are willing to accept continuing change in the balance of numbers between white and non-white populations, and between Muslims and non-Muslims, and if immigrants can successfully integrate into European society and enjoy equal access to all that it offers, then all will be well. But this is not what is happening now, nor is it likely to happen for decades to come. Racism and religious intolerance have already fed into the rise of Islamic extremism and have helped spawn right-wing anti-immigrant political parties (as further discussed in Chapter 7). So, while immigration may help boost population numbers, it seems that the trade-off will be increased social, economic, and political tensions.

At the heart of concerns about the implications of population implosion is the growing imbalance between workers and retirees: thanks to a combination of declining fertility rates, improved health care, and growing life expectancy, Europeans are aging. Between 1960 and 2006, the percentage of the population aged sixty-five and older rose in most western European countries from about 9–12 to about 15–18, leaving them with a bigger proportion of older residents than in Australia, Canada, New Zealand, or the United States (but not Japan—see Fig. 6.2). The median age of the world's population in 2000 was nearly twenty-seven, but in Europe it was thirty-eight and is projected to rise to forty-nine by 2050. In 2007, 16.1 per cent of the population of Europe was aged sixty-five or over, compared to 12.5 per cent in North America, 9.9 per cent in Latin America, 6.6 per cent in Asia, and 3.4 per cent in Africa.[14] Europe in 2005 had 35 people of pensionable age for every 100 of working age; by 2050 the ratio is projected to rise to 75:100, and in some countries it may reach parity.

How can Europe continue to sustain its generous welfare provisions when relatively few people are working? Fundamental economic logic suggests that adjustments will need to be made to those provisions, either through a reduction in benefits, greater restrictions on the amount of time

149

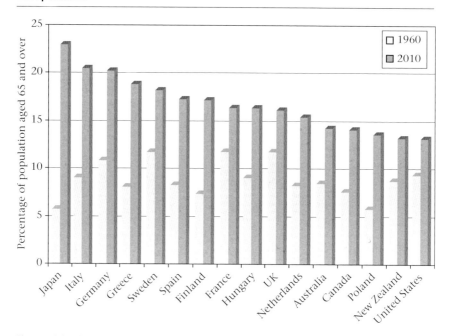

Figure 6.2 The aging of the population

Source: OECD Factbook 2009, http://www.oecd.org (retrieved September 2009).

that individuals can claim benefits, increased taxation in order to cover increased costs, cutting government expenditures in other areas, or through the privatization of key services. But consider also an alternative set of possibilities:

- Improvements in health care will continue not just to help people live longer but also potentially to live better, thereby reducing some of the load on the health-care system.

- The costs of social security could be reduced by greater reliance on personally invested retirement accounts, which would supplement the often low income offered through state pensions.

- Labour shortages might increase the demand for skilled workers, who will earn more and thus pay more in taxes.

- The continued shift to often higher-paid service jobs will give Europeans more income and raise the tax base needed to pay for social security.

- A more effective response to unemployment problems will increase the number of taxable workers.

- There will be less pressure on government to provide jobs, schools, hospitals, houses, roads, energy, and infrastructure, thereby allowing more government spending to be diverted to social security.

In other words, rather than presenting Europe with a new balance of payments problem, the need to respond to the numbers disparity between workers and retirees might oblige European governments to develop a new social model in which the efforts of a smaller labour force are used more efficiently, and in which there will be a recalculation of how health care and welfare are managed. Certainly, the pressures for a review of policy are greater in Europe than in other advanced economies.

The second problem often tied to demographic change in Europe is that of declining productivity. The argument runs that growing populations mean greater economic dynamism and greater national productivity and much of the economic data suggest that American workers, for example, have for years now been handily outstripping their European peers. But much depends upon the time-frame considered, and upon how the data are compiled and interpreted. For example, Pontusson suggests that if output is calculated according to purchasing power parity on the basis of output per hour, Europeans hold their own in relation to other capitalist economies (see Fig. 6.3). A study by American economist Robert Gordon suggests that at least part of the reason why European GDP appears to be lower than American GDP is that Europeans do not have to spend as much on health care, education, transport, and security as Americans. He also calculates that between 1950 and 2002, growth in European productivity outstripped that in the United States, growing by 3.3 per cent annually, compared to 2 per cent annually in the United States.[15] Another study concludes that while the gap between the United States and the EU-15 in overall levels of per capita gross domestic product remained almost unchanged between 1970 and 2000 (workers in the EU-15 consistently produced 30 per cent less than workers in the United States), the gap between the two in GDP per hour closed markedly: in 1970, EU-15 workers were producing 35 per cent less than US workers, but by 2000 they were producing only 9 per cent less.[16]

Concerns about productivity only make sense if we continue to define economic health purely in terms of output as measured by gross domestic product. But economists have long wondered about the utility of GDP as a benchmark, and one alternative to the standard measures of economic progress is the Genuine Progress Indicator developed by the American think tank Redefining Progress in 1995. This takes production and consumption data and adjusts them for factors such as income distribution,

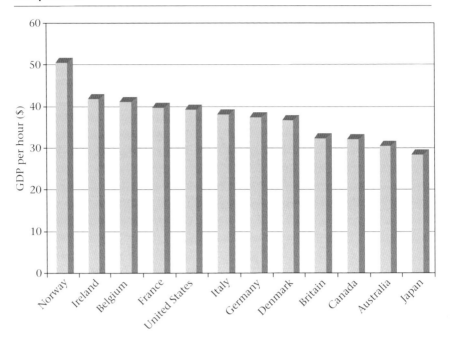

Figure 6.3 Economic productivity

Source: Jonas Pontusson, *Inequality and Prosperity: Social Europe vs. Liberal America* (Ithaca, NY: Cornell University Press, 2005), 12. Calculations by author using OECD data, expressed in US dollars at purchasing power parities, multiplying average annual hours worked and the total number of people employed. Figures are for 2002.

adds factors such as the value of household and volunteer work, and subtracts factors such as the costs of crime and pollution.[17] Thus, health care, education, the environment, public safety, and personal well-being can be factored into calculations of economic and social progress, allowing us to measure progress in both quantitative and qualitative terms. From this perspective, declining or stabilizing population numbers may offer Europe an opportunity unavailable at the moment to most of the rest of the world. In other words, Europeans might use their demographic trends to show that production and consumption can achieve a more equitable balance, and offer Europeans a life in which the effort they invest in work can meet needs while also allowing workers more time to enjoy the benefits of their productivity.

As we saw in Chapter 5, sustainability is at the heart of Europeanist thinking. In turn, reduced consumption is at the heart of sustainability, and smaller populations are at the heart of reduced consumption. The matter of the earth's carrying capacity has been the subject of speculation since 1650, when the British physician William Petty wrote of the multiplication of human population, but concluded that it would take 2,000 years for that capacity to be reached. Nearly 150 years later, greater public impact was achieved by the warnings of the British classical economist Thomas Malthus outlined in his *Essay on Population*, written in 1798–1803. He argued that because the natural rate of population growth was exponential, while that of food production was arithmetical, unless population growth was checked, population numbers would outstrip the available food supply and there would be widespread famine. But Malthus did not take into account the possibility that changes in science might allow the world to continue feeding and supplying a growing population. Nor, many years later, did Paul Ehrlich, whose 1968 book *The Population Bomb* was written against a background of rapidly growing population, leading him to warn that millions would face starvation in the 1970s and 1980s, that the limits of human capability to produce food by conventional means had nearly been reached, that attempts to increase food production would cause environmental deterioration and reduce the earth's capacity to produce food, that population growth could lead to plague and nuclear war, and that the only solution lay in a change in human attitudes.[18]

How far can we continue to support a growing population? The answer depends in part on the balance between population and resources: more people means more production and consumption, and unless they are sustainable, the balance between demand and supply will inevitably tip in the wrong direction. The answer also depends on the quality of production and the effects of consumption; unless carefully regulated and controlled, one will lead to greater pollution and the other to ongoing waste. In addition, more people means more demand for schools, health-care services, infrastructure, transport and energy networks, the maintenance of law and order, and the provision of core social services. The United States is often touted as the world's most dynamic economy, and its growing population is portrayed as one of its clear advantages over Europe, and yet it is instructive that even the world's wealthiest country is unable to provide the education, health care, and infrastructure that its people need, to deal with a growing gap between the affluent and the poor, or to always pursue sustainable development policies successfully.

Consider the prospects for Britain, the only major European country that fits with the 'positive' model of a growing population. Eurostat projects that the British population will reach 77 million by 2060, overtaking that of Germany, currently by a large margin the most populous country in Europe. Britain is already overcrowded, with a population density of about 250 people per square kilometre. While this is much less than the Netherlands (more than 390), Japan, or India (about 340), and is slightly above the figure for Germany, it is twice the figure for France or China, three times the figure for Spain, and nearly eight times the figure for the United States or for Europe as a whole.[19] Britain's cities are already crowded, its roads ever busier with traffic, its rush hours often a nightmare of congestion, its property prices unrealistically high before the 2008 crash, and its people must live in small houses and drive small cars that they must fit into small parking spaces. While changes in technology and consumption patterns will minimize the environmental impact of a rising population, rarely considered is the psychological impact of dealing on a daily basis with so many people. Rather than being something that Britons should welcome, perhaps it is something they should fear.

Bigger populations supposedly mean bigger markets, more production, more consumers, bigger militaries, and more political and economic influence in the world. But bigger populations also mean greater demand for resources and services, more pressures on the environment, more traffic on roads, expanding cities, more overcrowding, and social dysfunction. A smaller population promises more benefits than costs for Europe. Reductions in the labour force will increase the pressure for technological change, which will help make European workers more efficient and see more automation of industry. Except during economic downturns, workers will be able to negotiate higher salaries, providing them with more disposable income, allowing them to spend more and helping boost the European marketplace. Europeans will also be able to save and invest more, helping strengthen European economies. They will also pay more in taxes, helping governments raise the funds needed to take care of retirees, and the number of people living in poverty will likely decline. In short, then, the European model of declining population numbers may have many advantages over the fascination that most other parts of the world seem to have with growth.

The family: no longer traditional

The term *family* is cocooned in myth. It is often assumed in the West, for example, that the standard family unit is a parent or parents living together with their children in what sociologists call a nuclear or conjugal arrangement. Equally common is the myth that the family has long been the typical sub-unit of society, and—for social conservatives, at least—that the ideal family lives according to 'traditional' values. The latter are rarely defined, but are routinely exploited to defend arguments that a family should consist of a husband and wife in a monogamous relationship, with children living according to a code of respect, discipline, abstinence, censorship, and religious faith. For them, the family is a source of ethical guidance, and the 'decay' of the family is associated with the decay of society.

The reality, of course, is quite different. Families come in multiple forms and sizes, and are based on such varied norms and principles that it is impossible to pin down many consistent features, and indeed the family values that are claimed as traditional—and therefore as archetypical—are anything but that. And even if we assume that the nuclear family is an ideal, or a benchmark against which all families might be measured, it is clear that nowhere in the world is society moving so clearly and so rapidly away from that benchmark as in Europe. So substantial have been the changes in the last few decades that the structure of European families has taken on a quite distinctive character, which can be summarized thus: fewer marriages, fewer children, more children born outside marriage, and smaller households. What exactly is happening, and what are the implications?

First, fewer Europeans are getting married, their ages at marriage are rising, and divorce rates are growing. Until perhaps the 1960s, a heterosexual marriage was considered a core social relationship, as well as the norm for European households, and Europeans would commonly marry in their late teens or early twenties. But as more women went on to higher education and to work, and as cohabitation became more socially acceptable, so couples delayed marriage and delayed starting families. Where it was once usual to marry in the early twenties, the average age for first marriages in 2006 in the EU-27 was thirty-one for men and twenty-eight for women, rising as high as 33–34 in Sweden and Denmark, while remaining as low as 27–29 in much of eastern Europe.[20] Europe is not that different from many other parts of the world in this regard—averages in Australia, Canada, Japan, New Zealand, and the United States are all in the range 28–30—but where Europe stands out is in the way marriage trends contribute to the other demographic changes that have redefined notions of the family.

Second, not only is the fertility rate among Europeans declining (see earlier in this chapter), but more children are being born outside marriage. In 1960, no more than 2–5 per cent of western European children were born outside marriage, the highest rates being in Austria (12 per cent) and Sweden (11 per cent). By 2000, nearly one-third of babies in the EU-25 were born outside marriage, and even more in Denmark, Latvia, France, Britain, and Finland (all 40–45 per cent) and in Sweden (55 per cent). Only in Greece and Cyprus were the percentages still in single figures.[21] Birth outside marriage is often associated with poverty, hence the concerns that the non-marital birth rate among blacks and Hispanics in the United States is more than twice the rate among whites (although the gap is closing). But while the link with poverty is still present in Europe, birth outside marriage is increasingly a deliberate choice on the part of parents.

Finally, household structure is changing. Where once the nuclear family was widespread in Europe, single-parent households have become more usual, as have households containing couples without children, and households where the parents are unmarried. This is true also of the United States, where households with nuclear families are now outnumbered by single-person households and adult-only households, but the change has been more marked in Europe. Two-third of households in the EU-25 in 2005 had no children at all (in Germany and Austria, a remarkable three-quarters of households were childless), and only 17 per cent had two children or more. Single-parent households accounted for 13 per cent of all those with children, rising as high as 16 per cent in Germany, 18 per cent in Belgium, and 24 per cent in Britain.[22]

Although there are similar trends under way in other industrialized countries,[23] they began in Europe, they are most marked among Europeans, and when identified in other societies it is usual to see the discussion turn to how those societies are becoming 'more like Europe'. The changes have also more fundamentally altered the European demographic landscape than has been the case elsewhere. For example, large families are still relatively common in the United States, where the 'traditional family values' argument has had a greater political impact, and where there are fewer worried conversations about the decline of the family (except among African-Americans, where the nuclear family is a thing of rarity) or about falling fertility rates. The decline of the European family is all the more ironic given the expansion of social policies that have made having children easier and less expensive, including maternity and paternity leave, improved access to day care, free or subsidized education and health care, shorter working weeks, more holiday time, and other benefits that reduce the conflict between work and family time.[24]

Along with changes in the definition of the 'traditional' family, new assumptions are also being made in Europe about homosexuality, with growing support for same-sex marriages and civil unions. Homosexual acts are illegal throughout most of the Middle East, South Asia, and eastern and southern Africa, and are subject to large fines, or even the death penalty in Iran, Nigeria, Pakistan, Saudi Arabia, Sudan, and several other countries. But when asked in a 2003 poll if homosexuality was a way of life that should be accepted by society, more than three-quarters of Germans, French, Britons, and Italians agreed, compared to just over half of Americans.[25] A 2007 Eurobarometer poll found that while only 44 per cent of respondents were in support of the recognition of same-sex marriages, there was generally greater tolerance in western Protestant states than in eastern and/or Catholic states. Among the Dutch, the Danes, and the Swedes, support was in the range 69–82 per cent, but in almost every eastern state it was in the range 10–20 per cent.[26]

Denmark in 1989 was the first country in the world to recognize a same-sex civil union, the Netherlands in 2001 was the first country to allow same-sex marriage, and Spain in 2005 was the first country to give same-sex marriages equal rights with heterosexual marriages. As of late 2009, Belgium, Norway, and Sweden also allowed same-sex marriages (along with Canada and South Africa), while fourteen European countries (along with five non-European countries and parts of four non-European countries) recognized some form of same-sex civil union or partnership. European tastes stand once again in notable contrast to those in the United States, where same-sex marriages are legal in six states, and civil unions in nearly a dozen more, but the reaction against these trends has been marked and substantial. The Defence of Marriage Act was passed in 1996, defining a marriage as a union between a man and a woman, more than two dozen states have passed constitutional amendments preventing the recognition of same-sex marriages, most have also made illegal the recognition of any kind of same-sex union, and calls have been made for an amendment to the US Constitution that would prevent same-sex marriages.

Working to live

As noted in Chapter 5, Europe has developed and explored the concepts of post-industrialism and welfarism further and more deeply than any other society on earth. This is reflected in the structure and priorities of the European marketplace, and in the provision of extensive and often generous welfare provisions. Often overlooked in the debate, however, and yet reflective of some of the core qualities of Europeanism, is the question of how individuals should balance their work and personal life. While residents of much of the rest of the world seem either to live to work, or to work simply to survive, Europeans have transformed the idea of working to live into a fine art. They are working fewer hours, they are producing more with those hours, they have developed a host of leisure-friendly laws and policies, and the additional time that they have free to spend at home or on holiday gives them more time to relax. Polls reveal that most are satisfied with the results: in almost every western European country, 80–90 per cent of respondents in 2005 agreed that their working hours fitted well with their family and other social commitments outside work. Only in Spain, Italy, and several eastern European countries were the numbers lower.[27] A 2007 Eurobarometer poll found that nearly half of respondents felt that more importance should be given to spare time than to work.[28]

The case of Japan offers a particularly stark contrast with that of Europe. Japanese urban culture is noted for a work ethic that values loyalty, selflessness, obligation, honour, and the placing of company needs above personal needs. The government has tried and failed for years to place limits on long working hours and overtime, which have resulted in fatigue, higher rates of work-related suicide, and a combination of stress and other health problems leading to *karoshi* (death from overwork).[29] The contrasts between Europe and the United States are also stark. The Puritan ethic of industry and individualism provides a compelling foundation for the search for the American dream, in pursuit of which Americans are encouraged to work hard, take personal responsibility, and seek always to better themselves. For low-paid American workers, the pressures to work longer hours in order to pay their bills and to offset declining job security offered by employers are almost irresistible, while leaders of business and industry are urged on by the pressures of capitalism, consumption, power, and often greed. How American perceptions will change as a result of the 2007–9 global economic crisis we must wait and see, but crisis or not, for most working Americans there are three rules of thumb: your social life revolves around a combination of the workplace, the family, and the church; you have little leisure time (because you work long hours with short vacations); and you use what little free time you have intensively (you work hard, so you play hard as well).

Europeanist attitudes are quite different. For most working Europeans, the three rules of thumb are thus: your social life revolves around the workplace and the community; you have more government-mandated time to relax; and you use your free time less energetically. Among liberal democracies at least, Europe is notable for the amount of free time workers are afforded by their employers. The average number of hours that workers spend on the job in most liberal democracies has been falling steadily in

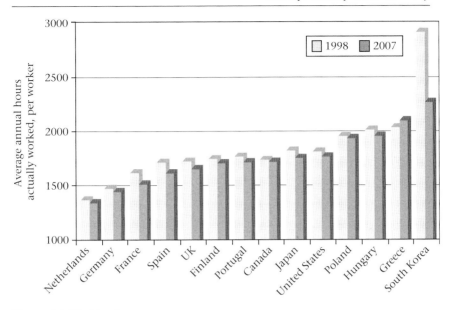

Figure 6.4 Working hours

Source: OECD Factbook 2009, http://www.oecd.org (retrieved September 2009).

recent decades, but nowhere so markedly as in Europe. In 2007, western European workers were each spending about 1,400–1,700 hours per year at work, and although numbers were higher in eastern European states, they are now declining there as economic priorities change and workers become wealthier. By contrast, Japanese and American workers spent nearly 1,800 hours per year at work, and South Koreans were in a class of their own at just over 2,300 hours (see Fig. 6.4). The average American was working 23 per cent longer than his or her French counterpart and 33 per cent longer than his or her German counterpart. In addition to working fewer hours per week, Europeans also have more paid vacation. While most American workers are limited to ten to twelve days per year, and there is pressure for them not to take all those days as a block, many European workers enjoy as many as twenty-five to thirty paid days off per year, and often take most of them as a block. As though generous mandated leave is not enough, Europeans also typically have eight to ten public holidays, while Americans have six (although federal government employees have ten).

Some of the differences can be explained by the impact that European labour unions have had on bringing changes in working conditions, and by voter support for socialist and social democratic political parties that are sympathetic to changes in the demands of the workplace. While the typical

159

American worker is expected to work forty to forty-two hours per week, and has plenty of opportunities for overtime and pressures to take work home with them, workers in France enjoy a legislated thirty-five-hour working week, and EU workers more generally are subject to a 1993 EU working time directive which capped the number of working hours at forty-eight per week, although it allowed opt-outs for countries that wished to set higher limits. One of the last remaining holdouts is Britain, which has resisted attempts to remove the opt-outs, as a result of which workers show less conviction that working life is getting better.[30] Perhaps unsurprisingly, polls find that fewer Britons associate work with happiness than is the case almost anywhere else in the European Union.

Europeans have developed a wide array of benefits and opportunities for workers that often astonish their American peers: generous parental leave for both parents (up to fifty-two weeks at full pay in Denmark, or fifty-two weeks at reduced pay in Finland), breastfeeding leave, reduced working hours to raise children, paid sick days, study leave, and even the right to a sabbatical or leave to set up a business (in France). And while Europeans take their national health-care programmes mainly for granted, they represent an additional substantial benefit: neither workers nor employers need worry about paying health insurance premiums (unless they opt for private health care), and even the most complex medical and surgical procedures are available at only a nominal charge. In the United States, by contrast, health insurance premiums are growing faster than the rate of inflation, such that the average for an employer's health plan covering a family of four in 2007 was just over $12,000. In 2005, the United States spent 15 per cent of its gross domestic product on health care, compared to between 7 and 10 per cent in most European countries.[31]

What explains the European attitude toward work? Ferguson argues the link between secularism and the changing work ethic, reminds us of Max Weber's argument that modern capitalism was born out of Christian asceticism, and concludes that we are witnessing the simultaneous decline of Protestantism and its work ethic. He also points to the large differences in the number of days lost to strikes in Europe compared to those in the United States. In all, he concludes, this explains why the US economy 'has surged ahead of its European competitors in the past two decades. It is not about efficiency. It is simply that Americans work more.'[32] Critics of Europe's secularization like to make the point that while a Godless Europe may appear at least superficially to be progressive and non-judgemental, the longer-term prognosis is not good. The combination of an absence of faith, the declining place of the family, and falling birth rates will create a society, claims Weigel, that is unsustainable. Europeans are becoming hedonists.[33] For critics of Europe, making the link between the decline and fall of the Roman Empire, and the trends now under way in Europe, is irresistible. Or at least it was until the economic collapse of 2008, most commonly blamed on the willingness of American banks to lend to home-buyers who had overreached themselves and were unable to afford the large payments on their mortgages. Growth in the American market (often measured in terms of housing starts, or new houses built) was impressive, but it was built in part on a foundation of unrealistic credit.

While there is no denying the correlation of figures measuring declining religious affiliation and changing work ethic, there is just as close a correlation between poverty and work ethic: as a general rule, the citizens of wealthier states tend to work less than those of poorer states. This is evident in the data for Europe, where—when asked in 2005 how many hours they usually work in their main job each week—only 10–25 per cent of Scandinavians, Germans, Britons, the French, the Dutch, and Belgians said more than forty hours, compared to 25–40 per cent of Italians, Spaniards, and Portuguese, and 40–55 per cent of Poles, Czechs, Slovaks, Romanians, and Greeks.[34] Of course there is poverty in western Europe, but there is also less pressure for middle-class workers to put in extra hours in order to help make up the shortfall, for at least two reasons.

First, generous welfare systems mean that Europeans are able to work less because many of their basic needs are met by the state. While Americans must worry about large health insurance premiums, being saddled with large medical bills, or using retirement income to pay for vitally-needed drugs or medical procedures, Europeans have none of these concerns (although they must expect to pay more taxes in order to meet the costs of government programmes). Meanwhile, the wide availability of free or subsidized education in Europe means no need to pay expensive school fees in order to keep their children out of sometimes inferior state schools, and no need for them to save for their children's university education. Both the latter are options that are faced as a matter of routine by most middle-class American parents.

Second, there are broader explanations coming out of the inevitable effects of post-industrialism. In the feudal and industrial eras, workers earned a minimal living by labouring on the land or in soulless and exploitative factories. They worked simply to feed, clothe, and house themselves, and there was little leisure time, and few ways to use what little such time they had. But in the post-industrial era, not only do many people now pursue careers—working for the pleasure of engaging in whatever activity they feel suits their particular interests and skills—but work and leisure have increasingly coincided. People work in order not just to sustain themselves, but also to feel personally fulfilled, and to give them the income that they need to make the most of their leisure time, for which there are now numerous options.

Furthermore, to go back to Ferguson's point about the productivity that comes with the American Protestant work ethic—perhaps Americans work more, but at what cost? Workplace pressures in the United States have been implicated in increased stress and depression, a rise in workplace violence, increased levels of absenteeism, rising numbers of claims for worker compensation (for injury or ill-health), and the break-up of the family. They may even factor in the slightly shorter life expectancy of Americans, which stood at seventy-eight years in 2006 compared to 79–81 years in most western European states.[35]

In short, then, Europeans are working fewer hours, but they are doing more with those hours, in part because the measure of personal worth and success is no longer tied so securely to work, and in part because unremitting labour has been balanced by a new emphasis on enjoying the fruits of that labour. Such outcomes have been long predicted as an inevitable result of industrialization, automation, and changes in patterns of consumption, which would lead to other activities gaining importance at the expense of labour. Work is still a critical measure of self-worth for Europeans, and a financial necessity, and polls find that only family ranks above work in the priorities set by Europeans. It would be wrong to suggest that Europeans value self-development over good pay and job security, but they have moved further along the road to this post-modern principle than workers in the United States, and certainly than those in poorer countries where self-development rarely factors in worker calculations.

Criminal justice: an emphasis on rights

If one of the qualitative measures of a society is how it treats its most vulnerable members—be they children, the elderly, the poor, or the disabled—another is surely the way in which it deals with crime and criminals. What does society define as a crime, what does it consider reasonable punishment, how tolerant is its criminal justice system, and does it stop at punishment or does it also try to address the root causes of crime and to rehabilitate offenders? There are differences in the nature of European legal systems, such as those between the English common law system and the French civil law system, and between the Dutch inquisitorial system and the English accusatorial system. There are also differences in the culture of criminal justice systems, the Dutch having a reputation for being relatively tolerant while the English and Welsh have a reputation for being harder and more punitive.[36] However, Europeanization is leading to change as national criminal justice systems adapt to fit the requirements of EU law, and as European states work together to deal with terrorism and transnational crime. Demands have been particularly great on eastern European states as they have moved away from Soviet-style criminal justice to the greater rights afforded under Western legal traditions.

Comparisons with the United States bring out several of the core qualities of the European model of criminal justice. Whitman makes a distinction between what he describes as the harshness of the American criminal justice system and the 'dignity and mildness' found in the continental European model. In the United States, he argues, criminal law consistently tries to treat all alike (more so than is the case in Europe), but shows less respect for individuals—persons do not matter as much as they do in Europe. In the case of Europe, he argues, mildness is reflected in the emphasis placed on victims' rights and in encouraging mediation between offenders and victims as a way of avoiding criminal prosecution. Non-violent offenders who are routinely imprisoned in the United States serve no time in Europe while violent offenders in the United States serve longer terms than is the case in Europe. Europe targets a smaller class of offenders (mainly those that have committed violent acts), and prison conditions are (with some exceptions) generally better in Europe (and usually less crowded) than is the case in the United States.[37] Also, pre-trial terms of detention are rare and short compared to those in the United States, where—in spite of constitutional guarantees to a speedy trial—detention is frequent and terms are often long. Europe may have travelled too far down the road of mildness however: polls find that a large majority (84 per cent) of residents of the European Union feel that there is too much tolerance and that criminals should be punished more severely.[38] Ironically, many Americans would agree, in spite of the already large prison populations found in the United States.

The European model is also distinctive for its relatively low levels of litigiousness. In resolving disputes, Europeans are more willing to negotiate than to confront through the law, and they are also more inclined to resign themselves to misfortune than to attempt to achieve resolution through legal means. Indeed, in their social relationships, they reflect many of the same qualities found in Europeanist attitudes towards relations among

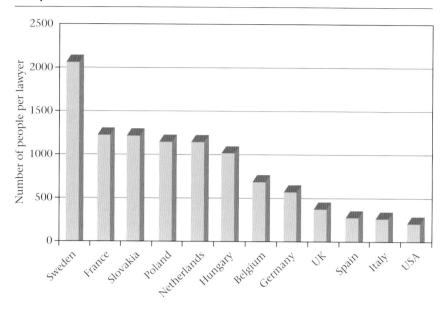

Figure 6.5 Numbers of lawyers

Source: US figure (for 2008) calculated from American Bar Association website at http://www. abanet.org; European figures (for 2008) from Council of Bars and Law Societies of Europe website at http://www.ccbe.eu. Both retrieved September 2009.

states, including engagement and soft power (see Chapter 8). There have been signs of change in some areas, notably in the insurance industry, where there has been anecdotal evidence of an increase in litigiousness that has led to worries about higher liability claims of the kind that have plagued the 'compensation culture' of the United States.[39] There have also been concerns that Europeans are turning increasingly to class action suits made possible by changes to the law in several countries, and may be further encouraged to sue for compensation if American-style contingency fees (where lawyers are paid only if successful) are made more widely available. Whether the European Union is moving towards the American model, or whether entrenched institutions and cultures will prevent that happening, is actively debated.[40] But, for now at least, Europeans are less inclined to take legal action in cases of dispute, in which they are encouraged by the relatively low numbers of lawyers in most European states (see Fig. 6.5).

The effects of the different criminal justice cultures of Europe compared to those in other states are reflected in the figures on prison populations: as a function of total population size, the number of prisoners in most

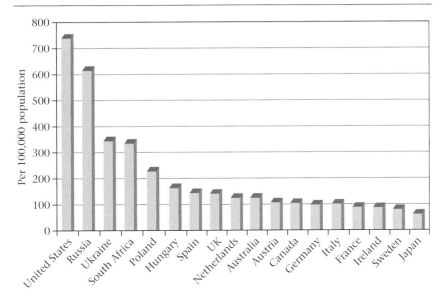

Figure 6.6 Prison populations

Source: OECD Society at a Glance, http://www.oecd.org (retrieved January 2009). Figures are for 2006.

continental European states is quite low, typically in the range 80–130 prisoners per 100,000 people. Figures are higher for Britain with its combination of longer terms for more serious offences and its greater number of prisoners either on remand or serving shorter terms for less serious offences, and for most eastern European states with their heritage of Soviet-style criminal justice. But even though European prison populations have been growing since the 1990s as a result mainly of a change in attitude towards the use of imprisonment, Europe generally is quite distinct from the United States and Russia, where the prison population is as much as six to nine times greater (see Fig. 6.6). In terms of the quality of life in prisons, requirements under the European Convention on Human Rights and the Convention for the Prevention of Torture and Inhuman or Degrading Treatment or Punishment have helped promote the rights of detainees and have mainly prevented a reduction in the quality of prisons even as prison populations have grown. This has not always had the desired effects, to be sure, as reflected in the dire conditions that prevail at many French prisons, a problem that has only recently been actively addressed.

The character of the contemporary European criminal justice model has been determined and homogenized in large part by pressures not only from the European Court of Justice, but also from the Council of Europe and the

European Court of Human Rights, the latter acting through its oversight of the European Convention on Human Rights (ECHR). In force since 1953, the convention prohibits torture and 'inhuman or degrading treatment or punishment' without exception or limitation, provides that everyone has the right to liberty and security of person, protects the right to a fair trial (including a presumption of innocence and the right to a public hearing before an independent and impartial tribunal within reasonable time), protects against discrimination based on gender, race, colour, language, religion, and other criteria, and includes the right to an effective remedy before national authorities for violations of rights under the convention.

Europeanist values have been reflected most clearly in recent decades in the response to international terrorism. Concerns have risen in the past about the extent to which anti-terrorist actions—such as those in Northern Ireland in the 1980s—have been allowed to interfere with individual human rights. But now that all European states except Belarus have signed the ECHR, they are also subject to what the convention says about individual rights, which means that they may not put terrorists beyond the law.[41] The European response to terrorism was also reflected in the deep political and public opposition to the policies of the Bush administration in the United States on extraordinary rendition, torture, and the holding of terrorist suspects at Guantanamo Bay. While several European governments were complicit in supporting American policy, there was widespread condemnation when this was publicly admitted. A majority of Americans see the war on terrorism as a struggle against evil, but the European view is more nuanced, with more consideration paid to the root causes of terrorism and the need to address them.

7

Values: Multicultural and Secular

Earlier chapters of this book have wrestled with the challenges of defining terms such as *state*, *nation*, *society*, and *political culture*. This chapter is focused on another troublesome term: *values*. Contemporary discussions about values in liberal democracies have been heavily influenced—some might even say hijacked—by ideology, with conservatives claiming owner-ship of 'traditional' values such as family, respect, religion, marriage, and hard work, and liberals objecting to the notion of 'traditional' values and portraying many of the related debates as an attack on freedom of choice. But there is more to an understanding of values than ideology alone. Values are driven also by ethics, morality, and culture, and are collectively fash-ioned by a complex set of pressures and influences that include economic development, civil liberties, political stability, communal wealth, religious and social attitudes, and history. Value systems provide lenses through which more focus can be provided to the assessment of states, societies, and governments, and offer reference points that can help impose order on what might otherwise appear disorderly. They shed light on the norms, conditions, and goals that determine approaches to politics, society, family, community, work, and other core aspects of human existence.

Most studies of values will typically include such concepts as democracy, freedom, equality, and human dignity. The European Values Study—which has been assessing European values since the early 1980s—places more em-phasis on citizenship, family, religion, the workplace, society, and well-being. Yet another means of conceptualizing collective values is offered by the World Values Survey (WVS), which has undertaken comparative studies since 1990 using a two-dimensional assessment: community-based 'secular-rational' va-lues driven by opinions on religion, patriotism, authority, obedience, and family, and individual-based 'self-expression' values driven by opinions on freedom, expression, non-conformity, self-direction, and human trust.

The authors of the WVS argue that societies de-emphasizing religion, patriotism, authority, and family values are strong on secular-rational values (while the opposite holds true in societies where these values are emphasized), and that individuals who value liberty, conformity, and trust in others are strong on self-expression (and vice versa). Societies at the strong end of both scales are characterized by choice, while societies at the weak end of both scales are characterized by constraint. On the basis of its findings, the WVS has constructed a cultural map of the world which places most of Europe at the strong end of both the secular-rational and self-expression scales, with the notable exception of most ex-communist states (which are strong on secular-rational values but weak on self-expression), and of Ireland, Poland, Portugal, and Romania (which are weaker on the secular-rational scale).[1]

Values were at the core of the arguments made in Chapters 5 and 6, which suggested that Europeanism is associated with preferences for state regulation of markets and social welfare with a view to promoting economic equality and opportunity. But when it comes to questions of how far the state should be allowed to make moral decisions for individuals, or to define personal choices, Europeans are less tolerant of government. The tightening of security in response to international terrorism has resulted in something of a reversal of late, but this has not impinged upon core European preferences in regard to such issues as gender equality, abortion, homosexuality, access to alcohol and drugs, euthanasia, censorship, and religion. On these and related matters, Europeanism represents positions that are liberal and progressive, and that often stand in notable contrast to the values of other societies, particularly in the Islamic world. This chapter explores European values by focusing on three ethical and moral issues in which the particular qualities of Europeanism are most clearly pronounced: multiculturalism, secularism, and opposition to capital punishment. It ends with an assessment of the rather more nebulous notion of life satisfaction, assessing the match between public policy and private priorities.

Multiculturalism

Europe has always been a multicultural society, a region of invaders and immigrants who have repeatedly moved across cultural and political borders to blend ideas and philosophies. This is often forgotten, however, for two main reasons. First, the state and the nation have both long exerted a strong grip on European imaginations, drawing attention away from the multicultural qualities of Europe as a whole. Second, the limited social mobility offered first by feudalism and then by the class pressures of industrialization ensured that it was not until relatively recently, mainly since the end of the Second World War, that most Europeans began personally to experience different cultures. They have since become more conscious of the diversity of the region in which they live: the conflicting pressures of integration and devolution have raised questions about the relative influence of European, state, and national identity; the influx of new workers from former colonies and nearby states—notably Arabs to France, Turks to Germany, and South Asians and West Indians to Britain—has increased Europe's ethnic and religious diversity; and the single market has created new patterns of internal migration, whose scale and implications became newly important in the wake of the influx of eastern European workers to the west following EU enlargement.

Multiculturalism has always represented something of a double-edged sword in European calculations. On the one hand, the movement of intellectuals, ideas, and culture across borders has been one of the distinctive glories of European identity, where individuals from multiple different cultures have contributed to the common pool of European culture: just as Shakespeare, Goethe, and Voltaire are all a part of European literature and language, so Aristotle, Mill, and Marx are all a part of European political philosophy; da Vinci, Picasso, and Hockney are all a part of European art; and Beethoven, Verdi, and the Beatles are all part of the European musical heritage. On the other hand, xenophobia, racism, and intolerance have always been the ugly side of European thinking, generating centuries of discrimination against the Jews and the Roma, accounting for the more unpleasant aspects of colonialism, reaching a nadir with the Holocaust, and rearing its head again in contemporary racism and intolerance for religious minorities, particularly Muslims.

Multiculturalism is usually understood to suggest that the identities of different groups within a society should be respected and maintained, the extreme version of this view being that all cultures are of equal value and that all aspects of each culture must be accepted by the others. The opposite view is to reject or ignore the differences and to work to assimilate minorities into society, denying and quashing their distinctive qualities and values. The middle-range approach is the American- or Brazilian-style melting-pot philosophy (through which attempts are made to fuse multiple nationalities, races, and cultures). Although much of the recent debate on multiculturalism has focused on race, Europe has a long and often overlooked tradition of multiculturalism arising from the diversity of European nations, and a Europeanist habit of integrating core values and features from almost every new group with which its dominant cultures have come into contact. Given the myths that surround much of what is regarded as national culture, it is difficult any more to be sure of what constitutes a feature of the home culture and what does not. So rather than speaking of the integration of alien cultures into the home culture, the arrival of new groups in Europe in the post-war era has simply continued to build upon a long tradition of multiculturalism, and has added new layers of complexity to the definition of the home culture.

Even though nineteenth-century nationalism was based on the idea of breaking existing states and empires into nation-states, where each nation had its own sovereign state, many European states remained both multi-national and multicultural, and remain so today. The consequences are reflected in the contemporary data: according to Pan and Pfeil, there are 337 ethnic and national minorities in Europe, to which 105 million people—or one in seven Europeans—belong. Within the EU states alone there are more than 160 ethnic minorities, the number having been greatly increased by eastern enlargement. About one in ten EU citizens speaks a minority language, and all but the smallest of European states has at least three indigenous national minorities, and in most cases many more.[2] Attempts may have been made to standardize and promote dominant languages during the nineteenth century, but minority languages and cultures have persisted regardless.

The character of multiculturalism in Europe changes according to the manner in which the term is applied and understood. In most of the debates, it is restricted mainly to immigrants; that is, to the racial and religious minorities who have been relatively recent arrivals in Europe. And yet these minorities make up only a small part of the bigger picture: focusing just on the European Union, only about 25 million of its legal residents (3–4 per cent of the population) belong to a racial minority. This is a small figure in comparison to the United States (where racial minorities make up 23 per cent of the population) or Canada (16 per cent), and it pales by comparison to the multi-ethnic qualities of Russia, India, or China. But European multiculturalism is about far more than race or religion, and includes at least five additional groups of minorities:

• National minorities who live in one state but are the kin of national majorities in neigh-bouring states. These include ethnic Hungarians in Romania, Slovakia, and Ukraine, ethnic Germans in Romania, Poland, and Hungary, ethnic Romanians in Ukraine, ethnic Albanians in Kosovo and Macedonia, Greeks and Turks in Cyprus, Turkish Muslims in Bulgaria, ethnic Poles in Belarus and Lithuania, ethnic Czechs in

Slovakia and vice versa, and ethnic Ukrainians in Poland. There are an estimated 25 million members of such minorities, along with 23 million Russians living in Soviet successor states.

- Transnational minorities that are divided among two or more states but do not form a majority in any. These include the Basques and Catalans of Spain and France, and the Frisians of Germany and the Netherlands.

- Indigenous minorities living within a single state, including the Scots and the Welsh of Britain, the Corsicans and Bretons of France, and the Galicians of Spain.

- Foreigners legally resident in Europe, including citizens of one European state living in another. Some of these are ethnic minorities, but by no means all. According to Eurostat, there were nearly 29 million foreigners legally resident in the EU member states in 2007, accounting for nearly 6 per cent of the population (see Table 7.1).

- Foreigners illegally resident in Europe. The exact numbers are unknowable, but estimates place the total at between 4 and 8 million, with perhaps as many as 500,000 more arriving each year. Reflecting similar debates in the United States, there is increased pressure on European leaders to work to reduce illegal immigration and to address related concerns about crime and strains on social services.

The debate about multiculturalism in Europe tends to overlook most of these groups except the last, and yet they are the clearest evidence that

Table 7.1. Europe's ten biggest immigrant populations

	Legal residents with foreign nationality (millions)	Percentage of population	Percentage of population with favourable view of immigrants
Germany	7.3	8.8	38
Spain	4.6	10.6	64
UK	3.7	6.1	45
France	3.6	6.0	49
Italy	2.4	4.2	36
Switzerland	1.5	20.5	n/a
Belgium	0.9	8.9	38
Greece	0.9	8.0	45
Austria	0.8	10.0	37
Netherlands	0.7	4.2	56
EU-27	28.9		

Source: Data on legal residents from Eurostat at http://epp.eurostat.ec.europa.eu (retrieved March 2009); figures are for 2007. Percentage of population calculated by author. Data on favourable opinions from Eurobarometer 69, November 2008.

multiculturalism is a core part of the Europeanist landscape, and not one that necessarily causes problems. National, transnational, and indigenous minorities make demands for the preservation of their languages and religions, and may campaign for greater autonomy, but their presence does not always lead to conflict (other than in such cases as the Basques and the division in Northern Ireland). Multiculturalism has always been a fact of life for Europeans, who have long lived in close proximity to people who speak different languages, belong to different religions, enjoy different cuisines, and hold different moral standards and traditions. The rise of states, rather than imposing territorial boundaries around those separate cultures, usually had the opposite effect of bringing multiple cultures and nationalities under a common state authority, drawing additional attention to cultural differences. The rise of the European Union has further emphasized multiculturalism as Europeans have been freer to travel, and as the media have more actively reported events and stories in other European states. All along, core aspects of multiculturalism—including the right to practise different religions, to celebrate holidays associated with different cultures, to run businesses catering to cultural minorities, and to join religious and cultural organizations—have mainly survived unchanged.

If there has been a rhetorical shift against multiculturalism in Europe, it has been driven less by culture than by a complex mix of race and religion, and more specifically by the rising number of Muslims of non-European extraction. While Europeans have long moved across cultural borders without sparking urgent public debates about the need for new arrivals to learn the local language or to undertake citizenship tests, these earlier waves of cultural exchange involved people who were both white and predominantly Christian. But the foundations of diversity have been changed since the Second World War by the influx of non-white immigrants, and later of Muslims from North Africa, the Middle East, and South Asia. While multiculturalism was not seen as a threat to identity in the immediate post-war years, there has more recently been a backlash, its origins traceable to the arrival of the first waves of non-white immigrants in the 1950s and 1960s, and being given a fillip by the terrorist attacks in New York, Madrid, and London in 2001, 2004, and 2005. Muslims make up only about three per cent of the population of Europe, and Islamic militants make up only a tiny proportion of that minority, and yet most of the questions posed about the health of European multiculturalism have focused on this small part of the bigger picture. The exaggerated nature of much of the debate is reflected in the themes explored by commentators in books with titles such as *While*

Europe Slept: How Radical Islam Is Destroying the West from Within, Londoni-stan, and *The Coming Balkan Caliphate.*[3]

With new questions posed on what multiculturalism has meant for state and national identity, there have been charges that multiculturalism in Europe is an illusion, bound to fail because of the poor record in assimilating Muslims. Walter Laquer bemoans the 'last days of Europe', arguing that the region is threatened by a collision between falling birth rates and uncontrolled immigration. Few immigrants from Asia, Africa, or the Middle East have any desire to be integrated into European society, he warns, generating a continent-wide identity crisis. Immigrants have congregated in ghettoes, and widespread educational failure has combined with religious or ideological disdain for the host country, and with resentment and xenophobia among native Europeans, to create growing political and social tensions and extremist violence.[4] Christopher Caldwell makes similar arguments, suggesting that Europe became a multi-ethnic society 'in a fit of absence of mind', and notes that while governments have done much to accommodate the newcomers, public opinion is reacting against these efforts.[5]

Evidence of the reaction is identified in the institution of language and civics training or tests for new immigrants or citizens in Britain, Denmark, France, and Germany, the ban on the wearing of Muslim headscarves in some parts of Europe, and the adoption in the Netherlands of an explicit policy of assimilation. These trends are sometimes contrasted with policy in Canada, where efforts are made to make immigrants feel welcome, and where multiculturalism is constitutionally protected: the Canadian Charter of Freedoms and Rights includes the proviso that it be 'interpreted in a manner consistent with the preservation and enhancement of the multicultural heritage of Canadians'. At the darker end of the scale is the support given to European anti-immigrant political parties, particularly in Austria, Belgium, France, Germany, and the Netherlands, and growing tensions between Europeans and Muslim extremists, which reached their nadir in the bomb attacks on Madrid and London. For Caldwell, the Islamic challenge stems from the strength and self-confidence of Islam, which contrasts with the insecurities, malleability, and relativism of European culture; but this rather overlooks the deep divisions within Islam, its sensitivity, and the rapidity with which it takes offence, and gives little weight to the idea that Europeanism is a growing political, economic, and social force.

Writing about the dispute over headscarves in France, Bowen argues that it conceals underlying concerns as varied as the role of religion in schools, the development of separate communities, the threats posed by radical Islam, and gender discrimination.[6] The rise of Islam certainly poses challenges to notions of European secularism, with the need to meet demands for separate schools and a recognition of cultural norms regarding the family and the place of women in society while at the same time protecting the principles of liberal democratic modernity. Ironically, Islam is often criticized by Europeans for its treatment of women, and yet racial and religious discrimination is alive and well in Europe, as reflected in the findings of a Pew Global Attitudes Survey in 2008 that found negative views towards Muslims and Jews that were notably higher in Europe than in the United States, and were growing. Almost half of Spaniards had unfavourable opinions about Jews, as did 36 per cent of Poles and 20–5 per cent of Germans and French, compared to just 7–9 per cent of Americans and Britons. As for Muslims, about half of Spaniards, Germans, and Poles had unfavourable opinions, as did 38 per cent of French and 23 per cent of Americans and Britons.[7]

Although most western Europeans by large majorities believe that the cities or areas in which they live are good places for racial or ethnic minorities to live,[8] discrimination against those minorities is well documented, and has been rising in those parts of the European Union where records are kept. According to the EU Agency for Fundamental Rights, incidents of racist crime rose between 2000 and 2006 in the eleven EU member states that collected data, and incidents of anti-Semitic crime grew between 2001 and 2006 in three of the four countries that collected data. It also notes that in twelve member states, there were no sanctions available for cases of ethnic discrimination, and that Britain alone had more sanctions available than all other EU member states combined. The brunt of discrimination is directed at visible minorities, refugees, asylum seekers, and the Roma.[9] At the same time, it is important to distinguish racial and religious intolerance from economic concerns; the primary concern of many middle-class white Europeans is not that they must share suburbs, schools, and shopping centres with non-whites, but rather that they must share them with the poor and the under-educated people who they fear may undermine the quality of life that the middle class has worked hard to achieve. The response to social division then is not to focus on the assimilation or fusion of race or religion or culture, but to focus on the fusion of wealth and opportunity.

Religion: the secular exception

Few values so clearly define Europe as secularism. So weak a role does religion now play in the lives of most Europeans that the American

Catholic author George Weigel has been moved to describe Europe as a 'post-Christian' society, the legal scholar Joseph Weiler has written of a 'Christophobic' Europe, and Pope Benedict XVI has appealed to Europeans to rediscover their faith.[10] The church is still a presence in such state matters as education, organized religion still has a strong following in Ireland and Poland, and true secularism (where the state promotes neither religion nor irreligion[11]) applies only in a few European states. As a general rule, however, religious factors no longer drive political and social choices in Europe, and in no other part of the world does organized religion today play so marginal a role in public life.[12] For Katzenstein, 'secular liberalism is deeply engrained in the self-understanding of most Europeans and in the interpretation of most scholars of European politics'.[13]

Peter Berger uses the term 'Eurosecularity' to describe the European case,[14] whose exceptional nature is emphasized by the growth of religion in most other parts of the world. He argues that non-Europeans are as religious as they have ever been, and in some cases more religious than ever; the evidence lies not only in the resurgence of Islam and of Evangelical Protestantism but also of Catholicism, Eastern Orthodox Christianity, Judaism, Hinduism, and Buddhism. Most of the world, he concludes, 'is bubbling with religious passions'. He notes that while the United States is often described as a highly religious society in contrast to Europe, and that this claim is used to illustrate its exceptional qualities, it is Europe that is the exceptional case and America that conforms to the more usual trends in other parts of the world.[15] In short, in a world where religion is at least holding its own, and is in many cases growing, the decline of religion in Europe—and its strong secular preferences—makes it almost unique in the world.

As noted in Chapter 1, the decline of mainstream religion in Europe can be traced back at least to the Enlightenment, but it became a topic for wider public reflection only during the second half of the twentieth century, when church attendance fell, expressions of faith became more uncommon, and agnosticism and atheism were both more openly admitted and less immediately criticized. But just why all this has happened is open to conjecture. Some have argued that citizens of wealthy and democratic societies, where life is more predictable and stable, feel less need for the reassurances provided by religion. Others have argued that the doubts many Europeans feel about organized religion today are a reaction against the dominating role that it once played in directing and limiting the choices Europeans made, and in sparking war and conflict, or at least being used to justify war and conflict.

Secularism is also often portrayed as the inevitable consequence of the European model of modernization; as Crouch puts it, modernization has brought secularization, consistent with nineteenth-century rationalist arguments about the incompatibility of religion and science.[16] But this argument has fallen out of fashion in light of the extent to which even modern societies retain many of their religious qualities and values.[17] Davie argues that Europeans find it hard to believe that what happens today in Europe will not happen tomorrow elsewhere in the world; hence they tend to believe that as the world modernizes it will also secularize. But she finds little evidence for this, and argues that secularization has not followed modernization in the US, Latin America, or sub-Saharan Africa. The European model, she concludes, is not one for export, but is 'something distinct, [that is] peculiar to the European corner of the world and needs to be understood in these terms'.[18]

The relative marginalization of religion in Europe today is reflected in the findings of survey research:

- A 2005 Eurobarometer poll, for example, found that while 62 per cent of residents of the EU-25 expressed belief in a God, the numbers were significantly (and not surprisingly) higher in Catholic and Greek Orthodox societies, including Malta, Cyprus, Greece, and Poland (80–95 per cent), and lowest in western Protestant states such as Britain, France, Germany, and the Scandinavian states (31–47 per cent) (see Fig 7.1).

- A Gallup poll in 2000 found that while nearly half of all North Americans and one-third of Latin Americans attended religious services at least once per week, the same was true of only 20 per cent of western Europeans and only 14 per cent of eastern Europeans. While 87 per cent of Latin Americans and 83 per cent of North Americans considered God important in their lives, only 49 per cent of Europeans made the same claim.[19]

- When asked by a Pew Global Attitudes poll in 2003 if it was necessary to believe in God in order 'to be moral and have good values', 58 per cent of Americans agreed, compared to 38 per cent of Poles, 33 per cent of Germans, 27 per cent of Italians, 25 per cent of Britons, and 13 per cent of French.[20]

- A Gallup poll on irreligion in 2007–8 asked respondents if they thought religion was important, and found that most Europeans felt it was not (in the range of 50–90 per cent, except in Austria, Ireland, Greece, Portugal, Italy, and Poland), in contrast to the United States (33 per cent said it was not), most Latin American states (10–30 per cent), and most African and Muslim states (0–20 per cent).[21]

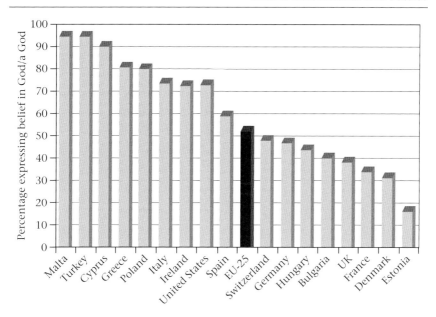

Figure 7.1 Belief in God

Source: European figures from *Eurobarometer Social Values, Science and Technology* poll, June 2005. US figure from Harris Poll at http://www.harrisinteractive.com (conducted 31 October 2006; data retrieved April 2009).

Although about 88 per cent of western Europeans and 84 per cent of eastern Europeans claim to belong to a religious denomination,[22] the affiliations of most are not strong. For Gerda Hamberg, many Europeans 'belong without believing',[23] meaning that, when pushed, they will admit to belonging to the religion with which their family has traditionally identified, but they will rarely attend church except for christenings, weddings, and funerals. For Grace Davie, many other Europeans 'believe without belonging',[24] meaning that they do not so much challenge belief in God as participation in organized religion. They also engage in 'vicarious religion', meaning that religion is followed by an active minority on behalf of an inactive majority that approves of the action of the minority. For example, church leaders are expected to embody and project moral codes on behalf of others, even when those others no longer believe.[25]

If belief in a God is one thing, allowing religion to influence one's life or individual choices is quite another. Not everyone is agreed on the significance of the survey data, however, or on the extent to which secularization has taken hold in Europe; a Eurobarometer poll in 2007, for example, found that residents of the EU were split on the importance of religion in society:

46 per cent felt that it was too important, but 48 per cent disagreed.[26] It has also been argued that religious issues have become more politicized of late in Europe.[27] We have only to look, for example, at the effects of the growth in the Muslim population of Europe, which has challenged claims of secularism: if religion is not important in the lives of Europeans, then why the fuss among 'Christians' over Islam, and over headscarves and the banning of religious symbols in schools? The enlargement of the European Union outside the original western European arena has, in the view of Grace Davie, revealed a particular irony: 'Whether consciously or not, the effective barriers to entry coincide with a geographical definition of Christendom'.[28] Europeans may no longer believe, runs the logic, but Christianity is still part of the definition of their identity. Or is it? Concerns about the Islamization of Europe are surely based less on religious objections than on cultural and racial factors. It is not so much the threat that Islam poses to Christianity, but instead the fact that so many Muslims are Arab, Middle Eastern, or North African. Hence the issue is non-white immigration, not religion.

There has also been conjecture that levels of faith will not continue to decline in Europe so much as undergo a shift in focus: immigration from North Africa and the Middle East will combine with higher birthrates among Muslims and lower birthrates among non-Muslims to lead to a process of Islamization, the alarmist view being that Europe will become part of 'Eurabia', an anti-Christian, anti-Western, anti-American, and anti-Semitic cultural and political appendage of the Muslim world.[29] In 2004, European Commissioner Frits Bolkestein predicted a world in which the United States was the only superpower, China was an economic giant, and Europe was Islamicized.[30] George Weigel has written of 'a Europe in which the muezzin summons the faithful to prayer from the central loggia of St. Peter's in Rome, while Notre Dame has been transformed into Hagia Sophia on the Seine—a great Christian church become an Islamic museum'.[31]

But the prospects for Islamization have been overstated. Jenkins notes that discussions about the prospect of Muslim dominance in Europe assume that Islam will be immune to the cultural and social arrangements that have 'gutted the continent's Christian heritage'. However, he argues, 'both Christianity and Islam face real difficulties in surviving within Europe's secular cultural ambience in anything like their familiar historical forms', and Islam, like Christianity, has instead had to adapt.[32] The repeated claim that Islamization will be accompanied by anti-Americanism and anti-Semitism assumes that European Muslims will necessarily be radical in their approach. But—as noted earlier in this chapter—European Muslims are a small minority, and radicals are a minority within that minority; furthermore, they are concerned less with extending the boundaries of Islam within Europe than with factional and doctrinal struggles in the Middle East.[33] It is more likely that while Islam will continue to grow in Europe, it will become integrated into mainstream European society in much the same way as Judaism, Hinduism, and Buddhism have, and that it will not fundamentally challenge the dominant societal place of secularism.

The role of religion in Europeanist ideas briefly became a matter for wider public debate in 2003–4 as a consequence of attempts made to include a reference to the Christian heritage of Europe in the preamble to the still-born EU Constitution. The states most in favour of that inclusion were Catholic Italy, Ireland, Poland, and Portugal, which argued that Christianity had been a dominant influence on European civilization, and that the Judeo-Christian heritage was therefore a core European value. The opposition was led by Protestant Britain and Sweden, which argued that European integration was not about religion, that giving undue prominence to religion was potentially divisive, that it would give offence to non-Christians and those without faith, and that it might even prohibit the admission of non-Christian states such as Turkey.[34] Weigel notes the irony in the fact that while the writing of the constitution was driven by the historical memory of Europe, and by the emphasis placed by Europeans on freedom, tolerance, and equal civil rights, the ultimate deletion of any reference to Europe's Christianity amounted to a refusal by Europe to recognize its Christian past. He wondered as a result whether Europe could give an account of itself while denying the very moral tradition through which its culture had arisen.[35]

Further light is shed on the role of religion in Europe by considering what is absent from public discourse rather than what is present, and here again comparisons with the US case are instructive. Unlike Americans, Europeans rarely interpret national history in terms of God's preferences, nor do they routinely call on God to bless either Europe or their particular states, nor do they routinely suggest that either Europe or individual European states are favoured by God. Fundamentalists and the religious right are rarely part of calculations about support for political parties or discussions about voter turnout in Europe, religious leaders rarely become important political figures, there is rarely any discussion in Europe about the religious affiliation or faith of candidates for (or holders of) high public office, there is little expectation that political leaders should also be moral leaders and should openly declare their faith, religion rarely comes up in discussions about public policy, and few Europeans would hesitate to vote for a candidate who was openly atheist or agnostic (assuming that the issue even came up in discussions).

One area in which Eurosecularity is on clear display is in the relationship between religion and science. Hutton notes that 'Europe has for long accepted that reason and science are the twin underpinnings and driving forces of Western society; that religious faith cannot trump or obstruct science but must seek reconciliation with it'.[36] But the same cannot be said of the United States, as reflected—for instance—in the debate over evolution versus creationism (the latter being the belief that humans, the earth, and the universe were created by a Supreme Being or deity, literally as described in the Bible). At least until recently, the debate had been largely resolved in Europe in favour of evolution, and even the Catholic Church has acknowledged that the origins and development of the human race are explained by evolution. But a solid majority of Americans disagree: a 2007 Gallup poll found that two-thirds of Americans believe that creationism is definitely or probably true, while 44 per cent believe that evolutionary theory is definitely or probably false.[37]

While the numbers are almost exactly reversed in Europe, there have been some recent signs of attempts to introduce creationism into schools, and a 2006 poll in Britain found that 39 per cent of those asked believed in creationism or intelligent design (an alternative developed by creationists in the United States as a means of circumventing limits placed on the teaching of creationism by arguing that certain features of the universe and of life on earth are best explained by an intelligent cause).[38] Alarmed at such trends, the Council of Europe was prompted in 2007 to pass a resolution urging its forty-seven member governments to 'firmly oppose' the teaching of creationism on an equal footing with evolution. The Council described creationism as a threat to human rights, as a source of confusion to students, and as a handicap to scientific research, and associated opposition to the theory of evolution with 'religious extremism' which was itself 'closely allied to extreme right-wing political movements'.[39]

Eurosecularity is also reflected in attitudes towards public policies in which religious belief plays a role, including abortion and euthanasia. Abortion is legal everywhere in Europe except Ireland, Malta, and Poland, although limitations are imposed in some countries, which allow it only in cases of rape, threats to the health of the mother, foetal defects, and socioeconomic factors. It is also legal through much of Asia, and in Canada, the United States, and South Africa. But it is either illegal or carries a heavy social stigma in most of Latin America, Africa, and the Middle East. It also continues to generate much controversy in the United States, where attempts have been made to overturn the 1973 Supreme Court decision *Roe vs. Wade* that made it legal. Abortion is often an issue in American national elections, and demonstrations against clinics providing abortions have occasionally turned violent.

On euthanasia, the contrasts are again most obvious between Europe and the United States. Euthanasia is legal in only five European states—Albania, Belgium, the Netherlands, Luxembourg, and Switzerland—but passive euthanasia (the removal of life-saving care, as distinct from the provision of the means to end a patient's life) is tolerated in Britain and Sweden, and there is majority public support for its legalization in several countries. Where opposition is strongest, as in Italy, Poland, and Spain, it tends to have mainly religious roots, with the same arguments about the sanctity of life that are made in debates about euthanasia in the United States. There, religious conservatives believe that end-of-life issues fall under the dominion of God, while religious liberals believe that individuals have the right to choose between life and death.[40] There were several headline-making cases in Italy in 2006–9 involving patients in a persistent vegetative state, and debates about whether or not they should be kept alive. Much of the discussion was couched in religious terms, with questions about the God-given right to life versus the right of law and science to bring life to an end. But such debates are relatively rare elsewhere in Europe.

Capital punishment: leading the way on abolition

Just as Europe is exceptional in its experience with secularism, so is it exceptional in its experience with capital punishment: few values more centrally define Europeanism today than opposition to the death penalty, which has been abolished in every European state except Belarus. Moreover, Europe has been active in pursuing abolition around the world, its demands being felt most strongly closest to home: any state aspiring to join either the Council of Europe or the European Union is required to abolish the death penalty as a precondition. Bulgaria, Cyprus, Estonia, Lithuania, Malta, and Poland all fell in line in 1997–2002 as they prepared for EU membership, as did Turkey in 2002 as part of its negotiations on membership. Further afield, the European Union has orchestrated attempts within the United Nations to introduce a global moratorium on the death penalty as a first step towards its worldwide abolition, and in 2007 hosted the first annual European Day Against the Death Penalty. Europe has been particularly aggressive in exerting pressure on the United States: it has lobbied both the federal government and state governments to change policy, it has refused to extradite criminals and terrorists to the United States if they face the death penalty, and it has even filed amicus briefs in US Supreme Court cases dealing with the execution of juveniles and the mentally disabled.[41]

Ironically, all this has happened in spite of European public opinion. The decision to abolish the death penalty in Germany in 1949, for example, went in the face of majority public opinion, and as late as 1970 opinion among Germans was still evenly divided; it was only in the 1980s that a majority came down in favour of abolition. The British too were slow to support abolition; the last execution in Britain was carried out in 1964, but 82 per cent of Britons continued to support capital punishment in 1975,[42] as do a slight majority even today. Most notable, though is the east–west divide in opinion on capital punishment: although there was little public debate in eastern Europe prior to its banning, the death penalty is supported by majorities in several countries. Political leaders in Poland and Hungary have called for its reinstatement, but have also recognized that this would be impossible given the requirements of the European Convention on Human Rights (see upcoming discussion). Given that capital punishment was used during the Soviet era for a wide variety of offences, and given the abuses of power by Soviet-era governments, it might be reasonable to assume that there would have been a public reaction against capital punishment after the fall of the Berlin Wall. In fact, support remains strong, in part, argues Smith, because of a desire for protection against the uncertainties of the transition to democracy and capitalism.[43]

The mismatch between public opinion and political action in Europe has prompted criticism from the United States, where there is some sensitivity to the manner in which Europeans are thought to be lecturing their moral superiority. That European governments have occasionally acted in spite of public opinion rather than in response has generated barbed comments about the quality of European democracy. Hence Marshall's suggestion that Europe does not have the death penalty 'because its political systems are less democratic, or at least more insulated from populist impulses' than is the case in the United States.[44] This latter point may well be true, but it must also be remembered that abolition has not been seriously opposed in Europe, that support for the death penalty is neither strongly held nor expressed, and that restoration only tends to briefly become a talking point following particularly heinous murders. In short, the public debate over capital punishment in most parts of Europe is, to all intents and purposes, dead.

By no means did Europe take the lead in abolishing capital punishment. US states such as Pennsylvania, Michigan, and Rhode Island were among the first to abolish it for murder (ironically, given that the United States remains today one of the most active users of the death penalty), Venezuela in 1863 was the first country in the world to abolish the death penalty for all crimes, and many other Latin American states removed it during the nineteenth century for crimes committed in peacetime.[45] Furthermore, formal abolition has come only recently to most European states (as late as the mid-1990s in Italy, Spain, Belgium, and Britain, for example—see Table 7.2).

The post-war lead on abolition was taken by the Council of Europe, under whose auspices the European Convention on Human Rights (ECHR) came into force in 1953. Protocol 6 of the convention (opened for signature in 1983) limited the death penalty to times of war or the 'imminent threat of war', abolition was made a precondition for membership of the Council of Europe in 1994, and it was made a precondition for membership of the European Union in 1998. The European Union also adopted a set of guidelines in respect to non-member states confirming that the European Union would work towards its abolition elsewhere.[46] Protocol 13 of the ECHR (opened for signature in 2002) provided for the total abolition of capital punishment, and while several European states still have not ratified, and the conservative Polish government in 2006 called for the reintroduction of the death penalty, it no longer exists in Europe. The last western European states to use it were Greece (1972), Spain (1975), and France (1977), and the last eastern European states were Latvia (1996) and Ukraine (1997). Latvia long held out on abolishing it for all crimes, but the coming into force in 2009 of the Treaty of Lisbon made the use of the death penalty under any circumstances illegal throughout the European Union. Belarus is the only European state to retain capital punishment, which is one reason why it has been turned down for membership of the Council of Europe.

While Europe has abolished the death penalty, it is still legal in 110 countries (although many have scrapped it in practice), including China, Cuba, India, Iran, Japan, South Korea, Nigeria, Pakistan, Saudi Arabia, and—perhaps most famously—the United States. China allows capital punishment for sixty-five crimes, ranging from murder to racketeering, corruption, the killing of pandas, and tax evasion, and while it officially admits to executing hundreds of its prisoners each year, true numbers may run into the thousands. Meanwhile, the United States remains the only liberal democracy apart from Japan to retain the death penalty. Not only can it be used against those who break federal law, and for capital crimes in thirty-eight of the fifty states, but the United States also allows the execution of juveniles, and is one of only seven countries in the world that

Table 7.2. Capital punishment in Europe

	Last used	Abolished for all crimes		Last used	Abolished for all crimes
Western Europe			Eastern Europe		
Iceland	1830	1928	Romania[a]	1989	1989
Germany	1948	1949	Slovenia	1957	1989
Austria	1950	1968	Croatia	1987	1990
Finland	1944	1972	Czech Republic	Unknown	1990
Sweden	1910	1972	Hungary	1988	1990
Portugal	1849	1976	Slovakia	1989	1990
Denmark	1950	1978	Macedonia	Unknown	1991
Luxembourg	1949	1979	Moldova	1989	1995
Norway	1948	1979	Poland	1988	1997
France	1977	1981	Bulgaria	1989	1998
Netherlands	1952	1982	Estonia	1991	1998
Ireland	1954	1990	Lithuania	1995	1998
Switzerland	1944	1992	Latvia	1996	1999[b]
Italy	1947	1994	Ukraine	1997	1999
Spain	1975	1995	Bosnia and		
Belgium	1950	1996	Herzegovina	Unknown	2001
UK	1964	1998	Serbia and		
Malta	1943	2000	Montenegro	1989	2002
Cyprus	1962	2002	Albania	1995	2007
Greece	1972	2004	Belarus	Retains death penalty	
			Kosovo	No information available	

[a] Abolished 1864, reinstated 1936.
[b] Abolished for ordinary crimes only.

Source: Roger Hood and Carolyn Hoyle, *The Death Penalty: A Worldwide Perspective*, 4th edn. (Oxford: Oxford University Press, 2008).

is known to have executed juveniles since 1990 (the others being the Congo, Iran, Nigeria, Pakistan, Saudi Arabia, and Yemen). Polls indicate that about two-thirds of Americans continue to support the death penalty, and although it has been suggested that there is a trend towards its eventual abolition in the United States,[47] it is rarely an issue in American public and political discourse.

Surprisingly little effort has been made to understand why Europe has become a death penalty-free zone. Zimring notes that states that suffered the most under totalitarianism and that lost the war—notably Germany, Italy, and Austria—were among the first to abolish the death penalty, perhaps because of a wish to restrict the powers of future governments to punish their citizens.[48] But why other countries supported abolition has been little studied. Looking at the United States, Moravcsik has suggested that at least four factors might explain why it remains one of only two liberal democracies to retain the death penalty: the prevalence of social and political violence in the United States, high levels of public support, the decentralization of political institutions (which leaves criminal justice mainly in the hands of the states, and makes it difficult to make national policy), and the existence of a concentrated conservative opposition.[49] By implication, then, the opposite presumably holds in Europe: it is less violent, there is more public support for abolition, political institutions are more centralized, and there is no concentrated conservative opposition. How do these suggestions hold up?

On the first count, crime rates do not vary as much between Europe and the United States as popular culture and media reports suggest. According to the UN Survey of Crime Trends, which has gathered international data since the early 1970s, the overall level of recorded crime in the United States has fallen since the 1990s, while it grew in the European Union and had even overtaken the United States by the late 1990s. On homicide rates, however, there is more of a differentiation: while the United States in the late 1990s was fractionally above the global average of 7 murders per 100,000 inhabitants, most European states (with the notable exceptions of Albania, Belarus, Ukraine, and the three Baltic states) were in the range 1–5 homicides per 100,000 people.[50] Gun crime is also far more common in the United States, a fact that might encourage greater support for the death penalty. Furthermore, Europe does not have the same culture of violence found in the United States, where the frontier mentality of individual accountability and retributive justice still has a strong hold on the public imagination, war and violent crime are popular themes in film and television drama, and war and militarism loom large in the national consciousness.

On the second count, transatlantic levels of public support for the death penalty are certainly quite different. In 1965, more Americans opposed the death penalty than supported it (47 per cent to 38 per cent) and between 1968 and 1976 no executions were carried out anywhere in the United States. But support then grew steadily to a peak of 75 per cent in 1997, since when it has fallen again and stood at 63 per cent in 2008.[51] The death penalty is not an issue that tends to ignite public and political passions on either side of the Atlantic, however; in the United States this is in large part because of the absence of an organized and vocal abolition movement, and in Europe it is in large part because most Europeans take its abolition as a fait accompli. In western Europe, support for its restoration ranges from a high of 56 per cent in Britain to lows of 29 per cent in Finland and 23 per cent in Italy.[52]

On the third count, there is little question that federalism can stand as a barrier to the making of national policy, and conversely that the kind of unitary systems of administration found in every European state except Austria, Belgium, Germany, and Switzerland make it easier to overcome local sensibilities. Attempts to abolish the death penalty nationally in the United States would set off battles within Congress and the Supreme Court in which the policies of pro-death penalty states would inevitably be allowed to stand. Furthermore, argues Bae, electoral politics plays a role in the US case: more public officials are elected in the United States than in Europe, including judges, attorneys-general, police chiefs, and prosecutors, and they are more fearful of expressing their opposition to capital punishment.[53] Meanwhile, Moravcsik argues, 'European political elites enjoy more "state autonomy" to pursue humane policies in the face of public opposition', and regional or single-issue politics is discouraged by parliamentary systems.

More importantly, there is greater opportunity in Europe for governments to encourage policy changes even in the face of public opinion. This can be dismissed as undemocratic, but it can also be interpreted as good leadership. Most Americans vote for individuals rather than parties, and elected representatives keep a close eye on the wishes of their electoral base and special interest groups. But more Europeans vote for parties rather than individuals, and are more willing to trust that parties will work in their best interests. Good leaders are not necessarily those who respond to public opinion, but those who are willing to encourage voters to consider alternative options. When British legislators in 1965 decided to vote for a moratorium on the death penalty, notes the columnist Polly Toynbee, it required that they be 'brave enough to stand up to public opinion, to cast their votes in the Commons and take the flak back in their constituencies for following their consciences. Was that undemocratic, or was it giving the leadership they [were] elected for?' Support for the death penalty in Britain, she concludes, has declined in recent decades because 'a generation of politicians has persuaded large numbers of people on the issue, through good leadership'.[54]

On the final count, Moravcsik is suggesting that there is not so much broad public support for the death penalty in the United States as there is strong support among American conservatives. The American South is notable both for being socially conservative and for being strongly supportive of—and the most active user of—the death penalty; according to US

Department of Justice figures, two-thirds of all executions in the United States between 1976 and 2004 took place in just eight Southern states (and more than half of *those* in Texas alone). There is stronger support for the death penalty among social conservatives in Europe, too, particularly in eastern Europe, but this is not an issue around which the activities of interest groups and social reform movements have been built. Many Europeans may personally support the reintroduction of the death penalty, but collectively they are prepared to do little to act upon their preferences.

Life satisfaction

Satisfaction and happiness are qualities that are difficult to quantify and measure, because we all have different definitions of what makes us happy. Much of the academic discussion to date has been dominated (and diverted) by economists, who like to link satisfaction with material wealth.[55] Their argument is that as liberal democracies have lifted themselves out of poverty, and as the quality of life has improved (when measured by such factors as income, job security, the provision of basic services, and a greater availability of consumer goods), so satisfaction might be expected to grow. While people are generally happier in wealthier societies than in poorer ones, polls have found that the number of people in the former who consider themselves either 'very happy' or 'not very happy' has remained fairly static in recent decades, in spite of the fact that incomes have doubled since the 1950s. Hence there apparently comes a point at which material wealth ceases to make much difference. Layard suggests that it is not so much absolute wealth that generates happiness as relative wealth, and that there has been a zero-sum competition for money and status; one person's increase in income is another person's psychological loss, and if the former spends more time at work, the latter is encouraged to do the same in order to keep up, and thus spends less time with family and friends, and does not enjoy his or her leisure time.[56] The competition for wealth and status has contributed to greater wealth, but it has also contributed to alcoholism, depression, and the break-up of marriages.

These arguments are as true of Europe as they are of the United States, Canada, Japan, Australia, and New Zealand. But, as we all know, money cannot always buy happiness, as indicated by the many instances of unhappy wealthy individuals and of happy but poorer individuals. The fascination with the link between happiness and wealth is an inevitable consequence of the mindset of economists, and it is offered slightly more support by the results of studies in the United States than of those in Europe, but if we define happiness more broadly, we find a somewhat different picture emerging.[57] There is probably a common pool of hopes and expectations from which the majority of the citizens of liberal democracies can draw in their quest for satisfaction: most of us seek good health, job security, meaningful work, supportive relationships, physical security, personal peace, and low levels of stress. But for others there are more complex requirements for happiness, including living in a community with shared values, being surrounded by a pleasant and liveable physical environment, intellectual challenge, a match between ambitions and achievements, being able to process and contextualize the bad news to which we are routinely exposed by the media (including crime, poverty, disease, and war), and satisfactory interactions with the numerous individuals with whom most of us have only fleeting contacts.

Some of the problems inherent in defining happiness and satisfaction, and in agreeing to the necessary conditions, are reflected in discussions about liveability theory, which argues that happiness depends to a large extent on the degree to which living conditions meet basic needs (however those are defined). Take, for example, the liveability ranking that the *Economist* uses to assess life in 131 of the world's major cities. It uses qualitative and quantitative factors grouped in five broad categories: stability, health care, culture and environment, education, and infrastructure, but uses only the judgement of the magazine's analysts and contributors, who almost certainly fit within a narrow socioeconomic and educational range, and thus will bring particular biases to their assessments. That cities in wealthy, progressive states do well in the ranking (Canadian, Australian, and western European cities dominate the top of the list) is of little surprise, as is the low ranking of cities in poor, overcrowded, or badly governed states (Asian and African cities fill out the bottom of the list).[58] But the survey takes little account of such factors as weather or social tolerance, and while Vancouver (which topped the list in 2008 and 2009) may be safe and clean and well-ordered, it does not enjoy good weather year-round and is considered dull and conservative by some. Conversely, while many large Asian cities may be chaotic and overcrowded and drenched in poverty, they are also full of life and colour and cultural dynamism. One person's hell can be another's paradise.

To the extent that it is possible to be sure, how do Europeans measure up in terms of happiness? One source of data is the European Values Survey (EVS), which reveals that the happiest Europeans are found in Belgium, Denmark, Iceland, Ireland, the Netherlands, and Switzerland (where forty to fifty per cent of respondents say they are 'very happy' with their lives), while the least happy are residents of the former Soviet states, Bulgaria, Romania, and Slovakia (where less than ten per cent say they are 'very happy'). Intriguingly, while the British and the French are moderately happy (in the 30–39 per cent range), Germans and Italians are not (in the 10–19 per cent range). Perhaps most surprisingly, given its long years of sectarian violence and its continued problems with informal religious and economic apartheid, Northern Ireland is the happiest region in Europe.[59]

If self-determination is another indicator of happiness, then Europeans generally are content, the vast majority agreeing that they have high levels of freedom and control over how their lives have turned out.[60] At the same time, surveys find that while Europeans may have high levels of life satisfaction and happiness, they are also pessimistic (or, perhaps, pragmatic) about their long-term prospects. The Eurobarometer poll carried out in the spring of 2008 (and thus, it must be said, as the dimensions of the economic crisis were beginning to be more widely felt and understood) found the following:

- Levels of personal satisfaction had not declined; between 1998 and 2008, about 80 per cent of those surveyed said they were satisfied with the lives they led, levels being highest in Scandinavia and lowest in Bulgaria, Hungary, Portugal, and Romania.

- Ironically, about 70–80 per cent believed that their personal situations would not worsen in the next twelve months.

- Majorities in most EU states felt that the economic outlook in their own countries was worse than in other countries, and 61 per cent felt that the lives of today's children would be more difficult when they were adults than the lives of today's adults.

- While levels of faith in national political institutions had fallen, trust in the European Union had fallen less sharply, and a majority felt that the European Union was headed in the right direction.[61]

European worries may be explained simply by the fact that, as individuals achieve higher levels of wealth, stability, and personal satisfaction, they become aware that they have more to lose. Some living in poverty, uncertainty, and deprivation will generally feel that their lives can surely not get much worse, and may be inclined to hope for an improvement. But some who have achieved success and contentment—particularly if they have risen from great poverty—may always have the nagging fear that they could well lose what they have if economic conditions decline (as they did during the 2007–9 economic crisis) or if their luck turns, that good health and happy relationships are built on fragile foundations, and that society faces countless challenges—crime, poverty, racism, social dysfunction, terrorism, and environmental decline—that may conspire to undermine the achievements so carefully built by education, hard work, good luck, and opportunity.

As to whether there is a distinctive Europeanist model of happiness, the jury is still out. The European Values Survey finds that most Europeans place family and strong personal relationships at the top of their rankings, followed by meaningful jobs, and then possessions and money; however, other studies find that Americans are not all that different, either in their levels or in their sources of happiness. In terms of defining what is likely to make an individual happier, large majorities of Europeans agree that less emphasis on money and material possessions would be 'a good thing', as would more emphasis on family life, on the development of the individual, and on the pursuit of a simpler and more natural lifestyle. Opinion is divided on the importance of work as a measure of happiness: eastern Europeans give it clearly greater value than western Europeans, but even between one-third and one-half of western Europeans believe that a decrease in the importance of work in their lives would be 'a bad thing'.[62]

Perhaps where Europeanism most clearly differs from other liberal democratic societies is in the role played by different factors in making happiness more likely. For example, Europe's generous social welfare schemes provide stronger safety nets than those available in the United States, Russia, China, or India. Its national health-care systems not only provide a guarantee of assistance for all, but also remove many of the stresses that Americans must face: in the United States, 46 million people (one in six Americans) lack health insurance, an estimated 70 per cent of personal bankruptcies are caused or hastened each year by large health-care bills, and an estimated 20,000 Americans die each year because they cannot afford needed health care. Europe's low-cost and heavily subsidized education systems similarly provide access for all, and even though university students must often pay fees for their courses, they do not accumulate the enormous debts that many American students incur, nor are they compelled to work their way through universities. Finally, Europeans place less emphasis than most other societies on the link between happiness and religion while North Americans, Latin Americans, Asians, and Africans will seek relief and solace in greater numbers in appeals to the spiritual. Europeans are more inclined to look to the temporal for their happiness.

8

Europe in the World: Towards Perpetual Peace

The conventional view in most debates about international relations is that power is best understood in terms of deliberate, state-based capabilities. The most powerful actors in the international system, so runs the logic, are states that can act alone, that have large militaries, and that are willing to use hard power in the form of force, coercion, threats, and sanctions. Certainly, much of the history of the Westphalian state system seems to have borne this out, but in the contemporary era of globalization an alternative view has been gaining some traction, given its clearest illustration by the case of Europe. This emphasizes the role of civilian and soft power in international relations, and the ability of actors (including, but not limited to, states) to exert influence through incentives, encouragement, example, and ideas. Lacking statehood and a large unified military, the European Union is often disregarded as a major actor in international relations, but this has not prevented a widening debate over the qualities of European power, encouraging us to consider the possibilities of a European model of influence in the new global era.

There has been a particularly vigorous academic debate about Europe's qualities as a normative power, or one which projects power through ideas and ideology, and through influencing the formation and development of opinions, values, and norms. Hence Rosencrance concludes that 'Europe's attainment is normative rather than empirical', and that there is a paradox in the way in which 'the continent which once ruled the world through the physical impositions of imperialism is now coming to set world standards in normative terms'.[1] Manners develops this idea with his suggestion that the European Union is different from other political forms, that its construction on a normative basis 'predisposes it to act in a normative way in world politics', and that 'the most important factor shaping the international role of the EU is not what it does or what it says, but what it is'.[2]

Almost everyone agrees that Europe's global role has changed since the end of the cold war, but almost everyone also agrees that its new role has not yet been translated into significant power or influence. Sceptics are quick to point to policy disagreements among European governments to Europe's lack of statehood, Europe's often marginal influence over responses to the world's most pressing security problems, the absence of a well-developed European common foreign and security policy, and the supposed lack of teeth behind that policy. They scoff that Europe has neither the military resources nor the level of political unity or conviction needed to be a true global power, that its positions on international issues are often more rhetorical than real, that it has for too long been a security consumer rather than a security producer, that it has become a global actor more by accident or default than by intention, and that it punches well below its economic weight. In debates about the prospects for new superpowers, Europe is routinely overlooked in favour of China and India, and even occasionally—and more remarkably—of Russia and Brazil.

But how we regard Europe as a global actor depends on how we understand power. If we continue to believe that it must rest on deliberate actions and be backed up by military capabilities, then true enough: there is little to impress or encourage in the European model. If, on the other hand, we acknowledge that the nature of power has changed in the era of globalization, and that control of the means of production is more important than control of the means of destruction, then the defining qualities of Europeanism become more clear; while realists place a premium on hard power and unilateralism, and emphasize national interests and security, the European model values soft power and multilateralism, and takes a liberal, post-modern view of the world that places a premium on globalization, diplomacy, and internationalism.[3] Europeans believe that states can and must cooperate and work together on matters of shared interest and highlight the importance of international organizations and international law. They long ago acknowledged that they are members of an international system, and while they are prepared to use threats and force to resolve problems where needed, they prefer to use diplomacy and to act by example. In short, Europeanism represents a redefinition of the dynamics of inter-state relations, projecting soft power options in a manner that raises questions about the value and efficacy of military power, and embracing the merits of positive peace.

Kantian Europe

Historically, Europe has been a region of almost constant war and violence. As noted in Chapter 1, there was rarely a time between the classical era and the end of the Second World War when one European power, state, community, or monarch was not at war with another or fending off an external invader, and life for residents of the region was routinely disrupted by often widespread and lengthy conflict: consider the death and destruction wrought by numerous Roman and Greek wars and campaigns, the Viking invasions, the Arab conquests, the Saxon wars, the Crusades, the Hundred Years' War (1337–1453), the struggle against the Ottoman Empire, numerous wars of religion in the sixteenth and seventeenth centuries (including the Thirty Years' War, 1618–48), the Eighty Years' War (1568–1648), the Nine Years' War (1688–97), the Great Northern War (1700–21), the War of the Spanish Succession (1701–14), the War of the Austrian Succession (1740–8), the Seven Years' War (1754–63), the Napoleonic wars (1803–15), and the First and Second World Wars.

In the decades prior to the Second World War, the world's greatest imperial and military powers were European. They were adept at using hard power to build and maintain influence, to compete for resources, and to protect their political and economic interests. In spite of the general peace that reigned in Europe between 1871 and 1914, the major powers asserted themselves through the continued construction of empires, and through arms races that built the military capacities of Germany, France, and Russia while at the same time ensuring Britain's domination of the oceans. It has been estimated that between 1880 and 1914, German arms expenditure more than quintupled, British and Russian expenditure trebled, and French expenditure almost doubled.[4] By the time of the outbreak of the Great War, Germany had seventy divisions with 1.5 million soldiers mustered along its western border, and the French had an army of 800,000. With just one trained army of 160,000—the British Expeditionary Force—Britain was a relatively small player in terms of land forces, although it had a navy second to none.

But the human, political, and economic costs of two world wars—followed immediately by the threat of nuclear war—sparked a reassessment of principles, priorities, and methods. States still had their own foreign policy interests, Britain and France still had large militaries, and European leaders mainly fell in with their respective American and Soviet controllers during times of cold war tension. But Europeans had clearly tired of war and conflict, and the general view after the Second World War was that all efforts possible should be directed at avoiding militarism and state-sponsored violence. Cold war struggles raised the constant possibility of fighting wars, but because the United States and the Soviet Union were the primary protagonists in those struggles, Europe—particularly western Europe—had the benefit of being able to focus on peacetime reconstruction rather then preparation for war. Democratic peace theory suggests that it is now almost inconceivable that European states will ever go to war with one another again, and where Europe was once one of the most violent regions on earth, it is today one of the most peaceful regions on earth, and the one that works hardest to project peaceful dispute resolutions internationally.

Europe's post-war evolution has pushed it closer than any other part of the world to achieving the condition of perpetual peace outlined by Kant (see Chapter 1). Europe does not yet have all the qualities he considered necessary: it still has standing armies, it is not a federation of free states, and not every European state has a republican constitution (defined by Kant as one making provision for a representative government with a separated executive and legislature). But no European peace treaties tacitly reserve the possibility of future war, no European states dominate their neighbours or attempt to project themselves onto other states, no national debts have been contracted with a view to the 'external friction of states', no states forcibly interfere with the constitutions of other states, the mutual confidence of states in a general European peace has long been established, there is almost free movement of people within the European Union, and the European Union is a league of nations.[5] Where Kant argued that the natural state of humans living side by side was one of war rather than peace (including not only open hostilities but the incessant threat of war), the natural state of today's Europe is one of peace rather than war. Europeans face external threats, to be sure, but they no longer threaten one another, nor do they pose a threat to others.

Kantian Europe stands in contrast to Hobbesian America or Russia. Writing at the time of the English Civil War, and 150 years before Kant, Thomas Hobbes argued in *Leviathan* that a strong central authority was required in order to avoid discord and war. In the state of nature that would exist without organized government, each person would feel that they had a right or licence to whatever they wanted, and in seeking either gain, safety, or reputation, men would engage in a 'war of all against all'. In order to address this problem, men should agree to a social contract with a sovereign authority to which individuals surrendered their natural rights in return for protection. But while individuals may have been able to resolve their differences, no civil power existed between nations, which therefore had the same rights to protect themselves—including going to war with other nations—as individuals had possessed in the state of nature. It is difficult not to read Hobbes and to think of American and Soviet perceptions during the cold war, or of the foreign policies of George W. Bush and Vladimir Putin.

The Hobbesian–Kantian dichotomy was revisited in 2003 by Robert Kagan in his essay *Of Paradise and Power*, which contrasted Europe's new personality with that of the United States.[6] Europeans and Americans no longer shared a common view of the world, he argued, and on major strategic and international questions, Americans were from Mars and Europeans from Venus. While Europe was moving beyond power into a world of laws, rules, negotiation, and cooperation, and was realizing the Kantian ideal of perpetual peace, the United States remained 'mired in history, exercising power in an anarchic Hobbesian world where international laws and rules are unreliable, and where true security and the defence and promotion of a liberal order still depend on the possession and use of military might'. This was not a transitory state of affairs, Kagan concluded, but was likely to endure. Most European intellectuals felt that the two sides no longer shared a 'strategic culture', and that the United States was dominated by a 'culture of death'. The United States was less patient with diplomacy, and saw the world as divided between good and evil, and between friends and enemies, while Europeans saw a more complex global system, and were more tolerant of failure, more patient, and preferred to negotiate and persuade rather than to coerce.

Controversy was sparked by Kagan's assertion that the differences do not arise naturally out of the character of Europeans and Americans, but are instead a reflection of the relative positions of the two actors in the world; their attitudes have been reversed as their roles have been reversed. When European states were great powers in the eighteenth and nineteenth centuries, and when nationalism coloured their views of one another, they were more ready to use violence to achieve their goals. But now that Europeans and Americans had traded places, they had also traded perspectives. When the United States was weak, argued Kagan, it used the strategies of the weak, but now that it was strong, it used the strategies of power.[7]

But what his argument does not explain is why Europeans have been so critical of the American use of force. It is not that Europeans do not use force because they have smaller armies than the Americans, but rather—notes Dworkin—that in the aftermath of the trauma of the Second World War they have 'turned away from foreign policies based on the pursuit of national interest and the balance of power', and have instead 'constructed a new legal order based on shared sovereignty and transparency'. It is not force that worries Europe so much as lawlessness, he argues: Europeans objected to US action in Iraq in 2003 not because they opposed the use of force, but because the United States was prepared to use force outside the law and without the clear backing of the UN Security Council; Europeans do not believe that hard power is unimportant, but rather that 'the use of military force is a blunt and destructive tool that should be used only as a last resort'.[8] Menon et al agree: Europeans, they argue, have not stumbled upon a new approach to international relations in which force plays only a limited role, but they have instead chosen deliberately to be militarily weak; Europe is not a continent of pacifists, but one where the 'just' causes of war are actively debated and where there are different opinions about the role of military force.[9]

Kagan was writing at a time of great turmoil in international relations, when the Bush administration was combatively pursuing its war on terrorism, painting the world in terms of good and evil, and arguing that the United States should be ready to use military force to encourage democratic change around the world, and be willing to downplay reliance on diplomacy, multilateralism, international organizations, and treaties. Against this uncompromising background, the Europeanist preference for diplomacy and multilateralism was much easier to identify, but the obvious question was whether Europe was different only from the America of Bush–Cheney neoconservatism or whether the principles of Europeanism pre-dated—and would outlive—the Bush administration. Time will almost certainly support the latter view: Europeans and Americans have long had a different view of the world, those differences re-emerged after the Second World War, they matured during the cold war, and they became more clear once the common project of opposing the Soviet Union had gone after 1991. The differences were made particularly clear by European criticism of the policies of the Reagan and Bush administrations, but this does not mean that they surface only during times of ideological disagreement with individual American administrations.

The post-war reinvention of Europe as a global actor has been slow and peppered with mistakes and false starts, upon which its critics have jumped with alacrity. Before the Second World War, it was national or state interests that prevailed over European interests, and western European states continued to act independently in the main until the late 1960s, when the six EEC member states agreed on European Political Cooperation (EPC), a process under which their foreign ministers would meet regularly to coordinate policy.[10] The results were mixed at best, with the Community playing a modest role in the Middle East conflict and in the convening of the 1973 Conference on Security and Cooperation in Europe, and being marginalized in the response to the 1979 Soviet invasion of Afghanistan. Reflecting on progress in October 1981, the foreign ministers of the by then ten EEC member states noted that in a period of increased world tension and uncertainty the need for a coherent and united approach to international affairs by Community members was greater than ever. However, the ten were 'still far from playing a role in the world appropriate to their combined influence', and it was thus their conviction 'that the Ten should seek increasingly to shape events and not merely to react to them'.[11]

The European role has matured since then, thanks to a combination of the expanded powers and reach of the European Union, the role of the new European marketplace in transforming European global economic influence, the end of the cold war, Europe's emergence from playing second fiddle to the Americans and the Soviets, and the cumulative effects of a process of trial and error which have taught Europe what is necessary and possible. European Political Cooperation was replaced under the Maastricht treaty by the Common Foreign and Security Policy (CFSP). Its goals may have been vague—safeguarding the common values, fundamental interests, independence, and integrity of the European Union; strengthening the security of the European Union; preserving peace and strengthening international security; and promoting international cooperation—but it nonetheless established targets. It was given more focus in 1999 when the four external relations portfolios in the European Commission were combined into one, and a new post of High Representative for the CFSP was created. The latter may not have become the European foreign policy minister that many hoped for, but the creation of the post was a key step forward.

Even as the embarrassment of the 1991 Gulf War was still fresh in the minds of policy-makers, and the Community was about to trip up again in the Balkans, progress was being made on the security front. In 1992 the Petersberg tasks were agreed, stating that multinational European military forces could be used in humanitarian and rescue operations, peacekeeping, and crisis management that might involve peacemaking only if necessary. Also in 1992 the Eurocorps was founded by France and Germany, and became operational as a 60,000-member joint defence force in 1995. Four years later the European Security and Defence Policy was launched, founded on the Petersberg tasks and on plans to create a 60,000-member European Rapid Reaction Force that could be deployed at sixty days' notice and sustained for at least one year in the field. It was to prove too ambitious, however, because Europe lacked the necessary air and sea transport and logistical support; by 2004 the EU was talking instead of creating smaller battle groups that could be deployed at 15 days' notice and sustained between 30 and 120 days in the field.

Meanwhile, the European Security Strategy was adopted in 2003, hopefully declaring that the European Union was 'inevitably a global player', and that it 'should be ready to share in the responsibility for global security'. Arguing that large-scale aggression against an EU member state was now improbable, it listed the key international threats as terrorism, the proliferation of weapons of mass destruction, regional conflicts, state failure, and organized crime. In contrast to the pervasive threats that had been posed by the cold war, noted the authors of the strategy, none of the new threats was 'purely military; nor can any be tackled by purely military means'. Instead, they concluded, a combination of political, economic, judicial, humanitarian, and military responses was needed, along with multilateral responses and 'an effective and balanced partnership with the USA'.[12]

There is a distinction to be made between negative peace, defined as a period when a war is neither imminent nor actually being fought, and positive peace, where the ordering of politics, economics, and society makes war unthinkable.[13] For much of its history, Europe has had to live with negative peace; alliances and the need to keep a watchful eye on the balance of power meant that Europeans long lived with the strong prospect of conflict or war, even during times of what seemed like extended peace. Today, war and the prospect of war are both considered unacceptable by most Europeans. Where war was once a means of uniting Europeans, today it is peace—or the abhorrence of war—that offers Europeans their best prospect of unity. It is telling that when asked in a 2008 poll to choose the value that they personally held most important, more Europeans opted for peace (45 per cent) than for human rights (42 per cent), respect for human life (41 per cent), democracy (27 per cent), individual freedom (21 per cent), and equality (19 per cent).[14]

The European abhorrence of war has combined with the habit-forming cooperation of the post-war era to establish the European Union as a new kind of international actor, based on a set of principles that give Europeanism a distinctive character and that have fundamentally changed the way in which business on international affairs is now pursued by Europeans, including those not yet within the European Union. Three principles, in particular, define the global perspective of Europeanism: a preference for the use of civilian power over military power, a belief in the merits of smart power over hard power, and support for multilateralism and for addressing problems through international laws and institutions. Realists influenced by the cold war view of the international system continue to find it hard to accept that these qualities have much more than a supporting role to play in the international arena. But Europeanists—and the emerging model of European power—suggest otherwise.

Civilian power Europe

In the ongoing debate about American power in the world, and about the prospects for Chinese power, the emphasis given to military resources tends to negate claims that Europe is a significant global actor. And yet Europe is well armed and equipped: data compiled by the International Institute for Strategic Studies find that Europe's forty states among them have nearly two million active service personnel (more than the United States), backed up by 12,000 artillery pieces, about 3,700 combat aircraft, more than 160 surface naval vessels (including five aircraft carriers, with four more on order), and more than 80 submarines (including eight tactical nuclear submarines).[15] If Europe had a unified command system, a single defence budget, and a common security policy, the European Union would be widely acknowledged as a military superpower. But even without that unity, the European military establishment—if measured by spending, personnel, firepower, and deployment capabilities, and given that China is less a global than a regional military power, and that the Russian military is currently in disarray—is the second-most powerful in the world after that of the United States.

Furthermore, individual European states are not unwilling to use their militaries: Britain and France have been engaged in multiple conflicts since 1945 (including Korea, Indochina, Malaya, Suez, Aden, Northern Ireland, the Falklands, Lebanon, the Gulf, the Balkans, Rwanda, Haiti, Iraq, and Afghanistan) and almost every EU member state—even the neutrals, such as Finland, Ireland, and Sweden—have committed troops to European, NATO, or UN peacekeeping operations. In 2007–9, all twenty-seven member states—along with eight European non-member states—had military personnel serving in the International Security Assistance Force in Afghanistan (although the numbers were often quite small, and the role they played was sometimes quite modest). Also, EU forces have been deployed to (mainly peacekeeping) operations in Bosnia, Kosovo, Macedonia, Chad, the Central African Republic, and the Democratic Republic of Congo. And the European Union launched its first joint naval operation in December 2008 when it sent a flotilla of ships to deal with piracy off the coast of Somalia. A small step, to be sure, but one with much significance.

In spite of all this, Europe now sees itself—and is mainly seen by others—as a civilian power. It poses a military threat to no one; it faces no immediate conventional military threats of its own, and it does not feel the need to use force or the threat of force to encourage change; instead, it offers the incentive of opportunities. It meets Maull's definition of a civilian power as one that prefers to focus on non-military and mainly economic means to achieve its goals, leaving the military as a residual safeguard, and emphasizing the importance of cooperation (rather than conflict) and of developing supranational structures to deal with critical international problems.[16] It also reflects the four main qualities of civilian power described by Smith: using economic, diplomatic, and cultural instruments to achieve objectives; preferring international cooperation, solidarity, and strengthening the rule of law; preferring the use of persuasion; and emphasizing democratic civilian control over foreign and defence policy-making.[17]

The possibilities of civilian power were recognized by NATO as long ago as 1956, when it acknowledged that security was more than a military matter, and that the strengthening of political consultation and economic cooperation, the development of resources, and progress in education and public understanding could all be 'as important, or even more important, for the protection of the security of a nation, or an alliance, as the building of a battleship or the equipping of an army'.[18] The European Community seemed to be following this logic when in 1970—at the launch of the process of European Political Cooperation—its leaders argued that a united Europe had the potential to promote international relations 'on a basis of trust'.[19]

The notion of civilian power was explored in 1972–3 by François Duchêne, who felt that nuclear competition had devalued purely military power and given more scope to civilian forms of influence and action.[20] Writing against the background of Vietnam, he suggested that the lack of military power was not the handicap that it once was, and that western Europe might become 'the first major area of the Old World where the age-old process of war and indirect violence could be translated into something more in tune with the twentieth-century citizen's notion of civilized politics'. Europe's influence should not be wielded along traditional lines, he argued; there was no point in trying to build a European superpower because it would need to be a nuclear, centralized state with a strong sense of collective nationalism, and the lack of military power could be an advantage for Europe because it promised to remove suspicions about European intentions and might allow it to act as an unbiased moderator. Military power should not be ignored, but Europe should avoid trying to achieve military dominance, and should instead try to act as a model of a new kind of inter-state arrangement that could overcome war, intimidation, and violence. It should be a force for the diffusion of civilian and democratic standards, Duchêne concluded, otherwise it might itself become the victim of a political agenda determined by stronger powers.

Such arguments were rejected in 1982 by Hedley Bull, who dismissed the concept of 'civilian power Europe' as a contradiction in terms, and argued that the capabilities of great powers were likely to be defined indefinitely by their military resources. The European Community, he argued, needed to become more self-sufficient in defence and security, for three main reasons: the divergence of transatlantic interests, the threat posed by the Soviet Union, and the need to remove obstacles to its own regeneration by removing its dependence on the United States. Rather than becoming a civilian power, western Europe needed to build its nuclear and conventional forces, allow West Germany to play a more positive role in western European security, develop a Europeanist approach to defence, and pursue careful coexistence with the Soviets and the Americans.[21]

But Bull's conclusions are not that surprising given the times in which he was writing: cold war tensions were high, the European Community was in the political and economic doldrums, the USSR was suffering under the unimaginative and conservative leadership of Leonid Brezhnev, the still relatively new Reagan administration was making Europeans nervous with its apparent escalation of the cold war, and no one could know that within eight years the USSR would collapse and the cold war would end. Twenty-five years on, the world is a quite different place: the cold war is over, Europe has been transformed, globalization has taken hold, and security threats have become less direct, more vague, and less open to military solutions. We may be living in what Dandeker describes as an era of 'unstable violent peace',[22] but Bull's arguments about why Europe needs to become more self-sufficient in defence no longer hold so true: the divergence of transatlantic interests has seen Europe moving further along the path to civilian power, the Soviet Union no longer exists (even if Russia still poses a threat of its own), and the level of European dependence upon the United States has declined.

We are also living in an era in which more questions are being asked about the utility of military power: it is costly to maintain, it diverts resources away from other more valuable uses, the doubts about the value of major war are numerous and troubling,[23] and the maintenance and use of force—rather than resolving disputes—often creates its own new problems. We have only to look at US policy in the Middle East, or Israeli policy towards Palestine, to see that those who feel threatened by force are more likely to resort to violence themselves than to capitulate. The Soviet Union built its enormous military in large part because it felt threatened first by the German and then by the American military machine, and why else would North Korea or Iran want to build nuclear programmes other than because they feel threatened by American power, or because they want a bargaining chip in their dealings with the United States? Certainly there is no conclusive evidence to suggest that these programmes are intended to be offensive. And as for the modern rise of international terrorism, it is best seen as an expression of the frustration with great power politics felt among the poor and the disenfranchised, hence the adage that war is terrorism by the rich while terrorism is war by the poor.

The rifts in the Atlantic alliance that have waxed and waned since 1945 have been placed under additional stress by the growing independence of European views on security. Bailes argues that with the weakening of the exclusive nature of US–European ties since the end of the cold war, it has become clear that Europe has strategic values of its own, including a multilateral and multifunctional approach to global problems, a preference for minimizing and legitimizing the use of force, and a readiness to absorb past enemies.[24] These values are reflected in the pronouncements of political leaders. Thus, in response to the 1986 US bombing of Libya following a terrorist incident, West German Chancellor Helmut Kohl commented that 'force is not a promising way of dealing with things'.[25] As the war on terrorism moved into high gear in 2003, French foreign minister Dominique de Villepin was moved to note that 'there is no military solution to terrorism. You need to have a political strategy'.[26]

European strategic values are reflected in the results of public opinion surveys. A Eurobarometer poll carried out in 2000 in the EU-15 asked Europeans which threats they feared most, and found the list topped by organized crime, an accident at a nuclear plant, and terrorism, each identified by 74–7 per cent of respondents. Meanwhile, military threats were identified by only 44–5 per cent of respondents. By 2008, war had slipped even further down the list; when asked which they thought was the most serious problem facing the world, 68 per cent identified poverty, 62 per cent climate change, 53 per cent international terrorism, and just 38 per cent armed conflict. Europeans expressed high levels of trust in the military in 2000, and high levels of support for the creation of a European Rapid

Reaction Force, but were also clear about how they felt a European army should be used: 71 per cent said it should be used for the defence of the territory of the EU, and 63 per cent for guaranteeing peace in the European Union, while only 18 per cent believed that it should intervene in conflicts in other parts of the world.[27]

Similarly, a 2002 survey in six European countries (Britain, France, Germany, Italy, the Netherlands, and Poland) found that while Europeans were concerned about terrorism and the proliferation of weapons of mass destruction, and favoured the European Union playing a more global role alongside the United States, they placed more weight on non-military approaches to international problems, regarding them as more important and possibly more effective. When asked whether they thought economic strength or military strength played a more important role in determining a country's power and influence in the world, large majorities (80–9 per cent) opted for economic strength. When asked under what circumstances they would support the use of European troops, more opted for helping out in areas struck by famine or upholding international law (80–8 per cent) than for bringing peace to a region beset by civil war (72 per cent) or ensuring the supply of oil (49 per cent).[28]

Interestingly, public opinion in the United States—which might be ex- pected to be more favourable to military action overseas than is the case in Europe—has recently been equivocal at best. In cases where the United States is seen to have only a modest stake in the outcome of a problem (as in Somalia, Haiti, Bosnia, or Kosovo in the 1990s), there are low levels of support for using ground troops in combat. But in regard to the war on terrorism, there is both majority support for military action and a high level of tolerance for high casualties.[29] An important determinant of the level of support for military force is the nature of the objective: American public opinion supports restraining aggressive adversaries, but is leery of involve- ment in civil wars, and is sensitive to the relative risk of different military actions, to the prospect of civilian or military casualties, to multilateral participation in the mission, and to the likelihood of success or failure of the mission.[30]

War and conflict continue to be realities that must be faced, and Europe continues to maintain a large military against the possibility that it will be needed for the security of Europe, for peacekeeping operations abroad, and even occasionally for peacemaking.[31] But while militaries are still impor- tant to the state identity of the United States, Russia, China, and India, and play an important role in the politics of numerous less developed countries, the role of the military in the European psyche has declined markedly since

1945. Civilian power Europe might have been a contradiction in terms in 1982, but today it is a core element of the meaning of Europeanism. The purpose of the military has been redefined; from a time when European armies regularly fought with each other, the European military today is mainly kept in reserve, sustained by the need for humanitarian and peace-keeping operations, and redefined as an international force for the promotion of democratic principles, rather than as a force for the projection of European power.

Smart power Europe

Recent debates about Europe's global role have made much of its association with soft power, meaning the ability to employ military, economic, diplomatic, and cultural tools in such a way as to encourage, attract, and lead by example. Although the concept is usually associated with the writings of Harvard political scientist Joseph Nye, in fact it is as old as organized society, and contemporary assessments can be traced back at least to the early 1970s, when Klaus Knorr made a distinction between two kinds of influence: coercive (where a state uses sanctions or the threat of restrictions against another state, and one loses or expects to lose while the other state gains) and non-coercive (where a state's choices are 'enriched rather than limited' by another state, and both states expect to gain).[32] At about the same time, Steven Lukes suggested that studies of power were too focused on observable behaviour and concrete decisions, and that perhaps it was time to look also at latent or covert power, or the way in which states could influence, shape, or determine the wants of other states. Put another way, strength, magnetism, wealth, and diplomatic skills might provide a state with power even when they were not deployed.[33]

This idea of non-coercive, latent, or covert power was given a new name and has attracted new attention since the 1990s as Nye's concept of 'soft power'. Nye contrasted the threats and inducements tied to military and economic power with the outcomes achieved by using intangible assets such as culture, political values, and policies that are seen as legitimate or as having moral authority. Soft power, Nye argues, is attractive power, providing leadership by example, shaping the preferences of others, co-opting rather than coercing, and encouraging others to want the outcomes you want.[34] Lacking a large unified military and the ability and willingness to take military action quickly and decisively, while at the same time being driven by the economic priorities of the civilian–industrial complex discussed in Chapter 5, the European Union has come to be associated with soft power. Meanwhile, the enormous military power of the United States, combined with the political influence of its military–industrial complex, brands it in the minds of many as a hard power. But the hard–soft power dichotomy is too stark; more useful as a means of grasping what Europe now represents is the idea that neither soft power nor hard power can be relied upon in isolation, but that the key lies in using them both in combination, through what has come to be known as smart power.

Nossel traces the roots of this idea to Wilsonian liberal internationalism, and defines it as assertive leadership using a combination of diplomatic, economic, and military means to advance a broad array of goals, including human rights, free trade, and economic development. While conservatives 'rely on military power as the main tool of statecraft', she asserts, 'liberal internationalists see trade, diplomacy, foreign aid, and the spread of . . . values as equally important'.[35] But she was making an appeal to American progressives to revive liberal internationalism as a means of articulating a distinct alternative to conservative views of the world, and while Joseph Nye has since championed the concept of smart power, and Hillary Clinton raised it several times during her confirmation hearings as Secretary of State in January 2009, it had already been at the heart of European calculations for many years.

The suggestion that Europeans have either a soft or a smart power advantage is routinely rejected by realists, who argue that Europe can achieve little in an anarchic world unless it is able and willing to maintain and deliver the military force needed to back up its economic interests. American critics in particular equate European soft power with weakness, pointing to a 'tradition' of appeasement running from Munich in 1938 to Iraq in 2003. They assert that Europe's advantages in this area are almost entirely reliant on the insurance provided by American security guarantees; without a large US military, they argue, Europe would not be in the position to take the moral high ground. They list the many instances where European soft power has not worked or has failed to make much difference, including Afghanistan, Iran, Israel, and Lebanon. They also argue that Europe has quietly exploited anti-Americanism to extend its soft power credentials, contrasting its 'good cop' reliance on peace and economic incentives with the 'bad cop' role of the United States. Soft power, argues the conservative American military historian Victor Davis Hanson, translates into Europe 'using transnational organizations and its own economic clout to soothe or buy off potential adversaries, while a formidable cultural engine dresses it all up in high sounding platitudes of internationalism and multilateralism'.

205

Meanwhile, he asserts, most of the 'international sins of the recent age ... were the work of European avatars of peace'.[36]

And yet the absence of a threat of violence from Europe, combined with the considerable economic opportunities that Europe can offer, may well encourage some of those adversaries to be more receptive to its suggestions than to those of the United States. Moravcsik argues that 'Europe can win without an army', and that talk about European defence schemes 'distract Europe from its true comparative advantage in world politics: the cultivation of civilian and quasi-military power'. He lists five ways in which he feels that Europe can wield a level of influence over peace and war as great as that of the United States: through the promise of membership of the European Union, through continuing to provide the lion's share of official development assistance, through continuing to bolster international peacekeeping operations, through support for monitoring by international institutions, and through continuing to champion multilateral responses to crises. Rather than criticizing US military power or hankering after it, he concludes, Europe should instead invest in complementing that power.[37]

In better understanding the significance and possibilities of smart power, three key principles must be borne in mind. First, military power is not necessarily hard, except where violence or the threat of violence is used to achieve an objective. The Europeans clearly have a large military, and defence spending has increased in several European states in recent years, but European military efforts are directed mainly at humanitarian and peacekeeping operations, which are soft power activities. Military power is only hard where the states that control it threaten to use it offensively, or are so belligerent in the way they define its defensive capacities that they are seen to pose a threat to others.

Second, even though the United States is often characterized as placing more emphasis on hard than soft power, and it has been adept in its use of the latter. The democratic ideals it espouses have long been inspirational, and it was the principal architect behind many of the international institutions that the Bush administration treated with so little regard. American culture helps promote American influence, and the United States has made notable contributions to humanitarian efforts, ranging from the Marshall Plan of the 1950s through to the international response to the 2004 Indian Ocean tsunami. Indeed, the United States is often not given credit for its application of soft opportunities, a problem that lies in large part in how the US role in the world is perceived by its enemies.

Finally, it is essential to note that in spite of its civilian and soft power credentials, Europe is both willing and able to use hard power where necessary. Its military actions were noted earlier in this chapter, but it has also employed hard options on the economic front. Thus more than two dozen countries were targeted by EU sanctions between 1982 and 2004, including Afghanistan, Argentina, Belarus, China, Croatia, Indonesia, Nigeria, and South Africa.[38] Meanwhile, the European Union has been active in taking its trading partners to the World Trade Organization in order to protect what it defines as its best economic interests. Just as the United States is often wrongly disparaged for talking loudly and carrying a small carrot (to mix metaphors), so Europe is often wrongly disparaged for talking softly and carrying a big carrot. The difference between the two actors lies in their relative use of coercion and encouragement to achieve their foreign policy goals.

Often touted as the shining example of European soft power at work has been the record of the European Union in reaching out to its neighbours. Although the creation of the European Coal and Steel Community was met with little enthusiasm outside the six founding states, European integration steadily exerted an irresistible attraction, such that all forty European states today except Belarus are either members of the club or have short-term aspirations to join. EU enlargement, argues Moravcsik, is 'perhaps the single most powerful policy instrument for peace and security in the world today'.[39] And for those states that do not qualify for membership of the European Union, access to the European market exerts almost as much influence. In reviewing the impact of Europe on its neighbours, Leonard notes that 'the European idea of democracy has not travelled in armoured convoys from the west. It is an ideal that inspires people to change themselves from the inside'.[40] All new or aspiring members have made institutional or policy changes that have strengthened their democratic and capitalist credentials. Thus while it was US leadership in the cold war that kept western Europe safe and prosperous, it has been European leadership that has since taken up the burden of providing opportunities and solidifying the gains.

A second example of European soft power has been its role in peacekeeping and peacebuilding. If the former is understood as a military deployment to keep warring factions apart or to monitor a ceasefire, the latter consists of military or civilian interventions aimed at creating effective security, police, and judicial institutions in the interests of transforming war-torn states into stable market democracies.[41] Europe provides more than 40 per cent of the budget for UN peacekeeping operations, far more than anyone else (the United States provides 26 per cent, Japan 17 per cent, and China 3 per cent), and while the vast majority of uniformed personnel in those operations in recent years have come from Asia and Africa, several European states have made their own large personnel contributions, including Italy, France, and Spain.[42] Since a commitment made in 2000, the European Union has also been working on a civilian crisis management force made up of members of national police forces; the first two EU police missions were set up in Bosnia and Macedonia in 2003, and in 2006 the European Gendarmerie Force was inaugurated, sending its first mission to Chad in 2008.

A third example of European soft power can be found in its role as the world's foremost supplier of official development assistance (ODA). There are many questions about the effectiveness of aid, it is true, and about how much it is undermined by the unfair trading practices of industrialized countries, but there is little question that it has contributed strongly to development progress, and that some ODA is preferable to none at all. In absolute terms, Europe (the European Union, Norway, and Switzerland) accounted for 64 per cent of net ODA provided by OECD member states in 2008, compared to the 22 per cent provided by the United States, and the 8 per cent provided by Japan (see Fig 8.1). It also does well in relative terms: in 1970, the UN General Assembly set a target of 0.7 per cent of gross national income (GNI) for donor countries, the only ones of which to

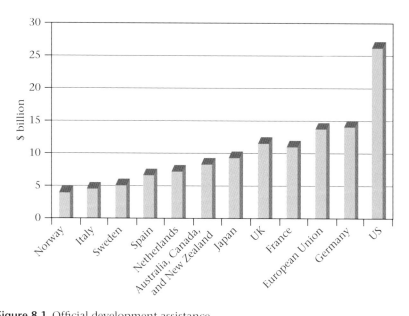

Figure 8.1 Official development assistance

Source: Organization for Economic Cooperation and Development at http://www.oecd.org/dac (retrieved September 2009). Figures are for 2008.

have so far met that target being Norway, Sweden, Luxembourg, the Netherlands, and Denmark, while eight more European countries are at least half-way to the target. Japan and the United States meanwhile give less than 0.2 per cent of GNI.[43] While apologists argue that the United States makes up for its shortfall with private philanthropy, the addition of private spending only pushes the US total up to 0.21 per cent of GNI,[44] and an estimated 40 per cent of private American spending goes to just one country: Israel.[45]

European aid also comes with relatively few political strings, and is directed primarily at civilian activities. Smith notes that the European Union prefers to use 'positive conditionality' in its aid policies, meaning that it encourages changes in the states with which it deals, promising benefits to those states in return for meeting conditions.[46] By contrast, a third of American ODA goes to just three countries (Iraq, Egypt, and Israel), 20–30 per cent of its aid (as noted in Chapter 5) is in the form of military assistance, and states with which the United States has an ideological difference of opinion—most notably Cuba—are denied American assistance. And while the Bush administration allocated $15 billion to the global fight against AIDS, it stipulated that the spending should be channelled to programmes that promoted abstinence rather than condom use, and that it could not be used for abortions or to treat prostitutes. It also refused to allow ODA to be used by groups that carried out or provided advice on abortions. True, this was an ideological decision that was reversed by the Obama administration, but it had greater support among conservative Americans than a similar policy would have had among conservative Europeans.

A final example of European soft power at work can be seen in its influence as an organizational model. The European Economic Community was the first attempt of the post-war era to promote regional integration, and has gone on to be the most successful. Other experiments in regional integration have followed in its wake, including the Council of Arab Economic Unity (1957), the Latin American Free Trade Association (1960), the Association of Southeast Asian Nations (1967), the East African Community (1967), the Caribbean Community and Common Market (1973), the Economic Community of West African States (1975), the South Asian Association for Regional Cooperation (1985), the Southern Cone Common Market (Mercosur) (1991), and the North American Free Trade Agreement (1994). In 2002, the African Union replaced the Organization of African Unity, and borrowed directly from the EU model, with its own equivalents of the European Commission, the Council of Ministers, the European Parliament, the European Court of Justice, the European Council, the

Committee of Permanent Representatives, and the European Central Bank. Not all these experiments have worked well, and some have even been disbanded, but the European Union has unquestionably been the pacesetter on the concept of regional integration.

Although there are several compelling examples of European soft power at work, Europe has become adept at balancing the stick and the carrot in such a way as to be better understood as a smart power. As noted, it will use military and economic threats where needed, but it prefers to avoid conflict and instead to pursue encouragement and cooperation. 'The great value of Europe's approach to international affairs', argues Everts, 'is that it seeks to create intensive webs of reciprocal obligations and exchange with other countries . . . [and] also tries to boost the capacity of international regimes to tackle new issues'. On a range of issues, from climate change to Iran, the International Criminal Court, landmines, and bio-weapons, 'the EU approach has produced real results—often in the face of US indifference and, sometimes, opposition'.[47] The possibilities of European smart power are not yet fully understood, because they have been so little studied and because we are still disinclined to define power in terms of the ambiguities of opportunity and example. But the drawbacks of hard power continue to mount, and the nature of international relations continues to change, obliging new attention to be paid to Europeanist values.

Multilateralism

The European Security Strategy included a call for an international order based on 'effective multilateralism', a phrase that sparked something of a minor firestorm of academic and political debate. If multilateralism is the philosophy that states should work together rather than in isolation, then—whether they work through direct intergovernmental contacts or through international organizations—the keys to effective multilateralism are rules, cooperation, and inclusiveness, and the building of a sustainable consensus among states.[48] Since the European Union is by definition a multilateral institution, Europeans are quite familiar with most of its possibilities and pitfalls. European institutions have had decades of experience of trial and error, and a proven track record of managing power rivalries among states, of encouraging states to work together on agreeing new laws and policies, and of making efforts to be inclusive and to engage. The results have not always been ideal, to be sure, but to the extent that we learn from our mistakes, Europeans have had much opportunity to learn.

Much of Kagan's thesis on Europe and America rests on what he regards as their differing attitudes towards international cooperation. 'Americans increasingly tend toward unilateralism in international affairs', he notes. 'They are less inclined to act through international institutions such as the United Nations, less likely to work cooperatively with other nations to pursue common goals, more sceptical about international law, and more willing to operate outside its strictures when they deem it necessary, or even merely useful'. By contrast, he claims, Europeans are quicker to appeal to international law, international conventions, and international opinion.[49] However, the reality is not quite that simple. On the economic front, multilateralism has been at the heart of the international financial and trading system that has been built with such care since 1945, while on the political front it has been promoted by the principles of the United Nations and a complex network of other international organizations, and by the construction of a system of international laws and treaties that are, by definition, multilateral in character. Thus Americans and Europeans have been subject to similar pressures. This does not mean, however, that they have approached the construction of the post-war system from similar philosophical positions, and in two areas in particular they have clearly been moving in different directions.

First, while American leaders since 1945 have had a tendency to see the world through a realist lens and to see threats in sometimes surprising places, their European counterparts have placed a premium on coopera-tion, and on the promotion of values rather than of interests. In their approach to numerous problems, including terrorism, arms control, non-proliferation, international trade, the environment, and human rights, Americans have emphasized self-interest while Europeans have worked to be more inclusive. On international terrorism, in particular, the contrasts are clear. While American neoconservatives have led a chorus of arguments that terrorists choose to strike because they envy the West and its freedoms, and that the only viable response is to meet violence with violence, Eur-opeans have been more inclined to seek out the underlying causes of terrorism. These may include criticism over the actions of Israel in the face of Palestinian demands for a state, the stationing of US troops in Saudi Arabia, or frustration among western European Muslims about their alienation. Whatever the cause, however, there are few Europeans who would advocate only a military response.

Second, the two sides have had a fundamentally different perception not only of the place and utility of military power but also of how the military should best be used. Above all, Europeans have been deeply reluctant to use their militaries other than in situations for which an international mandate—preferably one arranged through the United Nations—has been achieved. The British and the French in particular remember the international condemnation attracted by their venture into Suez in 1956, and the implications first of their failure to arrange international support for the invasion, and then of the political and financial pressure brought to bear by the United States. The United States not only has worked to build multinational coalitions wherever possible, as in Korea and during the 1990–1 Gulf crisis, but has also indicated its willingness to deploy its military even in the face of international opposition. Its lonely war against the North Vietnamese is a case in point, and another is offered by its willingness to invade Iraq in 2003 with or without the backing of the UN, and thus of the international community.

As the United States prepared in the opening months of 2003 to launch the invasion, most EU states rejected the idea of war without the backing of a UN Security Council resolution, and the Greek presidency issued a statement arguing that war was not inevitable, that 'force should be used only as a last resort', that it was 'committed to the United Nations remaining at the centre of the international order,' and that it believed the 'the primary responsibility for dealing with Iraqi disarmament lies with the [UN] Security Council'. Once the invasion was under way, the European Union demanded a central role for the UN in the rebuilding of Iraq. Indeed, the EU–UN relationship has become a key feature in the dynamics of international relations, Eide going so far as to suggest that the European Union is 'in many ways becoming the UN's main Western partner'.[50]

Patrick describes the American view on multilateralism as ambivalent at best, which he puts down to three particular features of the American experience: the belief that the United States is an exceptional society that is not only the one outlier on the rules that apply to other societies, but must also stand as an example and either encourage others to follow its lead or else go it alone; its domestic institutional structure, with the mandate shared between president and Congress making it harder for the United States to assume multilateral obligations; and its sheer power, which makes it more inclined to lead than to cooperate, and to pursue self-interest where needed.[51] On all the three counts, the European view is markedly different: there is no longer a prevailing sense of European exceptionalism, nor a sense that Europe has a mission to change others in its image; parliamentary government makes it easier for executives to win the support of legislatures for new treaties or strong positions in international organizations; and Europe's self-doubt about its power has combined with its habit of often conceding leadership to the Americans, and with the effects of the programme of European regional integration, to encourage it to work to achieve a consensus rather than rocking the boat.

European leaders are quite familiar with the adage that united we stand, divided we fall; not only is cooperation essential to the mission of regional integration, but the only way European states can really hope to influence the United States, China, or Russia is if they work together. And yet it has only been relatively recently, notes Maull, that the European Union has paid much attention to thinking through how multilateralism can best be promoted at a global level, the key qualification for success, he believes, being the ability to form and sustain broad-based coalitions.[52] For Brenner, effective multilateralism requires not only broad international support and legitimacy, but also the capacity to generate initiatives, and the political leadership to set the agenda, define deadlines, mobilize resources, and promote effective implementation.[53] As the tradition of European cold war deference to external powers fades into history, so the European Union in particular is showing its willingness and capacity to pursue all these qualities.

Additional evidence for European support of multilateralism can be found in Europe's role in the work of the United Nations, the World Trade Organization, NATO, and other international organizations, and in European support for international treaties. Supporting multilateral cooperation is 'a basic principle' of EU foreign policy, declared the European Commission in 2003, and the UN is regarded as the core channel for pursuit of that principle: the European Union should consider itself a 'driving force' in pursuing UN initiatives on sustainable development, poverty reduction, and international security (while also giving new impetus to UN reform).[54] Eide argues that one of the EU's greatest strengths in recent years has been 'its ability to co-opt, enhance and gradually reshape other international organizations'. After having seemed to be at odds with many of those organizations in the 1990s, he suggests, it has since come to be accepted as a positive force by reworking the capacities and goals of bodies such as NATO, the African Union, and the Organization for Economic Cooperation and Development. These advances 'have given the EU a strategic reach far greater than its . . . assets warrant'.[55]

The political reach of Europeanist methods and values is routinely underrated in large part because we live in a world where military power is still seen to trump other forms of power, in spite of the mounting evidence of the pitfalls of military options. We also still tend to see power in terms of state interests, and since states have a near-monopoly over the maintenance and deployment of military power, we find it hard to appreciate the possibility that suprastate arrangements might exert significant influence. Multilateralism, in particular, because it demands international agreement and thus the watering down of state positions in the interests of reaching collective agreement, is portrayed by hawks as weakness and as the start of the slippery slope to appeasement. But the new dynamics of the international system, in which interests are defined less in state or territorial terms, and increasingly in collective terms, fits centrally with—and has been most actively promoted by—Europeanist perceptions about the most effective means for managing and deploying influence. Those means place the emphasis on the tools needed to achieve a democratic and positive peace.

9
Conclusions: United in Diversity

A few years ago, an unofficial competition was held to develop a motto for the European Union. School pupils throughout the then-fifteen member states of the European Union submitted ideas, and in May 2000 the then-president of the European Parliament announced that the winning entry was 'United in Diversity'. It was hardly an original concept—almost every multicultural society claims some variation on the same theme as a guiding principle—but the motto joined a modest cluster of symbols that have come to represent European integration, ranging from the blue flag with the twelve gold stars to the adoption of 'Ode to Joy' as an anthem and the declaration of 9 May as Europe Day. Some have even suggested that the burgundy EU passport and the euro might also be considered contemporary symbols of Europe.

The promotion of these symbols, often adopted as a result of the ruminations of one committee or another in Brussels or Strasbourg, has met with mixed reactions. For those who admit to knowing little or nothing about the goals and structure of the European Union, they are the only visible (or aural) reminders of the existence of 'Europe'. For some, they are meaningful—if only symbolic, and perhaps somewhat contrived—representations of the European project, and a reminder of the direction in which most European states are now moving. For others, they have little or no meaning, and are dismissed as a waste of both time and money. For supporters of European integration, they are useful but do not go far enough. For the most eurosceptic, their growing visibility—at the expense, it is alleged, of national symbols—is a matter of dismay and regret, and representative not so much of the growing unity of Europe as of the declining sovereignty of the state.

But 'Europe' is not just a cluster of symbols. More substantially, the European project is reflected in the legislative and policy activities of the

European Union institutions: the European Council, the Commission, the Council of Ministers, the European Parliament, and the European Court of Justice. The European project has been advanced over the decades through a complex dynamic arising out of the work of these bodies and their interactions with the governments of the member states, the governments of aspirant member states, and the governments of all other states that have interacted with the collective representatives of the European Union. These interactions may not always have been satisfying, trouble-free, or productive, and the assessments of the European Union as an exercise in decision-making and democracy have been many and varied. Like the symbols, the institutions and the processes have their supporters, their detractors, their critics, and those who simply have little or no idea how they work or what purpose they serve.

But while committees adopt symbols, and leaders develop policies and approve laws, arguably more telling as an indicator of 'Europe' has been the growth of a European consciousness, and of a sense that there is a set of political, economic, and social norms, interests, and values that define Europe and the European experience, that explain European public preferences and proclivities, that drive the attitudes of Europeans towards each other and towards others, that guide European views about their place in the world, and that collectively might be understood as Europeanism. These norms, interests, and values apply not only to the residents of the member states of the European Union (even if integration has been a critical force in their development) but are also reflected to varying degrees in almost all of the forty sovereign states that today constitute Europe. Europeans may not always be conscious of what they have in common, and Europeanism as a concept is still remarkably under-studied, and yet— as this book has argued—most Europeans clearly hold shared views on a variety of issues, ranging from how societies should be ordered to the responsibilities of government, responses to critical problems, and the manner in which international relations should be managed. More importantly, these views are distinctive from those held by the residents of most other parts of the world.

The foundations of Europeanism lie in the evolving identities of Europeans, whose home has long been afflicted by crisis and conflict, who have had to adapt to the repeated redefinition of their political, social, and religious communities, and who have been repeatedly obliged to reconsider their affiliations accordingly. The waxing and waning of those affiliations accelerated during the nineteenth and twentieth centuries as nationalism and state power achieved new levels of prominence, sparking a cataclysmic

European civil war that was fought in two phases, interrupted by a nervous and temporary peace. This was capped in turn by Europe's post-war division under the leadership of external powers, a new and dismal role that represented the nadir of the long history of failure by Europeans to cooperate. It was now clear that Europe had to set aside nationalist tensions in order to ensure protection both from itself and from external threats, and if it was to be able to lead rather than being obliged always to follow. The end of the cold war meant a new focus on bringing the divided houses of Europe back together, an exercise that was given additional meaning and urgency by a new appreciation of how Europe differed with the world's last remaining superpower—the United States—on the ranking, understanding, and resolution of critical political, economic, and social problems.

As we have seen, Jürgen Habermas and Jacques Derrida were among the first to try defining what Europe meant in the new international environment, but their assessment was limited in both its geographical and its philosophical scope: they unnecessarily excluded Britain and eastern Europe from their calculations, and offered a modest menu of just six core qualities. This book has taken the stimulus they provided and has attempted to offer the debate new impetus and breadth by considerably expanding the discussion about the meaning and content of Europeanism, whose major constituent qualities are as follows:

- *Remodelled identities.* As European integration has progressed and its effects have spread from the economic to the political sphere, so too has European attachment to the state—whose modern lines first emerged in Europe—declined, encouraging Europeans to rediscover their national identities while also repudiating state-based nationalism, to rethink the meaning of citizenship and patriotism, and to begin the process of reinventing themselves as Europeans. The state is still seen to have extensive political, economic, and social responsibilities, but identity with the state, and with the self-interest of states, is on the wane.

- *Cosmopolitanism.* As associations with state and nation have been redefined, Europeans have gravitated towards the view that they might associate themselves with universal ideas and with the belief that all Europeans, certainly, and possibly even all humans, belong to a single moral community that transcends state boundaries or national identities. Europeanism since 1945 has pursued the idea that local and global concerns cannot be separated or divorced, and that rather than Europe or the world being separate from the community or state in

217

which each of us lives, the importance of the universal trumps that of the local.

- **Communitarianism.** In contrast to the liberal emphasis on individual rights, Europeanism supports a balance between the individual and community interests, emphasizing the responsibilities of government to all those who live under its jurisdiction. Europeans are open to the idea that society may be a better judge of what is good for individuals rather than vice versa, and to the argument that the state occasionally has a role in restricting individual rights for the greater good of the community.

- **The collective society.** Europeanism emphasizes the view that societal divisions will occur in spite of attempts to ensure equal opportunity, and accepts the role of the state as an economic manager and as a guarantor of societal welfare. The hold of social democracy remains strong in Europe, nowhere more so than in expectations regarding the advantages of government regulation of the business sector, and of the public delivery of social services.

- **Welfarism.** Europeanist notions of economic management hold that while individual endeavour is to be welcomed, applauded, and rewarded, the community—via the state—has a responsibility for working to ensure that the playing field is as level as possible, and that opportunity and wealth are equitably distributed. Europeans emphasize communal responsibilities and public welfare, are ready to criticize capitalism as the source of many social ills, have a broader conception of the idea of individual rights (believing that all should enjoy access to education, health care, and social security), and emphasize equality of results over equality of opportunity.

- **The civilian–industrial complex.** Post-war peace and economic re-construction have combined with changed European views about the role of the military in national calculations to emphasize the civilian over the military dimensions of economic activity. Europeanism means support for the idea that more time and investment should be expended upon meeting the needs of the consumer market than on military pro-duction, and that the political role of the defence industry should accordingly be limited.

- **Sustainable development.** At the heart of Europeanist thinking on the environment is the idea that development should be sustainable, meeting the needs of the present without compromising the needs of future generations. Europeans, who downplay unthinking consumption, are more conscious of the finite nature of resources, and more attuned to the place of humans within the biosphere.

- **Redefining the family.** Europeanism has meant a redefinition of the family: fewer Europeans are opting to marry, their ages at marriage are rising, divorce rates are growing, fertility rates are declining, more children are being born outside marriage, and single-parent households have become more usual, as have households containing couples without children, and households where the parents are unmarried. At the same time, new assumptions are being made about homosexuality, with support for same-sex marriages and civil unions.

- **Working to live.** As Europeans have adopted post-material values, so they have changed their views about work. They are working fewer hours, they are doing more with those hours, they have developed family-friendly laws and policies, and the additional time that they have free to spend at home or on holiday gives them a higher quality of life, and more time to enjoy their leisure.

- **Criminal rights.** In matters of criminal justice, Europeanism means a greater emphasis on individual rights, and a preference for resolving disputes through negotiation rather than confrontation through the law.

- **Multiculturalism.** Europe has a long and often overlooked tradition of multiculturalism arising from the diversity of European societies, and a Europeanist habit of integrating core values and features from new groups with which its dominant cultures have come into contact. Given the myths that surround much of what is regarded as national culture, it is difficult any more to be sure what constitutes a feature of home culture and what does not. The arrival in Europe of new groups in the post-war era has continued to build upon the tradition of multiculturalism, and has added new layers of complexity to the definition of home culture. Racism and religious discrimination, however, have not gone away.

- **Secularism.** While religion continues to grow in most of the rest of the world, in Europe its role is increasingly marginalized: church attendance has fallen, expressions of faith have become more uncommon, agnosticism and atheism are more openly and widely admitted, religion plays only a marginal role in politics and public life, and secularism drives Europeanist attitudes towards science and towards public policies in which religious belief plays a role, including abortion and euthanasia.

- **Opposition to capital punishment.** Europeanism opposes capital punishment, which is prohibited in all European Union and

Council of Europe member states, and European governments have worked to achieve a global moratorium on the death penalty as a first step towards its worldwide abolition.

- ***Perpetual peace.*** Post-war Europeanism identifies closely with a rejection of violence, war, and conflict as a means of resolving disputes, allowing the region to make progress along the path to achieve the Kantian condition of perpetual peace. Europeans face external threats, to be sure, but they no longer threaten one another, nor do they pose a threat to others. The ordering of politics, economics, and society in contemporary Europe has made inter-state war in the region—once all too frequent—all but unthinkable.

- ***Civilian power.*** Europe is well armed and willing to use its military if needed, but it does not feel the need to use force or the threat of force to encourage change. Instead, Europeanism emphasizes the benefits of civilian power, focusing on non-military and mainly economic means to achieve goals, leaving the military as a residual safeguard, to be used mainly in peacekeeping rather than peacemaking, and emphasizing the importance of cooperation (rather than conflict) and of developing supranational structures to deal with critical international problems.

- ***Smart power.*** In contrast to its long history of militarism and war, Europe today is a region in which threats and coercion (hard power) are balanced against incentives, diplomacy, and encouragement (soft power) to produce an emphasis on smart power (balancing the stick and the carrot).

- ***Multilateralism.*** Europeanism has eschewed national self-interest in favour of cooperation and consensus, of the promotion of values rather than interests, of reliance on international rules and agreements, and of building coalitions and working through international organizations to resolve problems.

Paradoxically, few Europeans are actively aware of what they have in common, the focus of their conscious self-identification remaining with the nation, the state, or a combination of the two. As we have seen, only a small minority think of themselves as European, and when travelling outside their home state the vast majority will—if asked—describe themselves as citizens of their respective states rather than as Europeans. In legal terms, they are all citizens of a state rather than citizens of Europe. And yet the arguments made in this book—and the supporting evidence offered— suggests that most Europeans subconsciously think and act much alike, and that the coincidence of their opinions is not limited or restricted by national or state lines. Regional integration under the auspices of the European Union has been both a cause and an effect of the coalescing of European opinion since 1945 on a wide range of political, economic, and social matters, but Europe is much more than the European Union. More revealing as a means to understanding the dynamics of contemporary Europe is the set of norms, values, and perceptions that its people hold in common, and thus it is essential that more consideration be given to understanding the content and parameters of Europeanism.

Notes

Introduction

1. Address by Václav Havel, President of the Czech Republic, before Members of the European Parliament, Strasbourg, 16 February 2000.
2. European Commission, *First Report on the Consideration of Cultural Aspects in European Community Action* (Luxembourg: Commission of the European Communities, 1996), 102.
3. Ales Debeljak, 'Elusive Common Dreams: The Perils and Hopes of a European Identity,' in *Ny Tid*, 28 August 2001. Reproduced by *Eurozine*, http://www.eurozine.com.
4. Address by Václav Havel, President of the Czech Republic, before the Members of the European Parliament, Strasbourg, 8 March 1994.
5. Address by Václav Havel, President of the Czech Republic, before the Members of the European Parliament, Strasbourg, 16 February 2000.
6. Dominique Strauss-Kahn, quoted in *Le Monde*, 26 February 2003.
7. Jürgen Habermas and Jacques Derrida, 'February 15, or What Binds Europe Together: Plea for a Common Foreign Policy, Beginning in Core Europe,' in *Frankfurter Allgemeine Zeitung*, 31 May 2003. Reproduced in Daniel Levy, Max Pensky, and John Torpey (eds.), *Old Europe, New Europe, Core Europe* (London: Verso, 2005).
8. Gerard Delanty and Chris Rumford, *Rethinking Europe: Social Theory and the Implications of Europeanization* (London: Routledge, 2005), 36–7.
9. European Commission, *Eurobarometer* 69, November 2008.

Chapter 1

1. Philipp Blom, *The Vertigo Years: Europe 1900–1914* (London: Weidenfeld & Nicolson, 2008).
2. Jean-Baptiste Duroselle, *L'Idee d'Europe dans l'histoire* (Paris: Denoel, 1965), 261.
3. Michael Heffernan, *The Meaning of Europe* (London: Arnold, 1998), 9.
4. Anthony Pagden, 'Europe: Conceptualizing a Continent', in Anthony Pagden (ed.), *The Idea of Europe: From Antiquity to the European Union* (Cambridge: Cambridge University Press, 2002), 34.

5. Anthony Pagden, 'Introduction', in Anthony Pagden (ed.), *The Idea of Europe: From Antiquity to the European Union* (Cambridge: Cambridge University Press, 2002).

6. Gerard Delanty, *Inventing Europe: Idea, Identity, Reality* (Basingstoke and New York: Palgrave Macmillan, 1995), 18–19; Pim den Boer, 'Europe to 1914: The Making of an Idea', in Kevin Wilson and Jan van der Dussen (eds.), *The History of the Idea of Europe* (London: Routledge, 1995).

7. Tim Cornell and John Matthews, *Atlas of the Roman World* (Oxford: Phaidon, 1982).

8. David Hay, *Europe: The Emergence of an Idea* (Edinburgh: Edinburgh University Press, 1957), 25.

9. David Dunkerley, Lesley Hodgson, Stanislaw Konopacki, Tony Spybey, and Andrew Thompson, *Changing Europe: Identities, Nations and Citizens* (London: Routledge, 2002), 112.

10. Derek Heater, *The Idea of European Unity* (London: Continuum and New York: Palgrave Macmillan, 1992), 10; Derek Urwin, *The Community of Europe*, 2nd edn. (London: Longman, 1995), 2.

11. Anthony Pagden, 'Introduction', in Anthony Pagden (ed.), *The Idea of Europe: From Antiquity to the European Union* (Cambridge: Cambridge University Press, 2002), 4–5.

12. Gerard Delanty, *Inventing Europe: Idea, Identity, Reality* (Basingstoke and New York: Palgrave Macmillan, 1995), 42.

13. Derek Heater, *The Idea of European Unity* (London: Continuum and New York: Palgrave Macmillan, 1992), 6.

14. Pim den Boer, 'Europe to 1914: The Making of an Idea', in Kevin Wilson and Jan van der Dussen (eds.), *The History of the Idea of Europe* (London: Routledge, 1995).

15. David Dunkerley, Lesley Hodgson, Stanislaw Konopacki, Tony Spybey, and Andrew Thompson, *Changing Europe: Identities, Nations and Citizens* (London: Routledge, 2002), 115.

16. Derek Heater, *The Idea of European Unity* (London: Continuum and New York: Palgrave Macmillan, 1992), 30–5; Martin van Creveld, *The Rise and Decline of the State* (Cambridge: Cambridge University Press, 1999), 85.

17. Martin van Creveld, *The Rise and Decline of the State* (Cambridge: Cambridge University Press, 1999), 1–2.

18. Charles Tilly, 'Reflections on the History of European State-Making', in Charles Tilly (ed.), *The Formation of National States in Western Europe* (Princeton, NJ: Princeton University Press, 1975), 12.

19. David Dunkerley, Lesley Hodgson, Stanislaw Konopacki, Tony Spybey, and Andrew Thompson, *Changing Europe: Identities, Nations and Citizens* (London: Routledge, 2002), 26–7.

20. Eric Jones, *The European Miracle: Environments, Economies and Geopolitics in the History of Europe and Asia*, 3rd edn. (Cambridge: Cambridge University Press, 2003), 104.

21. Quoted in David Hay, *Europe: The Emergence of an Idea* (Edinburgh: Edinburgh University Press, 1957), 123.
22. Eric Jones, *The European Miracle: Environments, Economies and Geopolitics in the History of Europe and Asia*, 3rd edn. (Cambridge: Cambridge University Press, 2003), 107.
23. William Penn, 'An Essay Towards the Present and Future Peace of Europe by the Establishment of an European Dyet, Parliament, or Estates (1693)', in *The Political Writings of William Penn* (Indianapolis, IN: Liberty Fund, 2002), chapter 12. At http://oll.libertyfund.org/title/893/77004 (retrieved January 2009).
24. For assessments of the long-term implications of his arguments, see James Bohman and Matthias Lutz-Bachmann (eds.), *Perpetual Peace: Essays on Kant's Cosmopolitan Ideal* (Cambridge, MA: MIT Press, 1997).
25. Pim den Boer, 'Europe to 1914: The Making of an Idea', in Kevin Wilson and Jan van der Dussen (eds.), *The History of the Idea of Europe* (London: Routledge, 1995), 63–5.
26. Anthony Pagden, 'Introduction' to Anthony Pagden (ed.), *The Idea of Europe: From Antiquity to the European Union* (Cambridge: Cambridge University Press, 2002).
27. Calculated from Angus Maddison, *The World Economy: Historical Statistics* (Paris: OECD Development Centre, 2003); David Kenneth Fieldhouse, *The Colonial Empires: A Comparative Study from the Eighteenth Century* (London: Weidenfeld & Nicolson, 1966), 178; Paul Bairoch, 'International Industrialization Levels from 1750 to 1980', in *Journal of European Economic History* 11:1/2, 1982, 269–333; figures quoted in Paul Kennedy, *The Rise and Fall of the Great Powers* (New York: Vintage Books, 1987), 154.
28. Eric Jones, *The European Miracle: Environments, Economies and Geopolitics in the History of Europe and Asia*, 3rd edn. (Cambridge: Cambridge University Press, 2003), 239.
29. For a brief and accessible survey of nineteenth-century European nationalism, see Timothy Baycroft, *Nationalism in Europe 1789–1945* (Cambridge: Cambridge University Press, 1998).
30. Hugh Seton-Watson, *Nations and States: An Enquiry into the Origins of Nations and the Politics of Nationalism* (Boulder, CO: Westview Press, 1977), 5.
31. John Breuilly, *Nationalism and the State*, 2nd edn. (Chicago: University of Chicago Press, 1994), 2.
32. Benedict Anderson, *Imagined Communities: Reflections on the Origins and Spread of Nationalism* (London and New York: Verso, 2006), 6.
33. Ernest Renan, in a speech titled 'What Is a Nation?' Given at the Sorbonne in March 1882, translated by and quoted in Timothy Baycroft, *Nationalism in Europe 1789–1945* (Cambridge: Cambridge University Press, 1998), 31–2.
34. Stuart Woolf (ed.), *Nationalism in Europe: 1815 to the Present: A Reader* (London: Routledge, 1996), 59.
35. Ernest Gellner, *Thought and Change* (London: Weidenfeld & Nicolson, 1964), 169.

36. David Dunkerley, Lesley Hodgson, Stanislaw Konopacki, Tony Spybey, and Andrew Thompson, *Changing Europe: Identities, Nations and Citizens* (London: Routledge, 2002), 44.

37. John Breuilly, *Nationalism and the State*, 2nd edn. (Manchester: Manchester University Press, 1993).

38. Michael Billig, *Banal Nationalism* (London: Sage, 1995).

39. David Dunkerley, Lesley Hodgson, Stanislaw Konopacki, Tony Spybey, and Andrew Thompson, *Changing Europe: Identities, Nations and Citizens* (London: Routledge, 2002), 52.

40. Eric Jones, *The European Miracle: Environments, Economies and Geopolitics in the History of Europe and Asia*, 3rd edn. (Cambridge: Cambridge University Press, 2003), 127.

41. David Dunkerley, Lesley Hodgson, Stanislaw Konopacki, Tony Spybey, and Andrew Thompson, *Changing Europe: Identities, Nations and Citizens* (London: Routledge, 2002), 25.

42. Jonathan Sperber, *The European Revolutions, 1848–1851* (Cambridge: Cambridge University Press, 2005), 90–1.

43. Benedict Anderson, *Imagined Communities: Reflections on the Origins and Spread of Nationalism* (London and New York: Verso, 2006), 86.

44. For discussion, see John Breuilly, *Nationalism and the State*, 2nd edn. (Manchester: Manchester University Press, 1993), chapters 4 and 5.

45. David Dunkerley, Lesley Hodgson, Stanislaw Konopacki, Tony Spybey, and Andrew Thompson, *Changing Europe: Identities, Nations and Citizens* (London: Routledge, 2002), 29.

46. Timothy Baycroft, *Nationalism in Europe 1789–1945* (Cambridge: Cambridge University Press, 1998), chapter 6.

47. Brian Bond, *War and Society in Europe, 1870–1970* (Montreal: McGill-Queen's University Press, 1998), 13.

48. Timothy Baycroft, *Nationalism in Europe 1789–1945* (Cambridge: Cambridge University Press, 1998), chapter 7.

49. Peter Bugge, 'The Nation Supreme: The Idea of Europe 1914–1945', in Kevin Wilson and Jan van der Dussen (eds.), *The History of the Idea of Europe* (London: Routledge, 1995), 86.

50. Benedict Anderson, *Imagined Communities: Reflections on the Origins and Spread of Nationalism* (London and New York: Verso, 2006), 113.

51. Harold Nicolson, *Peacemaking, 1919* (London: Constable, 1934), 187.

52. See Gerhard L. Weinberg, *A World at Arms: A Global History of World War II*, 2nd edn. (New York: Cambridge University Press, 2005), chapter 1; Correlli Barnett, *The Collapse of British Power* (London: Pan, 2002).

53. Sally Marks, *The Illusion of Peace: International Relations in Europe, 1918–1933*, 2nd edn. (Basingstoke: Palgrave Macmillan, 2003), 156–60.

54. Ben Rosamond, *Theories of European Integration* (Basingstoke: Palgrave Macmillan, 2000), 21.

55. Peter Bugge, 'The Nation Supreme: The Idea of Europe 1914–1945', in Kevin Wilson and Jan van der Dussen (eds.), *The History of the Idea of Europe* (London: Routledge, 1995), 102.

56. Trevor Salmon and Sir William Nicoll (eds.), *Building European Union: A Documentary History and Analysis* (Manchester: Manchester University Press, 1997), 9–14.

Chapter 2

1. Jack S. Levy, *War in the Modern Great Power System, 1495–1975* (Lexington, KY: University Press of Kentucky, 1983), 16–18.

2. Christopher Thorne, *The Far Eastern War: States and Societies, 1941–45* (London: Unwin, 1986), 211–12.

3. Winston Churchill, speech at the University of Zurich, 19 September 1946.

4. Michael Heffernan, *The Meaning of Europe* (London: Arnold, 1998), 3.

5. Winston Churchill, speech at Westminster College, Fulton, Missouri, 5 March 1946.

6. John Gillingham, 'Jean Monnet and the European Coal and Steel Community: A Preliminary Appraisal', in Douglas Brinkley and Clifford Hackett (eds.), *Jean Monnet: The Path to European Unity* (New York: St. Martin's Press, 1991), 131–7.

7. Jean Monnet, *Memoirs* (Garden City, NY: Doubleday, 1978), 222.

8. John Hume, Nobel Lecture in Oslo, 10 December 1998, at http://nobelprize.org.

9. Bruno Coppieters, Michel Huysseune, Michael Emerson, Nathalie Tocci, and Marius Vahl, 'European Institutional Models as Instruments of Conflict Resolution in the Divided States of the European Periphery'. Centre for European Policy Studies Working Document No. 195, July 2003.

10. For a review of the costs of war, see Tony Judt, *Postwar: A History of Europe Since 1945* (New York: Penguin, 2005), 14ff.

11. Alan S. Milward, *The Reconstruction of Western Europe 1945–51* (Berkeley: University of California Press, 1984).

12. Alan S. Milward, *The Reconstruction of Western Europe 1945–51* (Berkeley: University of California Press, 1984), 46–8.

13. Tony Judt, *Postwar: A History of Europe Since 1945* (New York: Penguin, 2005), 86–91.

14. Barry Eichengreen, 'Mainsprings of Economic Recovery in Post-war Europe', in Barry Eichengreen (ed.), *Europe's Post-War Recovery* (Cambridge: Cambridge University Press, 1995), 16–20.

15. Articles 4–6 of the Convention for European Economic Cooperation, quoted in Michael Palmer et al., *European Unity: A Survey of European Organizations* (London: George Allen & Unwin, 1968), 81.

16. Alan S. Milward, *The Reconstruction of Western Europe 1945–51* (Berkeley: University of California Press, 1984), 208.

17. Tony Judt, *Postwar: A History of Europe Since 1945* (New York: Penguin, 2005), 352–3.

18. Roger Morgan, 'The Transatlantic Relationship', in Kenneth J. Twitchett (ed.), *Europe and the World: The External Relations of the Common Market* (London: Europa, 1976).

19. Credit is usually given to Herbert Giersch in *The World Economy in Perspective: Essays on International Trade and European Integration* (Aldershot: Edward Elgar, 1991), 260–74.

20. D. C. Watt, *Survey of International Affairs 1962* (London: Oxford University Press, 1970), 137.

21. US Information Agency polls reproduced in Richard L. Merritt and Donald J. Puchala (eds.), *Western European Perspectives on International Affairs* (New York: Praeger, 1968), 250–3.

22. See Frank Costigliola, 'Kennedy, the European Allies, and the Failure to Consult', in *Political Science Quarterly* 110:1, Spring 1995, 105–23.

23. Quoted by Richard J. Barnet, *The Alliance: America, Europe, Japan; Makers of the Post-war World* (New York: Simon & Schuster, 1983), 264.

24. The US–Israel relationship is reviewed in John J. Mearsheimer and Stephen M. Walt, *The Israel Lobby and U.S. Foreign Policy* (New York: Farrar, Straus and Giroux, 2006). Interestingly, there is little literature on the Europe–Israel relationship.

25. Robert Schuman, Declaration of 9 May 1950.

26. Tony Judt, *Postwar: A History of Europe Since 1945* (New York: Penguin, 2005), 158.

27. US Information Agency poll reproduced in Richard L. Merritt and Donald J. Puchala (eds.), *Western European Perspectives on International Affairs* (New York: Praeger, 1968), 283.

28. European Commission figures quoted by Christopher Layton, *Cross-Frontier Mergers in Europe* (Bath: Bath University Press, 1971), 3.

29. Brian White, *Understanding European Foreign Policy* (Basingstoke: Palgrave Macmillan, 2001), ch. 4.

30. Jacques Delors, 'European Integration and Security', in *Survival* 33:2, Spring 1991, 99–109.

31. *New York Times*, 25 January 1991.

32. *Economist*, 'War in Europe', 6 July 1991.

33. For details, see Sophie Meunier, *Trading Voices: The European Union in International Commercial Negotiations* (Princeton, NJ: Princeton University Press, 2005).

34. Klaus Heidensohn, *Europe and World Trade* (London and New York: Pinter, 1995), 133–8.

35. World Trade Organization, Dispute settlement database, http://www.wto.org (retrieved January 2009).

36. EOS-Gallup Europe, 'International Crisis Survey', January 2003.

37. European Commission, *Eurobarometer* polls, various years, 1992–2007.

38. Eurobarometer Flash Poll 151, 'Iraq and Peace in the World', October 2003, http://ec.europa.eu/public_opinion/flash/fl151_iraq_full_report.pdf. The other countries named were Afghanistan, Pakistan, Syria, Libya, Saudi Arabia, India, and Somalia.

39. European Commission, *Eurobarometer* polls, various years, 2003–8.
40. European Commission, *Eurobarometer* 63, Spring 2005, and *Eurobarometer* 66, September 2007.
41. European Commission, *Eurobarometer* 66, September 2007.
42. Worldviews survey undertaken by the Chicago Council on Foreign Relations and the German Marshall Fund, 2002. Taken in six European states (Germany, Britain, France, Italy, Poland, and the Netherlands).
43. *Economist*, 'Can Europe's recovery last?', 14 July 2007.
44. Hubert Védrine, with Dominique Moïsi, *France in an Age of Globalization* (Washington, DC: Brookings Institution Press, 2001), 2.
45. European Commission, *Eurobarometer* 69, November 2008.

Chapter 3

1. See, for example, Joseph A. Camilleri and Jim Falk, *The End of Sovereignty?* (Aldershot: Edward Elgar, 1992), and Kenichi Ohmae, *The End of the Nation State: The Rise of Regional Economics* (New York: Free Press, 1995) or *The Next Global Stage: Challenges and Opportunities in Our Borderless World* (Upper Saddle River, NJ: Wharton School Publishing, 2005).
2. Ernst-Otto Czempiel, *Global Changes and Theoretical Challenges: Approaches to World Politics for the 1990s* (Lanham, MD: Lexington Books, 1989), 132.
3. Jan Aarte Scholte, *Globalization: A Critical Introduction*, 2nd edn. (Basingstoke: Palgrave Macmillan, 2005), 136.
4. Susan Strange, *The Retreat of the State: The Diffusion of Power in the World Economy* (Cambridge: Cambridge University Press, 1996), 4, 73.
5. For a survey of the debate, see Georg Sørensen, *The Transformation of the State: Beyond the Myth of Retreat* (Basingstoke: Palgrave Macmillan, 2004).
6. Gerard Delanty and Chris Rumford, *Rethinking Europe: Social Theory and the Implications of Europeanization* (London: Routledge, 2005), 52–3.
7. Eric Hobsbawm and Terence Ranger (eds.), *The Invention of Tradition* (New York: Cambridge University Press, 2002).
8. Cris Shore, *Building Europe: The Cultural Politics of European Integration* (London: Routledge, 2000), 40, 41, 56–60.
9. Paolo Graziano and Maarten P. Vink (eds.), *Europeanization: New Research Agendas* (Basingstoke: Palgrave Macmillan, 2007), 7–8.
10. Thomas Risse, Maria Green Cowles, and James Caporaso, 'Europeanization and Domestic Change: Introduction', in Maria Green Cowles, James Caporaso, and Thomas Risse (eds.), *Transforming Europe: Europeanization and Domestic Change* (Ithaca, NY: Cornell University Press, 2001).
11. Georg Sørensen, *The Transformation of the State: Beyond the Myth of Retreat* (Basingstoke: Palgrave Macmillan, 2004), 111.
12. Minxin Pei, 'The Paradoxes of American Nationalism', in *Foreign Policy* 136, May/June 2003, 30–7.

13. Anatol Lieven, *America Right or Wrong: An Anatomy of American Nationalism* (New York: Oxford University Press, 2004).

14. John Breuilly, *Nationalism and the State* (Chicago: University of Chicago Press, 1993).

15. European Commission, *Eurobarometer* 66, September 2007.

16. European Commission, *Eurobarometer* 67, November 2007.

17. See Neil Fligstein, *Euroclash: The EU, European Identity, and the Future of Europe* (Oxford: Oxford University Press, 2008).

18. European Commission, *Eurobarometer* 61, Spring 2004.

19. European Commission, *Eurobarometer* 62, May 2005.

20. European Commission, *Eurobarometer* 67, November 2007.

21. European Commission, *Eurobarometer* 66, September 2007.

22. See, for example, *Eurobarometer* 66, September 2007, 112–17; *Eurobarometer* 67, November 2007, 84–6; and *Eurobarometer* 68, May 2008, 67–8.

23. Willem Maas, *Creating European Citizens* (Lanham, MD: Rowman & Littlefield, 2007), 106.

24. Timothy Garton Ash, *Free World: America, Europe, and the Surprising Future of the West* (New York: Random House, 2004), 190.

25. See Willem Maas, *Creating European Citizens* (Lanham, MD: Rowman & Littlefield, 2007), chapters 1 and 2.

26. Derek Heater, *What Is Citizenship?* (Cambridge: Polity Press, 1999), 4–6.

27. Ian Ward, *A Critical Introduction to European Law* (London: Butterworths, 1996), 40; Elspeth Guild, 'The Legal Framework of Citizenship of the European Union', in David Cesarani and Mary Fulbrook (eds.), *Citizenship, Nationality, and Migration in Europe* (London: Routledge, 1997), 30.

28. Étienne Balibar, *We, the People of Europe? Reflections on Transnational Citizenship* (Princeton, NJ: Princeton University Press, 2004).

29. European Court of Justice Case C-184-/99, *Rudy Grzelczyk v. Centre public d'aide sociale d'Ottignies-Louvain-la-Neuve* (2001), ECR I-6193.

30. Willem Maas, *Creating European Citizens* (Lanham, MD: Rowman & Littlefield, 2007), 95.

31. Igor Primoratz (ed.), *Patriotism* (New York: Humanity Books, 2002).

32. Harris Interactive, 24 June 2004, www.harrisinteractive.com/news. US figure is for 2002, all other figures are for 2004.

33. Pew Global Attitudes Project, *Views of a Changing World* (Washington, DC: Pew Research Center for the People and the Press, June 2003), T59.

34. Steven Johnston, *The Truth About Patriotism* (Durham, NC: Duke University Press, 2007).

35. Daniel Levy, Max Pensky, and John Torpey (eds.), *Old Europe, New Europe, Core Europe* (London: Verso, 2005), xv.

36. For a review of its core ideas and history, see Jan-Werner Müller, *Constitutional Patriotism* (Princeton, NJ: Princeton University Press, 2007), 16–21, 26ff.

37. Jan-Werner Müller, *Constitutional Patriotism* (Princeton, NJ: Princeton University Press, 2007), 6.

38. Mattias Kumm, 'Why Europeans Will Not Embrace Constitutional Patriotism', in *International Journal of Constitutional Law* 6:1, January 2008, 117–36. See also Craig Calhoun, 'Constitutional Patriotism and the Public Sphere: Interests, Identity and Solidarity in the Integration of Europe', in Pablo de Greiff and Ciaran Cronin (eds.), *Global Justice and Transnational Politics* (Cambridge, MA: MIT Press, 2002), 275–312.

39. See discussion in Justine Lacroix, 'For a European Constitutional Patriotism', in *Political Studies* 50:5, December 2002, 944–58.

40. Mattias Kumm, 'Why Europeans Will Not Embrace Constitutional Patriotism', in *International Journal of Constitutional Law* 6:1, January 2008, 117–136.

41. For background, see Martha C. Nussbaum, 'Kant and Cosmopolitanism', in James Bohman and Matthias Lutz-Bachmann (eds.), *Perpetual Peace: Essays on Kant's Cosmopolitan Ideal* (Cambridge, MA: MIT Press, 1997), and Daniele Archibugi, *The Global Commonwealth of Citizens: Toward Cosmopolitan Democracy* (Princeton, NJ: Princeton University Press, 2008).

42. See Chris Rumford, 'Introduction', in Chris Rumford (ed.), *Cosmopolitanism and Europe* (Liverpool: Liverpool University Press, 2007), and Ulrich Beck and Edgar Grande, *Cosmopolitan Europe* (Cambridge: Polity Press, 2007).

43. Daniele Archibugi, 'Principles of Cosmopolitan Democracy', in Daniele Archibugi, David Held, and Martin Köhler (eds.), *Re-imagining Political Community: Studies in Cosmopolitan Democracy* (Cambridge: Polity Press, 1998); Maurice Roche, 'Cultural Europeanization and the "Cosmopolitan Condition": European Union Regulation and European Sport', in Chris Rumford (ed.), *Cosmopolitanism and Europe* (Liverpool: Liverpool University Press, 2007); Gerard Delanty, 'What Does It Mean To Be a "European"?', in *Innovation: The European Journal of Social Sciences* 18:1, March 2005, 11–22.

44. For review of literature on cosmopolitan democracy, see Daniele Archibugi and Mathias Koenig-Archibugi, 'Globalization, Democracy and Cosmopolis: A Bibliographical Essay', in Daniele Archibugi (ed.), *Debating Cosmopolitics* (London: Verso, 2003). See also 'Cosmopolitan Manifesto', in *New Statesman* 11:496, 20 March 1998, 28–30. For a discussion about what cosmopolitanism has to offer political science, see Edgar Grande, 'Cosmopolitan Political Science', in *British Journal of Sociology* 57:1, March 2006, 87–111.

45. See discussion in Margaret C. Jacob, *Strangers Nowhere in the World: The Rise of Cosmopolitanism in Early Modern Europe* (Philadelphia: University of Pennsylvania Press, 2006), introduction; Thomas W. Pogge, 'Cosmopolitanism and Sovereignty', in *Ethics* 103:1, October 1992, 48–75. Simon Caney, *Justice Beyond Borders: A Global Political Theory* (Oxford: Oxford University Press, 2005), 6.

46. See Ulrich Beck, *The Cosmopolitan Vision* (Cambridge: Polity Press, 2006), and Ulrich Beck and Edgar Grande, *Cosmopolitan Europe* (Cambridge: Polity Press, 2007).

47. David Held, *Global Covenant: The Social Democratic Alternative to the Washington Consensus* (Cambridge: Polity Press, 2004), 171, 178.

48. Ulrich Beck, 'The Cosmopolitan Society and Its Enemies', in *Theory, Culture and Society* 19:1–2, April 2002, 17–44.

49. Martha C. Nussbaum, 'Kant and Stoic Cosmopolitanism', in *Journal of Political Philosophy* 5:1, March 1997, 1–25. See also Martha C. Nussbaum, *For Love of Country?* (Boston, MA: Beacon Press, 2002), in which her arguments in favour of cosmopolitanism over patriotism are discussed by multiple contributors.

50. Derek Heater, *What Is Citizenship?* (Cambridge: Polity Press, 1999), 136.

51. Simon Caney, *Justice Beyond Borders: A Global Political Theory* (Oxford: Oxford University Press, 2005), 10.

52. See, for example, Daniele Archibugi and David Held (eds.), *Cosmopolitan Democracy: An Agenda for a New World Order* (Cambridge: Polity Press, 1995); Jacques Derrida, *On Cosmopolitanism and Forgiveness* (London: Rutledge 2001); Luis Cabrera, *Political Theory of Global Justice: A Cosmopolitan Case for the World State* (New York, Routledge, 2004); Gillian Brock and Harry Brighouse (eds.), *The Political Philosophy of Cosmopolitanism* (Cambridge: Cambridge University Press, 2005); Patrick Hayden, *Cosmopolitan Global Politics* (Aldershot: Ashgate, 2005); Robert Fine, *Cosmopolitanism* (London: Routledge, 2007).

53. Robert Firth, 'Cosmopolitan Democracy and the EU: The Case of Gender', in *Political Studies* 56:1, March 2008, 215–36.

54. Jeremy Rifkin, *The European Dream: How Europe's Vision of the Future Is Quietly Eclipsing the American Dream* (New York: Jeremy P. Tarcher/Penguin, 2004), 358.

55. John Hume, Nobel Lecture, in Oslo, 10 December 1998, at http://nobelprize.org.

56. Mary Kaldor, 'Cosmopolitanism Versus Nationalism: The New Divide?', in Richard Kaplan and John Feffer (eds.), *Europe's New Nationalism: States and Minorities in Conflict* (New York: Oxford University Press, 1996).

Chapter 4

1. See, for example, Larry Siedentop, *Democracy in Europe* (New York: Columbia University Press, 2001), Vivien A. Schmidt, *Democracy in Europe: The EU and National Polities* (New York: Oxford University Press, 2006), and Simon Hix, *The Political System of the European Union*, 2nd edn. (Basingstoke: Palgrave Macmillan, 2005).

2. See William Outhwaite, 'European Transformations', in Gerard Delanty (ed.), *Handbook of Contemporary European Social Theory* (London: Routledge, 2006), 284.

3. Emile Durkheim, *The Division of Labour in Society* (Toronto: Macmillan, 1933); Gabriel A. Almond and Sidney Verba, *The Civic Culture: Political Attitudes and Democracy in Five Nations* (Princeton, NJ: Princeton University Press, 1963), and *The Civic Culture Revisited* (Boston: Little, Brown, 1980).

4. Ekavi Athanassopoulou, 'Same Words, Different Language: Political Cultures and European Integration', in Ekavi Athanassopoulou (ed.), *United in Diversity? European Integration and Political Cultures* (New York: I. B. Tauris, 2008), 9.

Notes

5. See, for example, Roger Eatwell, *European Political Cultures: Conflict or Convergence* (London: Routledge, 1997), and Ekavi Athanassopoulou (ed.), *United in Diversity? European Integration and Political Cultures* (New York: I. B. Tauris, 2008).

6. Brian Girvin, 'Change and Continuity in Liberal Democratic Political Culture', in John R. Gibbins (ed.), *Contemporary Political Culture: Politics in a Postmodern Age* (London: Sage, 1989).

7. See discussion in introduction to Simon Hix and Klaus H. Goetz (eds.), *Europeanised Politics? European Integration and National Political Systems* (London: Frank Cass, 2001).

8. For a review of the literature, see Kevin Featherstone, 'Introduction: In the Name of "Europe"', in Kevin Featherstone and Claudio M. Radaelli (eds.), *The Politics of Europeanization* (Oxford: Oxford University Press, 2003).

9. Peter Mair, 'The Limited Impact of Europe on National Party Systems', in Simon Hix and Klaus H. Goetz (eds.), *Europeanised Politics? European Integration and National Political Systems* (London: Frank Cass, 2001).

10. Klaus H. Goetz, 'European Integration and National Executives: A Cause in Search of an Effect?', in Simon Hix and Klaus H. Goetz (eds.), *Europeanised Politics? European Integration and National Political Systems* (London: Frank Cass, 2001).

11. Lisa Conant, 'Europeanization and the Courts: Variable Patterns of Adaptation among National Judiciaries', in Maria Green Cowles, James A. Caporaso, and Thomas Risse (eds.), *Transforming Europe: Europeanization and Domestic Change* (Ithaca, NY: Cornell University Press, 2001).

12. Gabriel A. Almond, Russell J. Dalton, and G. Bingham Powell (eds.), *European Politics Today*, 2nd edn. (New York: Longman, 2002), 32ff.

13. Gabriel A. Almond, Russell J. Dalton, and G. Bingham Powell (eds.), *European Politics Today*, 2nd edn. (New York: Longman, 2002), 42ff.

14. See Robert D. Putnam, *Bowling Alone: The Collapse and Revival of American Community* (New York: Simon & Schuster, 2000).

15. Richard Balme and Didier Chabanet, *European Governance and Democracy: Power and Protest in the EU* (Lanham, MD: Rowman & Littlefield, 2008), 47–50.

16. See discussion in Jenna Bednar, John Ferejohn, and Geoffrey Garrett, 'The Politics of European Federalism', in *International Review of Law and Economics* 16:3, September 1996, 279–94.

17. See discussion in Michael Burgess, *Comparative Federalism: Theory and Practice* (London: Routledge, 2006).

18. Alexis de Tocqueville, *Democracy in America* (first published 1835–40).

19. See Amitai Etzioni, *The Spirit of Community: Rights, Responsibilities and the Communitarian Agenda* (London: Fontana Press, 1995).

20. Tony Blair, in speech to the Labour Party Conference, Blackpool, 1998.

21. Philip Selznick, *The Communitarian Persuasion* (Baltimore, MD: Johns Hopkins University Press, 2002), 4.

22. Amitai Etzioni, 'Introduction', and 'The Responsive Communitarian Platform: Rights and Responsibilities', in Amitai Etzioni (ed.), *The Essential Communitarian Reader* (Lanham, MD: Rowman & Littlefield, 1998), x, xix.

23. Robert D. Putnam, *Bowling Alone: The Collapse and Revival of American Community* (New York: Simon & Schuster, 2000), 19.

24. Amitai Etzioni, 'Introduction', in Amitai Etzioni (ed.), *The Essential Communitarian Reader* (Lanham, MD: Rowman & Littlefield, 1998), xii.

25. Elizabeth Frazer, *The Problems of Communitarian Politics: Unity and Conflict* (New York: Oxford University Press, 1999), 21.

26. Peri K. Blind, 'Building Trust in Government in the Twenty-First Century: Review of Literature and Emerging Issues'. Paper presented to 7th Global Forum on Reinventing Government, Vienna, 2007.

27. European Commission, *Eurobarometer* 69, November 2008.

28. Gallup poll, February 2008, at http://www.gallup.com (retrieved May 2009).

29. Gallup poll, April 2009, at http://www.gallup.com (retrieved May 2009).

30. Benjamin Jervis Goold, *CCTV and Policing: Public Area Surveillance and Police Practices in Britain* (Oxford: Oxford University Press, 2004).

31. See Florian Pichler and Claire Wallace, 'Patterns of Formal and Informal Social Capital in Europe', in *European Sociological Review* 23:4, September 2007, 423–35; Heiner Meulemann (ed.), *Social Capital in Europe: Similarity of Countries and Diversity of People? Multi-level Analyses of the European Social Survey 2002* (Leiden: Brill, 2008).

32. For discussion, see Peter A. Hall, 'Institutions and the Evolution of European Democracy', in Jack Hayward and Anand Menon (eds.), *Governing Europe* (Oxford: Oxford University Press, 2003).

33. Vivien A. Schmidt, 'National Patterns of Governance Under Siege: The Impact of European Integration', in Beate Kohler-Koch and Rainer Eising (eds.), *The Transformation of Governance in the European Union* (London: Routledge, 1999).

34. Wolfgang C. Müller, Torbjörn Bergman, and Kaare Strøm, 'Parliamentary Democracy: Promise and Problems', in Kaare Strøm, Wolfgang C. Müller, and Torbjörn Bergman (eds.), *Delegation and Accountability in Parliamentary Democracies* (Oxford: Oxford University Press, 2006), 4.

35. James Bryce, *Modern Democracies* (New York: Macmillan, 1921), ii: 469.

36. See Jean Blondel and Ferdinand Muller-Rommel (eds.), *Cabinets in Western Europe*, 2nd edn. (Basingstoke: Palgrave Macmillan, 1997), and *Cabinets in Eastern Europe* (Basingstoke: Palgrave Macmillan, 2001), and Kaare Strøm, Wolfgang C. Muller, and Torbjorn Bergman (eds.), *Cabinets and Coalition Bargaining: The Democratic Life Cycle in Western Europe* (Oxford: Oxford University Press, 2008).

37. For discussion of the majoritarian/consensual dichotomy, see Arend Lijphart, *Patterns of Democracy: Government Forms and Performance in Thirty-Six Countries* (New Haven, CT: Yale University Press, 1999).

38. See discussion in Gordon Smith, 'The Decline of Party?', in Jack Hayward and Anand Menon (eds.), *Governing Europe* (Oxford: Oxford University Press, 2003).

39. See discussion in Peter Mair, 'The Limited Impact of Europe on National Party Systems', in Klaus H. Goetz and Simon Hix (eds.), *Europeanised Politics? European Integration and National Political Systems* (London: Frank Cass, 2001).

40. Yves Mény, Pierre Muller, and Jean-Louis Quermonne, 'Introduction', in Yves Mény et al., *Adjusting to Europe: The Impact of the European Union on National Institutions and Policies* (London: Routledge, 1996), 10–11.

Chapter 5

1. Will Hutton, *The World We're In* (London: Abacus, 2003), 53–8.

2. Gérared Cornilleau, 'Welfare', in Alberto Martinelli (ed.), *Transatlantic Divide: Comparing American and European Society* (Oxford: Oxford University Press, 2007).

3. Werner Sombart, *Why Is There No Socialism in the United States?* (London: Macmillan, 1976).

4. Michel Albert, *Capitalism v. Capitalism: How America's Obsession with Individual Achievement and Short-Term Profit Has Led to the Brink of Collapse* (New York: Four Walls Eight Windows, 1993).

5. Jonas Pontusson, *Inequality and Prosperity: Social Europe vs. Liberal America* (Ithaca, NY: Cornell University Press, 2005), 17.

6. Gøsta Esping-Andersen, *The Three Worlds of Welfare Capitalism* (Princeton, NJ: Princeton University Press, 1990), 26–7.

7. André Sapir, 'Globalization and the Reform of the European Social Models.' Paper presented to ECOFIN Informal meeting, Manchester, 9 September 2005.

8. European Commission, *Eurobarometer* 69, November 2008, 34–40.

9. Frida Ghitis, 'No European Unity in Financial Crisis Response', in *World Politics Review*, 9 October 2008.

10. Bruno Waterfield, 'Return of the East–West Divide: European Union in Chaos as Global Recession Deepens', in *Daily Telegraph*, 15 March 2009.

11. 'Ducking Change, the European Way', in *Economist*, 22 April 2006.

12. John Gelissen, 'Popular Support for Institutionalised Solidarity: A Comparison Between European Welfare States', in *International Journal of Social Welfare* 9:4, October 2000, 285–300.

13. Clyde Prestowitz, *Rogue Nation: American Unilateralism and the Failure of Good Intentions* (New York: Basic Books, 2003), 236–7.

14. James Truslow Adams, *The Epic of America* (Boston: Little, Brown and Company, 1931), 404.

15. Jeremy Rifkin, *The European Dream: How Europe's Vision of the Future Is Quietly Eclipsing the American Dream* (New York: Jeremy Tarcher/Penguin, 2004), 3.

16. Data from multiple sources compiled by Karlyn Bowman, 'European Views (Opinion Pulse)', in *American Enterprise* 13:8, December 2002, 62.

17. Pew Global Attitudes Project, 'Views of a Changing World', June 2003, at http://people-press.org/reports/pdf/185.pdf, T42 (retrieved March 2009).

18. The figures were 95 per cent of Britons and Russians, 94 per cent of Poles, 90 per cent of Germans, 89 per cent of Italians, and 87 per cent of French. Pew Global Attitudes Project, 'Views of a Changing World', June 2003, at http://people-press.org/reports/pdf/185.pdf, T55 (retrieved March 2009).

19. The figures were 32 per cent of Americans, 35 per cent of Canadians, 48 per cent of Britons, 54 per cent of French, 63 per cent of Poles, 66 per cent of Italians, and 68 per cent of Germans. Pew Global Attitudes Project, 'Views of a Changing World', June 2003, at http://people-press.org/reports/pdf/185.pdf, T7 (retrieved March 2009).

20. OECD, *Growing Unequal? Income Distribution and Poverty in OECD Countries* (Paris: OECD, 2008).

21. Will Hutton, *The World We're In* (London: Abacus, 2003), 54.

22. See discussion in James W. Russell, *Double Standard: Social Policy in Europe and the United States* (Lanham, MD: Rowman & Littlefield, 2006), 48–9.

23. Alberto Alesina and Edward L. Glaeser, *Fighting Poverty in the US and Europe: A World of Difference* (New York: Oxford University Press, 2004).

24. All data from Stockholm International Peace Research Institute at http://www.sipri.org (retrieved January 2009).

25. Larry Nowels, '"Foreign Aid": Understanding Data Used to Compare Donors', CRS Report for Congress, 7 June 2006; U.S. Overseas Loans and Grants, Obligations and Loan Authorizations (the 'Greenbook') at http://qesdb.cdie.org/gbk/index.html.

26. See discussion in Terrence Guay and Robert Callum, 'The Transformation and Future Prospects of Europe's Defence Industry', in *International Affairs* 78:4, October 2002, 757–6.

27. *Fortune* Global 500 list of biggest corporations, at http://money.cnn.com/magazines/fortune (retrieved January 2009).

28. Defense News Top 100, at http://www.defensenews.com/static/features/top100/charts/top100_08.php (retrieved January 2009).

29. Burkhard Schmitt, *From Cooperation to Integration: Defence and Aerospace Industries in Europe* (Paris: Institute for Security Studies, 2000).

30. World Commission on Environment and Development, *Our Common Future* (Oxford: Oxford University Press, 1987), 8.

31. See Susan Baker and John McCormick, 'Sustainable Development: Comparative Understandings and Responses', in Norman J. Vig and Michael G. Faure (eds.), *Green Giants: Environmental Policy of the United States and the European Union* (Cambridge, MA: MIT Press, 2004).

32. Figures for CO_2 emissions, municipal waste, and water consumption from OECD at www.oecd.org; figures are for 2005 or latest year available. Energy use figures from International Energy Agency at www.iea.org; figures are for 2003. Retrieved January 2009.

33. European Environment Agency press release, 'Europe Must Grasp the True Value of Biodiversity', 27 April 2009, at http://www.eea.europa.eu (retrieved May 2009).

34. See Norman J. Vig and Michael G. Faure (eds.), *Green Giants? Environmental Policies of the United States and the European Union* (Cambridge, MA: MIT Press, 2004).

35. See Jonathan Golub, *New Instruments for Environmental Policy in the EU* (London: Routledge, 1998).

36. Pew Global Attitudes Project, 'Views of a Changing World', June 2003, at http://people-press.org/reports/pdf/185.pdf, T105 (retrieved March 2009).

37. Pew Global Attitudes Project, 'Global Unease with Major World Powers,' 27 June 2007, http://pewglobal.org.

38. For an overview of the climate change issue, see Paul G. Harris, 'Europe and the Politics and Foreign Policy of Global Climate Change', in Paul G. Harris (ed.), *Europe and Global Climate Change: Politics, Foreign Policy and Regional Cooperation* (Cheltenham: Edward Elgar, 2007).

39. For details, see John McCormick, *Environmental Policy in the European Union* (Basingstoke: Palgrave Macmillan, 2001), 280–90.

40. European Environment Agency, *Annual European Community Greenhouse Gas Inventory 1990–2006 and Inventory Report 2008* (Copenhagen: EEA, 2008).

41. Energy Information Administration figures at http://www.eia.doe.gov (retrieved April 2009).

42. Eurobarometer, 'European's Attitudes Towards Climate Change', September 2008.

Chapter 6

1. See discussion in Gerard Delanty and Chris Rumford, *Rethinking Europe: Social Theory and the Implications of Europeanization* (London: Routledge, 2005), 106–9.

2. Anthony Giddens, 'The World Does Not Owe Us a Living! The Future of the European Social Model', in *Progressive Politics* 4:3, September 2005.

3. Anna Diamantopolou, Commission for Employment and Social Affairs. Comments to fringe meeting at the Labour Party Conference, Bournemouth, 29 September 2003. Available at http://www.easesport.org/ease/fichiers/File/social-dialogue/ad290903_en.pdf.

4. European Trade Union Confederation web site at http://www.etuc.org/a/111 (retrieved February 2009).

5. Commission of the European Communities, 'European Social Policy: A Way Forward for the Union'. White Paper COMM(94) 333 final, 27 July 1994.

6. Edward Bannermann, Policy Brief prepared in anticipation of March 2004 European Council Meeting in Barcelona (Brussels: Centre for European Reform, 2004).

7. See Eric Marlier, A. B. Atkinson, Bea Cantillon, and Brian Nolan, *The EU and Social Inclusion: Facing the Challenges* (Bristol: Policy Press, 2007).

8. Figures from the *Economist*, various issues, summer 2008.

9. Figures from the *Economist*, various issues, summer 2009.

10. Robert Samuelson, 'The End of Europe', in *Washington Post*, 15 June 2005.

11. George Weigel, 'Is Europe Dying? Notes on a Crisis of Civilizational Morale', in *Newsletter of the Foreign Policy Research Institute* 6:2, June 2005.

12. Niall Ferguson, 'A World Without Power', in *Foreign Policy* 143, July/August 2004, 32–9.

13. David Pearce and Francois-Carlos Bovagnet, 'The Demographic Situation in the European Union', in *Population Trends*, 119 (London: Office for National Statistics, Spring 2005).

14. United Nations Department of Economic and Social Affairs, Population Division, *World Population Ageing 2007* (Geneva: United Nations, 2008).

15. Robert Gordon, 'Two Centuries of Economic Growth: Europe Chasing the American Frontier', 17 October 2002, http://faculty-web.at.northwestern.edu/economics/gordon/355.pdf.

16. Oliver Blanchard, 'The Economic Future of Europe', Working Paper National Bureau of Economic Research, March 2004, http://papers.nber.org/papers/w10310.

17. See Redefining Progress web site at http://www.rprogress.org.

18. For details, see John McCormick, *The Global Environmental Movement* (Chichester: Wiley, 1995), 84–8.

19. See Eurostat web site at http://epp.eurostat.ec.europa.eu.

20. Eurostat press release 32/2008, 6 March 2008, at http://ec.europa.eu/eurostat.html.

21. Eurostat press release STAT/06/59, 15 May 2006, at http://ec.europa.eu/eurostat.html.

22. Eurostat press release STAT/06/59, 15 May 2006, at http://ec.europa.eu/eurostat.html.

23. See Ron J. Lesthaeghe and Lisa Neidert, 'The "Second Demographic Transition" in the US: Spatial Patterns and Correlates.' PSC Research Report No. 06–592, Population Studies Center, University of Michigan, March 2006.

24. See discussion in Neil Gilbert and Rebecca A. Van Vorhis, 'The Paradox of Family Policy', in *Society* 40:6, September/October 2003, 51–6.

25. The figures were 83 per cent of Germans, 77 per cent of French, 74 per cent of Britons, 72 per cent of Italians, and 51 per cent of Americans. Pew Global Attitudes Project, *Views of a Changing World* (Washington, DC: Pew Research Center for the People and the Press, June 2003), T65.

26. European Commission, *Eurobarometer* 66, September 2007.

27. Eurofound, Fourth European Working Conditions Survey 2005, at http://www.eurofound.europa.eu/ewco/surveys.

28. European Commission, *Eurobarometer* 66, September 2007.

29. *Economist*, 'Jobs for Life', 19 December 2007; Blaine Harden, 'Japan's Killer Work Ethic', in *Washington Post*, 13 July 2008.

30. See discussion in Madeleine Bunting, *Willing Slaves: How the Overwork Culture is Ruling Our Lives* (London: HarperCollins, 2004).

31. OECD in figures at http://www.oecd.org (retrieved December 2008).

32. Niall Ferguson, 'Why America Outpaces Europe (Clue: The God Factor)', in *New York Times*, 8 June 2003.

33. George Weigel, *The Cube and the Cathedral: Europe, America, and Politics Without God* (New York: Basic Books, 2005).

34. Eurofound, Fourth European Working Conditions Survey 2005, at http://www.eurofound.europa.eu/ewco/surveys.

35. World Bank Development Data, at World Bank web site: http://www.worldbank.org (retrieved March 2009).

36. Phil Fennell, Christoper Harding, Nico Jörg, and Bert Swart (eds.), *Criminal Justice in Europe: A Comparative Study* (Oxford: Clarendon Press, 1995).

37. James Q. Whitman, *Harsh Justice: Criminal Punishment and the Widening Divide Between America and Europe* (New York: Oxford University Press, 2003), particularly chapter 3.

38. European Commission, *Eurobarometer* 69, November 2008.

39. 'Survey Finds European Insurers Increasingly Concerned By Growing Tort Claims', in *Insurance Journal*, 14 September 2004.

40. See Daniel Kelemen, 'Suing for Europe: Adversarial Legalism and European Governance', in *Comparative Political Studies* 39:1, February 2006, 101–27.

41. See discussion in Colin Warbrick, 'The European Response to Terrorism in an Age of Human Rights', in *European Journal of International Law* 15:5, November 2004, 989–1018.

Chapter 7

1. See World Values Survey at http://www.worldvaluessurvey.org.

2. Christoph Pan and Beate Sibylle Pfeil, *National Minorities in Europe* (West Lafayette, IN: Purdue University Press, 2004). For a survey of diversity in Europe, see Panikos Panayi, *An Ethnic History of Europe Since 1945: Nations, States and Minorities* (Harlow: Longman, 2000).

3. Bruce Bawer, *While Europe Slept: How Radical Islam Is Destroying the West from Within* (New York: Broadway, 2007); Melanie Phillips, *Londonistan* (Washington, DC: Encounter, 2007); Christopher Deliso, *The Coming Balkan Caliphate: The Threat of Radical Islam to Europe and the West* (Westport, CT: Praeger, 2007).

4. See, for example, Walter Laquer, *The Last Days of Europe: Epitaph for an Old Continent* (New York: Thomas Dunne Books, 2007).

5. Christopher Caldwell, *Reflections on the Revolution in Europe: Immigration, Islam and the West* (London: Allen Lane, 2009).

6. John R. Bowen, *Why the French Don't Like Headscarves: Islam, the State, and Public Space* (Princeton, NJ: Princeton University Press, 2008).

7. Pew Global Attitudes Project, 'Unfavorable Views of Jews and Muslims on the Increase in Europe'. Survey released in September 2008, available at http://pewglobal.org (retrieved March 2009).

8. Zsolt Nyiri and Cynthia English, 'Is Europe a Good Place for Racial and Ethnic Minorities?' Gallup poll, 14 December 2007, at http://www.gallup.com (retrieved March 2009).

9. EU Agency for Fundamental Rights, *Annual Report 2008* (Vienna: FRA, 2008).

10. George Weigel, *The Cube and the Cathedral: Europe, America, and Politics Without God* (New York: Basic Books, 2005); J. H. H. Weiler, *Un' Europa cristiana: Un saggio esplorativo* (Milan: Biblioteca Universale Rizzoli, 2003) (quotations translated by Weigel); Pope Benedict XVI, *Europe: Today and Tomorrow* (San Francisco: Ignatius Press, 2007).

11. John Madeley, 'European Liberal Democracy and the Principle of State Religious Neutrality', in John Madeley and Zsolt Enyedi (eds.), *Church and State in Contemporary Europe* (London: Frank Cass, 2003).

12. J. Christopher Soper and Joel Fetzer, 'Religion and Politics in a Secular Europe: Cutting Against the Grain', in Ted G. Jelen and Clyde Wilcox (eds.), *Religion and Politics in Comparative Perspective: The One, the Few, and the Many* (Cambridge: Cambridge University Press, 2002).

13. Peter J. Katzenstein, 'Multiple Modernities as Limits to Secular Europeanization?', in Timothy A. Byrnes and Peter J. Katzenstein (eds.), *Religion in an Expanding Europe* (Cambridge: Cambridge University Press, 2006).

14. Peter Berger, Grace Davie, and Effie Fokas, *Religious America, Secular Europe? A Theme and Variations* (Aldershot: Ashgate, 2008).

15. Peter L. Berger, 'Reflections on the Sociology of Religion Today', in *Sociology of Religion* 62:4, Winter 2001, 443–54. See also Grace Davie, *Europe: The Exceptional Case. Parameters of Faith in the Modern World* (London: Darton, Longman and Todd, 2002).

16. Colin Crouch, 'The Quiet Continent: Religion and Politics in Europe', in *Political Quarterly* 71: Supplement 1, August 2000, 90–103.

17. See discussion in Peter J. Katzenstein, 'Multiple Modernities as Limits to Secular Europeanization?' in Timothy A. Byrnes and Peter J. Katzenstein (eds.), *Religion in an Expanding Europe* (Cambridge: Cambridge University Press, 2006).

18. Grace Davie, *Europe: The Exceptional Case—Parameters of Faith in the Modern World* (London: Darton, Longman and Todd, 2002), ix–x.

19. Gallup International, Gallup International Millennium Survey, 2000. Results at www.gallup-international.com.

20. Pew Global Attitudes Project, *Views of a Changing World* (Washington, DC: Pew Research Center for the People and the Press, June 2003).

21. Gallup WorldView 2007–8, at https://worldview.gallup.com (retrieved April 2009).

22. Gallup International, Gallup International Millennium Survey, 2000. Results at www.gallup-international.com

23. Gerda Hamberg, *Studies in the Prevalence of Religious Beliefs and Religious Practices in Contemporary Sweden* (Uppsala: Uppsala Academy of Sciences, 1990).

24. Grace Davie, *Religion in Britain Since 1945: Believing Without Belonging* (Oxford: Blackwell, 1994) and *Religion in Modern Europe: A Memory Mutates* (Oxford: Oxford University Press, 2000).

25. Peter Berger, Grace Davie, and Effie Fokas, *Religious America, Secular Europe? A Theme and Variations* (Aldershot: Ashgate, 2008), 39–40.

26. European Commission, *Eurobarometer* 66, September 2007.

27. See, for example, Andrew M. Greeley, *Religion in Europe at the End of the Second Millennium: A Sociological Profile* (New Brunswick, NJ: Transaction, 2003).

28. Grace Davie, 'Global Civil Religion: A European Perspective', in *Sociology of Religion* 62:4, Winter 2003, 455–73.

29. Bat Ye'Or, *Eurabia: The Euro-Arab Axis* (Madison, NJ: Fairleigh Dickinson University Press, 2005).

30. Quoted in Philip Jenkins, *God's Continent: Christianity, Islam, and Europe's Religious Crisis* (New York: Oxford University Press, 2007), 4.

31. Quoted in Tom Hundley, 'A Crucible for Secularism', in *Chicago Tribune*, 19 June 2006.

32. Philip Jenkins, *God's Continent: Christianity, Islam, and Europe's Religious Crisis* (New York: Oxford University Press, 2007), 3.

33. Alison Pargeter, *The New Frontiers of Jihad: Radical Islam in Europe* (Philadelphia: University of Pennsylvania Press, 2008).

34. For discussion, see Carole Tonge, 'A Christian Union?', in *New Humanist* 18:2, 1 June 2003, and Philip Schlesinger and François Foret, 'Political Roof and Sacred Canopy?' in *European Journal of Social Theory* 9:1, February 2006, 59–81.

35. George Weigel, *The Cube and the Cathedral: Europe, America, and Politics Without God* (New York: Basic Books, 2005), 69 ff.

36. Will Hutton, *The World We're In* (London: Abacus, 2003), 57.

37. Gallup poll, 1–3 June 2007. Results at http://www.gallup.com/poll/1690/Religion.aspx.

38. BBC Online, 'Britons Unconvinced on Evolution', 26 January 2006.

39. Council of Europe, Parliamentary Assembly, 'The dangers of creationism in education', Doc 11297, 8 June 2007.

40. See Amy M. Burdette, Terrence D Hill, and Benjamin E. Moulton, 'Religion and Attitudes Toward Physician-Assisted Suicide and Terminal Palliative Care', in *Journal for the Scientific Study of Religion* 44:1, March 2005, 79–93.

41. The case of capital punishment is central to Manners' characterization of the European Union as a normative power. See Ian Manners, 'Normative Power Europe: A Contradiction in Terms?' in *Journal of Common Market Studies* 40:2, June 2002, 235–58.

42. Franklin E. Zimring, *The Contradictions of American Capital Punishment* (New York: Oxford University Press, 2004), 23.

43. Craig S. Smith, 'In Europe, its East vs. West on the Death Penalty', in *New York Times*, 19 November 2006.

44. Joshua Micah Marshall, 'Death in Venice: Europe's Death-Penalty Elitism', in *New Republic* 223:5, 31 July 2000, 12.

45. Roger Hood and Carolyn Hoyle, *The Death Penalty: A Worldwide Perspective*, 4th edn. (Oxford: Oxford University Press, 2008), 11.

46. Roger Hood and Carolyn Hoyle, *The Death Penalty: A Worldwide Perspective*, 4th edn. (Oxford: Oxford University Press, 2008), 24–5.

47. See Michael L. Radelet and Marian J. Borg, 'The Changing Nature of Death Penalty Debates' in *Annual Review of Sociology* 26, 2000, 43–61.

48. Franklin E. Zimring, *The Contradictions of American Capital Punishment* (New York: Oxford University Press, 2004), 19.

49. Andrew Moravcsik, 'The New Abolitionism: Why does the U.S. practice the death penalty while Europe does not?' in *European Studies* (Council of European Studies), September 2001.

50. Mark Shaw, Jan van Dijk, and Wolfgang Rhomberg, 'Determining Trends in Global Crime and Justice: An Overview of Results from the United Nations Surveys of Crime Trends and Operations of Criminal Justice Systems', in *Forum on Crime and Society* 3:1–2, December 2003, 35–63.

51. Harris Interactive Poll, February 2008. Results at http://www.harrisinteractive.com.

52. Death Penalty Information Center polls, various dates. Results at http://www.deathpenaltyinfo.org/home.

53. Sangmin Bae, 'The Death Penalty and the Peculiarity of American Political Institutions', in *Human Rights Review* 9:2, April 2008, 233–40.

54. Polly Toynbee, 'Ignore the tabloids—The death penalty is a dead issue', in *Guardian*, 21 August 2002.

55. See David G. Blanchflower and Andrew J. Oswald, 'Well-Being Over Time in Britain and the USA', in *Journal of Public Economics* 88:7–8, July 2004, 1359–86; Carol Graham and Steffano Pettinato, *Happiness and Hardship: Opportunity and Insecurity in New Market Economies* (Washington, DC: Brookings Institution Press, 2002).

56. Richard Layard, *Happiness: Lessons From a New Science* (London: Penguin, 2005).

57. See Richard A. Easterlin, 'Explaining Happiness', in *Proceedings of the National Academy of Sciences* 100:19, 16 September 2003, 11176–83, and 'Building a Better Theory of Well-Being', in Luigino Bruni and Pier Luigi Porta (eds.), *Economics and Happiness: Framing the Analysis* (Oxford: Oxford University Press, 2005).

58. *Economist*, 'Urban idylls', 28 April 2008.

59. Loek Halman, Ruud Luijkx, and Marga van Zundert, *Atlas of European Values* (Leiden: Tilburg University, 2005), 117.

60. Loek Halman, Ruud Luijkx, and Marga van Zundert, *Atlas of European Values* (Leiden: Tilburg University, 2005), 121.

61. European Commission, *Eurobarometer 69*, November 2008.

62. Loek Halman, Ruud Luijkx, and Marga van Zundert, *Atlas of European Values* (Leiden: Tilburg University, 2005), 120.

Chapter 8

1. Richard Rosecrance, 'The European Union: A New Type of International Actor', in Jan Zielonka (ed.), *Paradoxes of European Foreign Policy* (The Hague: Kluwer Law International, 1998), 15–23.
2. Ian Manners, 'Normative Power Europe: A Contradiction in Terms?' in *Journal of Common Market Studies* 40:2, June 2002, 235–58.
3. See discussion in Janet Adamski, Mary Troy Johnson, and Christina M. Schweiss (eds.), *Old Europe, New Security: Evolution for a Complex World* (Aldershot: Ashgate, 2006).
4. Brian Bond, *War and Society in Europe, 1870–1970* (Montreal and Kingston: McGill-Queen's University Press, 1998), 52–6.
5. See discussion in James Bohman and Matthias Lutz-Bachmann (eds.), *Perpetual Peace: Essays on Kant's Cosmopolitan Ideal* (Boston: MIT Press, 1997).
6. Robert Kagan, *Of Paradise and Power: America and Europe in the New World* (New York: Alfred A. Knopf, 2003).
7. Robert Kagan, *Of Paradise and Power: America and Europe in the New World* (New York: Alfred A. Knopf, 2003), 8–11.
8. Anthony Dworkin, 'Europeans From Venus? A Review of Robert Kagan's *Of Paradise and Power*' at FindLaw.com, 25 April 2002.
9. Anand Menon, Kalypso Nicolaidis, and Jennifer Welsh, 'In Defence of Europe—A Response to Kagan', in *Journal of European Affairs* 2:3, August 2004, 5–14.
10. See Simon Nuttall, *European Political Co-operation* (Oxford: Clarendon Press, 1992).
11. Report on European Political Cooperation (London, 13 October 1981), in *Bulletin of the European Communities* 1981, Supplement No. 3, 14–17.
12. European Security Strategy, 'A Secure Europe in a Better World', 12 December 2003, Brussels. Available at http://consilium.europa.eu/uedocs/cmsUpload/78367.pdf.
13. See discussion in Michael Howard, *The Invention of Peace: Reflections on War and International Order* (London: Profile Books, 2000).
14. European Commission, *Eurobarometer* 69, November 2008.
15. International Institute for Strategic Studies, *The Military Balance 2009* (London: Routledge, 2009).
16. Hanns W. Maull, 'Germany and Japan: The New Civilian Powers', in *Foreign Affairs* 69:5, Winter 1990–1, 91–106.
17. Karen E. Smith, 'Still "Civilian Power EU"?' European Foreign Policy Unit Working Paper 2005/1.
18. NATO, Text of the Report of the Committee of Three on Non-Military Cooperation in NATO, approved 13 December 1956, at www.nato.int/docu/basictxt/bt-a3.htm.

19. *Bulletin of the European Communities* 3 (110 1970), 10.

20. François Duchêne, 'Europe's Role in World Peace', in Richard Mayne (ed.), *Europe Tomorrow: Sixteen Europeans Look Ahead* (London: Fontana, 1972), and François Duchêne, 'The European Community and the Uncertainties of Interdependence', in Max Kohnstamm and Wolfgang Hager (eds.), *A Nation Writ Large? Foreign Policy Problems Before the European Community* (London: Macmillan, 1973).

21. Hedley Bull, 'Civilian Power Europe: A Contradiction in Terms?' in *Journal of Common Market Studies* 21:1/2, Sept/Dec 1982, 149–64.

22. Christopher Dandeker, 'Flexible Forces for the Twenty-First Century', in Alise Weibull and Christopher Dandeker (eds.), *Facing Uncertainty* (Karlstad: Swedish National Defence College, 2000), 108.

23. See discussion in Michael Mandelbaum, 'Is Major War Obsolete?' in *Survival* 40:4, Winter 1988–9, 20–38, and in John Mueller, *Retreat From Doomsday: The Obsolescence of Modern War* (New York: Basic Books, 1989) and *The Remnants of War* (Ithaca, NY: Cornell University Press, 2004).

24. Alyson J. K. Bailes, 'US and EU Strategy Concepts: A Mirror for Partnership and Difference?' in *International Spectator* 39:1, January–March 2004.

25. Quoted by E. J. Dionne, 'West Europe Generally Critical of US', in *New York Times*, 16 April 1986.

26. Dominique de Villepin, '2004—Just Another year of Fighting Terrorism?' in *Globalist*, 2 January 2004.

27. Philippe Manigart, 'Public Opinion and European Defense'. Translation of paper presented to symposium on public opinion and European defence, Brussels, 3–4 April 2001, at http://ec.europa.eu/public_opinion/archives/ebs/ebs_146_en.pdf; Eurobarometer, 'European's Attitudes Towards Climate Change', September 2008.

28. World views survey undertaken by the Chicago Council on Foreign Relations and the German Marshall Fund, 2002. Taken in six European states (Germany, Britain, France, Italy, Poland, and the Netherlands), at http://www.worldviews.org/detailreports/europeanreport/html/intro.html.

29. Eric V. Larson and Bogdan Savych, *American Public Support for US Military Operations from Mogadishu to Baghdad* (Santa Monica, CA: RAND Corporation, 2005).

30. Richard Eichenberg, 'Victory Has Many Friends: US Public Opinion and the Use of Military Force, 1981–2005', in *International Security* 30:1, Summer 2005, 140–77.

31. As of January 2009 there were more than forty armed conflicts under way in the world, most of which were insurgencies, civil wars, or uprisings. The only inter-state conflicts were in Afghanistan, Iraq, Israel–Palestine, and Kashmir. Source: GlobalSecurity.org at http://www.globalsecurity.org/index.html (retrieved January 2009).

32. Klaus Knorr, *Power and Wealth: The Political Economy of International Power* (New York: Basic Books, 1973), 3–4.

Notes

33. Steven Lukes, *Power: A Radical View* (Basingstoke: Macmillan, 1974), 21–5.

34. Joseph S. Nye, 'Soft Power', in *Foreign Policy* 80, Fall 1990, 153–72; *Bound to Lead: The Changing Nature of American Power* (New York: Basic Books, 1991); *Soft Power: The Means to Success in World Politics* (New York: Public Affairs, 2004), 5–7.

35. Suzanne Nossel, 'Smart Power', in *Foreign Affairs* 83:2, March/April 2004, 131–43.

36. Victor Davis Hanson, 'Soft Power, Hard Truths: America Cannot Long Be Partners with a Weak and Self-righteous Europe', in *Wall Street Journal*, 27 February 2005.

37. Andrew Moravcsik, 'How Europe Can Win Without an Army', in *Financial Times*, 2 April 2003.

38. Joakim Kreutz, *Hard Measures by a Soft Power? Sanctions Policy of the European Union, 1981–2004* (Bonn: Bonn International Centre for Conversion, 2005).

39. Andrew Moravcsik, 'How Europe Can Win Without an Army', in *Financial Times*, 2 April 2003.

40. Mark Leonard, *Why Europe Will Run the 21st Century* (London: Fourth Estate, 2005), 101.

41. Roland Paris, *At War's End: Building Peace after Civil Conflict* (Cambridge: Cambridge University Press, 2004).

42. Data from UN peacekeeping web site at http://www.un.org/Depts/dpko/dpko/index.asp (retrieved January 2009). Figures as of 1 January 2009.

43. Organization for Economic Cooperation and Development data at http://www.oecd.org/dac (retrieved January 2009). Figures are for 2007.

44. Jeffrey Sachs, 'Can Extreme Poverty Be Eliminated?' in *Scientific American*, September 2005, 56–65.

45. For data and discussion, see David Roodman and Scott Standley, 'Tax Policies to Promote Private Charitable Giving in DAC Countries', Working Paper 82, Center for Global Development, Washington, DC, January 2006.

46. Karen E. Smith, 'Engagement and Conditionality: Incompatible or Mutually Reinforcing? in Richard Youngs (ed.), *New Terms of Engagement: Global Europe Report 02* (London: Foreign Policy Centre, 2005).

47. Steven Everts, 'A Word of Advice from Europe: Soft Power Works' in *National Interest*, 16 October 2002.

48. See discussion in John Gerard Ruggie, 'Multilateralism: The Anatomy of an Institution', *International Organization* 46:3, Summer 1992, 561–98; *Multilateralism Matters: The Theory and Praxis of an Institutional Form* (New York: Columbia University Press, 1993).

49. Robert Kagan, *Of Paradise and Power: America and Europe in the New World* (New York: Alfred A. Knopf, 2003), 4–5.

50. Espen Barth Eide (ed.), *Effective Multilateralism: Europe, Regional Security, and a Revitalised UN: Global Europe Report 01* (London: Foreign Policy Centre, 2004), 3. See also the essays in Katie Verlin Laatikainen and Karen E. Smith (eds.), *The European Union at the United Nations: Intersecting Multilateralisms* (Basingstoke: Palgrave Macmillan, 2006).

51. Stewart Patrick, 'Multilateralism and Its Discontents: The Causes and Conse-
    quences of US Ambivalence', in Stewart Patrick and Shepard Forman (eds.),
    Multilateralism and US Foreign Policy: Ambivalent Engagement (Boulder, CO:
    Lynne Rienner, 2002).
52. Hanns W. Maull, 'Europe and the New Balance of Global Order', in *International
    Affairs* 81:4, July 2005, 775–99.
53. Michael Brenner, 'Introduction', in Michael Brenner (ed.), *NATO and Collective
    Security* (London: Macmillan, 1998), 1–5.
54. Communication from the Commission to the Council and the European Parlia-
    ment, of 10 September 2003, 'The European Union and the United Nations: The
    Choice of Multilateralism', COM (2003) 526 final.
55. Espen Barth Eide (ed.), *Effective Multilateralism: Europe, Regional Security, and a
    Revitalised UN: Global Europe Report 01* (London: Foreign Policy Centre, 2004).

Index